Imperfect Passage

Imperfect Passage

A Sailing Story of Vision, Terror, and Redemption

MICHAEL COSGROVE

Skyhorse Publishing

Skyhorse Publishing books may be purchased in bulk at special discounts for sales promotion, corporate gifts, fund-raising, or educational purposes. Special editions can also be created to specifications. For details, contact the Special Sales Department, Skyhorse Publishing, 307 West 36th Street, 11th Floor, New York, NY 10018 or info@skyhorsepublishing.com.

Skyhorse® and Skyhorse Publishing® are registered trademarks of Skyhorse Publishing, Inc.®, a Delaware corporation.

Visit our website at www.skyhorsepublishing.com.

10 9 8 7 6 5 4 3 2 1

Library of Congress Cataloging-in-Publication Data is available on file.

Cover design by Brian Peterson

Paperback ISBN: 978-1-63220-500-1
Ebook ISBN: 978-1-63450-032-6

Printed in the United States of America

Michael Cosgrove will be donating a portion of his profits to the Navy Special Warfare Family Foundation.

Contents

Disclaimer

This book describes the author's experience while attempting to sail around the world and reflects his opinions relating to those experiences. Some names and identifying details of individuals mentioned in the book have been changed to protect their privacy.

Dedication

This book is respectfully dedicated to my wonderful grandchildren.

Kelsey Gupton
Karley Gupton
Alexander Mueller
Tara Mueller
Tristan Martinez
Riley Martinez
Ryan Geller
Max Geller
Mia Geller
Riley & Reece Burke

When you die, not all of you will die, because the printed words I leave behind constitute a kind of immortality. The desire for immortality explains all the extraordinary achievements, good and bad.

—Martin Amis on Christopher Hitchens

• • •

CHAPTER 1

The View from Sixty

A man is not old until regrets take the place of dreams.

—John Barrymore

I'M AFRAID TO LOOK DIRECTLY at the mast—not for the fear of the sixty-two-mile-per-hour winds that are ravishing my boat, and not because there's anything wrong with the mast itself, as far as I know. I don't want to look at it for the same reason a little boy averts his gaze when he has to walk past a cemetery: I'm afraid I'll see a ghost. The last time I looked, a minute ago, there was an old woman sitting there with her back against the mast, smoking a pipe and gazing at me with an unsettling detachment. I have not eaten nor slept in three days, forced to this by a raging storm in the northern Tasman Sea, set to be a slave to the helm. To relinquish control of the boat for even a minute in conditions such as these will mean my death, and I did not come out here seeking death.

I can't help it. I look at the base of the mast, and there she is: wrinkled face, clay pipe—what is she, a Quechua woman from Peru? When I look directly into her eyes, she seems friendly enough, and I feel a little foolish for being afraid. Maybe she's here to help me. "Please," I say, "take the helm, just for a little while." She stares at me for a moment as if she doesn't understand. Then she throws her head back and laughs, and then fades away.

Heartbroken, I turn away, just in time to see the lights of a massive freighter bearing down on me. In a panic, I yank the wheel around to avoid a collision, look over my shoulder where the ship was, and see nothing but the empty gray sea, boiling and folding over itself in infinity.

"Oh, shit, Cos," I say to myself, "this trip has, quite literally, driven you crazy."

• • •

It all started with a birthday, as these things sometimes will. Some of us happen to hit a birthday marking an age ending in zero, and suddenly, no matter our record of achievement in the decades previous, we discover that we have much more still to prove to the world (by which, of course, I mean prove to ourselves). It gives me no great pride to report that my seafaring adventure was born from a classic three-quarter-life crisis.

I should have been perfectly content with what I had accomplished in life, and in fact, I thought that I was. I had a beautiful family, a successful career, and a lovely home with never-ending views of the Pacific Ocean. I had worked hard my whole life, always holding down two or more jobs at one time. Growing up in Michigan, I had watched my parents toil for thirty-five dreary years at the local Ford Motor Company factory—so I knew what drudgery was, and I was determined not to let it creep into my life. I didn't mind working hard, which my folks had certainly instilled in me, but I sought fulfillment, not just security. Standing on the manicured lawn of my Southern California home, hitting golf balls into Bluebird Canyon—*my canyon*, I felt that I had arrived.

Then came my sixtieth birthday. The funny thing was, birthdays number forty and fifty had barely registered with me. Sure, they hadn't been causes for ecstasy the way birthdays are when you're a kid (Whoopee! One year closer to death!), but I had taken them in stride. Sixty was completely different.

In the days leading up to the milestone birthday, I was actually looking forward to getting to share this event with my loved ones. Sally, my fiancée of five years, had put together a party sure to be filled with laughter and joy. All four of my daughters, Kelly, Kerry, Kasey, and Katie, joined us with my eight grandchildren, four boys and four girls. Kelly and Kasey traveled from their homes in Colorado, and Kerry and Katie drove up the I-5 freeway from San Diego. A few of my closest friends also joined in the celebration.

As the party was getting under way, I stood and gazed appreciatively on the scene. Our wonderful Golden Retriever, Sedona, was milling about the backyard, sniffing curiously at the tables decked out with white tablecloths, fancy napkins, and party hats. There were colorful clusters of balloons floating above the tables, many of them with references to the over-the-hill gang. Behind the balloons, like a friendly old giant, lolled the great Pacific Ocean, from Dana Point to the Palos Verdes peninsula. A caterer was serving appetizers and a smartly dressed bartender stood ready to supply us with drinks. I was pleased to note that he was armed with a large bottle of Malibu Rum, which is my all-time favorite. All the rituals that mark a major milestone were in place.

Things proceeded nicely up until one single moment that is burned into my memory.

The moment that changed everything.
The moment that nearly ended my relationship.
The moment that nearly depleted my life savings.
The moment that would later have me peering through a howling storm at the ghost of an old woman sitting against the mast of my sailboat.

I had grabbed my youngest grandson, two-year-old Alexander, and pulled him up on my knee. "Let's open some presents, kid." Alex ripped into the wrapping paper with obvious delight, thrilled at the opportunity to shed the pristine bows and claim the center of attention. The first gift he opened was a dozen Titleist golf balls.

Without much forethought, I said, "Alexander, when you turn twenty, we're going to play a lot of golf together!"

And that was when Old Age first came into my life. It really was a presence I could feel, just as if the sneaky ugly bastard had crept across the lawn, laid his heavy cloak over my shoulders and hissed in my ear, "When Alexander is twenty, you will be eighty-two years old!"

Eighty-two years old. Jesus Christ. This lovely party had abruptly lost its glitter. It was hard for me to keep up with the conversations going on around me, as my internal dialogue became the only thing I could hear.

There's decidedly more sand at the bottom of the hourglass than there is at the top. Twenty years will go by in a twinkling. Time speeds up when you're old.

Visions came to me, none of them flattering: juice-stained shirts, an old fart staggering behind a walker, a helpless codger in a wheelchair, an ancient fool bending toward the utterances of the young with his predictable, "Ehh? What's that you say, sonnyboy?"

And golf? Hoo, boy. Playing golf at eighty is not an attractive picture. I had played with some octogenarians before, so I was familiar with how that goes. Here's a bit of science for you: men in their eighties are weak and slow. On one occasion, after I'd hit my drive 270 yards straight down the middle of the fairway, one of my older playing partners had squinted after the ball, waved his hand dismissively and said, "Hell, I don't take vacations that long." I wanted to tell Alex that we might not be playing much golf together when he was twenty after all. Maybe I wouldn't be able to climb out of my wheelchair. Shoot, I might not even remember his name.

I moved through the rest of my birthday celebration in a fog, clammy hands fumbling with the presents, dry mouth barely able to swallow cake, thanking everyone with overly loud parting remarks and gestures as though we were speaking through a layer of Plexiglas. Mind spinning, heart thumping, breath short . . . was this a panic attack?

Hell yes, it was—I ought to know. I have a Master's Degree in psychology. Not that the degree gave me any great insight into my own psyche, nor did it do anything to mitigate what I was feeling. What a wonderful surprise present to myself: my very first panic attack. I had never experienced anything like this before.

"You're okay. You're okay," I kept repeating to myself, then listed:

Excellent health

Beautiful fiancée

Happy and healthy children and grandchildren

Successful career

Every time I checked off another positive aspect of my life (nice golf game, lovely house), it instantly began to diminish and then disintegrate. It was all on the wane, winding down, utterly out of my control.

The awful thoughts continued long after the guests had gone home and the tables had been taken down. Sixty was hitting me hard. It was traumatic, much different from my previous birthdays. At forty and fifty, I had taken cold assessment of how much time I had left to live. But at sixty, it dawned on me for the first time that longevity wasn't so much a concern as the quality of life I would be experiencing in the years to come. The picture of myself doddering in a wheelchair with oatmeal dripping off my chin scared the hell out of me. Over and over in my head, I heard:

"Boy, you only have fifteen, maybe twenty years left . . . what do you want to do with the rest of your life?"

I tried to reason with myself. Everyone hits sixty at some point, if they're lucky!

Join the crowd.

Get in line.

Now it was my turn. *So, suck it up.* But what did that even mean? Go quietly off to the shuffleboard court with no complaining? There was no way I was going to let that happen . . . What I needed now was a new goal; a dream that would allow me to get the most out of my remaining vim and vigor. I needed a challenge and an accomplishment, something that would test me both physically and mentally. Without a *big* one, I feared that I would sink into the grips of depression.

In the following weeks, I was consumed by my search for a new mission. I lay awake at night, racking my brain, frequently being interrupted by a voice yelling at me, "You're quickly running out of time, boy! What do you want to do with the rest of your life?"

My first few ideas were lamely predictable: buy a bigger house, buy a flashy new car, buy *another* Harley. The only problem was that all these were just supporting a more passive lifestyle; *sitting* in my bigger house, in my fancier car, or on my second Harley. This wouldn't get me anywhere, except fatter, slower, more unsteady, and, unfortunately, more prepared for that final sitting-place . . . the wheelchair.

It was pretty astonishing how all of my accomplishments up to that point could so thoroughly shed their significance. Hey, I was the first in my family ever to graduate from college! *Whoopty-doo*. Went to graduate school, raised four daughters, and built my own business from nothing. *Yeah? And . . . ?* In my tortured state, all that striving in my thirties, forties, and fifties amounted to a hill of beans. The view from sixty required a total overhaul.

I then recalled that I had gone through a mild mid-life crisis in my forties. So mild I had all but forgotten it. It was nothing compared to what I was experiencing now, but I had, for a time, felt slightly adrift. At the time, I had taken great comfort in Gail Sheehy's groundbreaking book, *Understanding Men's Passages*, and found it to be a source of wisdom and good counsel. Now I rushed to the closest bookstore and was excited to see that Sheehy had written a sequel, called *New Passages*. Hoping she might have a few more tricks for this old dog, I yanked it off the shelf, found a comfortable chair, and quickly scanned through the table of contents.

Each chapter was dedicated to another decade of life, and Sheehy had used catchy, descriptive titles, like, "Tryout Twenties," "Turbulent Thirties," and so on. I almost fell out of my chair when I saw that the chapter that pertained to me, which was titled "Serene Sixties," no less, was the next-to-last chapter in the book! Another stark reminder of the approaching end.

Just the fact that Sheehy hadn't bothered to write about the eighties, or perhaps that she simply couldn't come up with a snappy phrase for them, basically said it all.

The "Easy Eighties?" I think not.
How about the "Aching Eighties."
The "Ehh, Sonnyboy Eighties."
The "Amen-It's-Over Eighties."
Have to write those down and send them to Sheehy for her inevitable sequel, *The Final Passage*.

I bought the damn book anyway and started taking notes:

- I am now up against a more insidious enemy than any I have ever faced: the incipient depression of aging. I will experience an exciting new barrage of confusing physical symptoms to which I will become increasingly susceptible.
- I may slip from benign stagnation into depression; slip further into isolation; dig myself into a tunnel of despair.
- Brain cells don't die off; rather, they shrink or grow dormant in old age, particularly from *lack of stimulation and challenge*.
- It becomes more difficult to lie to yourself as you get older, the late afternoon of life.

Looking over my notes now, it's obvious that I wasn't planning to go out quietly. I was determined to make my sixties the most rewarding decade of my life. Forget serene, I wanted spectacular. For the last thirty years, my identity had been wrapped up almost entirely in my four daughters and my work.

Now it was my turn.

I no longer needed to perform for others; I would answer only to myself. My new mantra would be, "Think young, stay young." If you're not busy living, you're busy dying. Go out and live your dream.

Ah, but what dream? Every day, I was hounded by the very question I had asked my dear girls, lo, those many years ago: "What do you want to be when you grow up?" I couldn't happily blurt out, "Firefighter! Teacher! Veterinarian!" as they had done. I became consumed with the question, "If you could do anything, anything at all, what would it be?" Whatever it was, it had to constitute an impressive legacy for my children and grandchildren to look proudly upon. *Something grand*, I told myself.

I decided to do some on-paper brainstorming. Unwilling to accept age limitations as a factor, and hell-bent on including all possibilities, for fear of overlooking the truly thrilling ones, I allowed my thoughts to run wild. Here's a partial list, starting with the most egregious long shots and slowly working toward the most practical:

> Okay, so I'll admit it: I had always hoped to play football for the Detroit Lions.
>
>> Not gonna happen (*Sixty-Year-Old So-So Athlete Tops NFL Draft Pick, film at 11:00*). But it flitted onto the list for a nano-second, glimmered there bravely, and then died away like the sorry thing it was.
>
> Take acting classes in Hollywood and become an actor.
>
>> In fact, I had done a bit of modeling and acting for a few years now, so this one wasn't terribly far-fetched. Only thing was my fantasy wasn't about playing the granddad in a TV commercial for Cheerios; it involved my standing on stage holding a golden statuette. Not bloody likely. . . .
>
> Improve my golf game and join the PGA senior tour.
>
>> Yeah, this one was kind of like acting. I had a little talent, but did I have that much talent?
>
> Move to Hawaii, buy a small farm, and raise exotic tropical flowers.
>
>> Sure, never mind that I didn't even like to do my own yard work or that living in Hawaii would mean even greater separation from my family. . . .
>
> Go back to school and finish my Ph.D.
>
>> For what? So I could wear it after my name like a medal?
>
> Learn a foreign language.
>
>> Certainly a commendable aspiration. But I pictured Alex saying to one of his friends after I was gone, "My grandfather was a remarkable achiever. At the age of sixty—*sixty*, I tell you— he . . . learned a little French."

This most certainly wasn't easy. Whatever I was seeking had to be big enough to challenge my very identity as a human being. Some of these dreams were too big . . . some were too small. Like Goldilocks before me, I needed to come up with one that was just right.

I was rather surprised when Sally informed me that this dilemma I was dealing with—onset of the Serene Sixties—is not unique to men. "Think about it," she said. "You feel like you've devoted so much of yourself to career and family? What sixty-year-old woman do you know who hasn't done that? We all question the sacrifices we've made and wonder whether it's all been worth it. We all look at the time we have left and ask ourselves what's still possible." It was comforting to hear that she understood where I was coming from . . . and yet, something about the three-quarter-life crisis makes a body feel very, very alone in its anguish.

· · ·

One evening, Sally and I were driving along the Pacific Coast Highway on our way home to Laguna Beach after having dinner in Corona del Mar. We stopped at Crystal Cove State Park to watch the sun set on the ocean. As we walked along the beach, holding hands and gazing at the radiant orange ball of fire slowly slipping into the water, I was struck with an epiphany. Sail around the world. *We will sail around the world!*

I stopped in my tracks, overcome with a childlike rush of enthusiasm. "I've got it. I have the answer," I blurted out, reaching for Sally's hands. "We'll sail around the world, honey!"

Sally looked searchingly into my eyes for a moment, and then burst out laughing. "Are you crazy? We're certainly *not* going to sail around the world. You know I get seasick. What would we do with Sedona? Besides, it's much too dangerous. We could die out there!"

Duly noted.

She had raised some excellent points. A slight change in wording was required.

I will sail around the world!

Truth be told, our relationship of seven years had reached a tenuous state. Things were shaky at best. We were growing apart and not doing anything to help put the love back into our lives. I knew we were in trouble when one night she said, "You don't look at me anymore when we kiss." Uh-oh.

Sally would be my fifth marriage. My first wife was my college sweetheart. She was eighteen years old and I was twenty-two when we found out that she was pregnant! "Oh, my God! How did this happen?" Well, it happened in the front seat of my 1956 Ford convertible. I remember it like it was yesterday. It was the first and only time we "did it" . . . in that car, anyway.

I was on a full-ride football scholarship, just finishing my second year at Trinidad State College, a small two-year school in Colorado. In 1962, if a girl got pregnant out of wedlock, it was still considered an almighty scandalous affair. Oh, and have I mentioned that her father was the school's president? Well we decided not to tell anyone that she was "PG." We were married in the living room of the president's home. Looking back now as the father of four daughters, I see how lucky I was that her old man didn't shoot me right there in his house. I was just another smart-ass football player and she was his baby.

The marriage lasted eighteen years and we had four beautiful daughters.

My next three marriages were all short, lasting a combined total of four years. I found it easy to fall in love, but nearly impossible to stay that way. For the next eight years, I subscribed to a rigorous program of "love 'em and leave 'em." Once the laughter stopped, I was gone in a flash.

Then Sally came into my life. I was instantly struck by her beauty: shoulder-length blonde hair, deep blue eyes, and a smile that could melt the hardest of hearts. I thought I was looking at Christie Brinkley or Cheryl Tiegs.

Sally had one son, Jeff, a college student at the time we met. Her husband of twenty-three years had died tragically in a single-car accident one year earlier. She was having a difficult time dealing with the sudden death of her high school sweetheart; when she confided in me that she had contemplated ending her own life, I was deeply shocked and dismayed. My heart hurt for her. She needed some help to work through her crisis, and with my past experience as a psychologist, I felt I might be able to provide some friendly—though unofficial—counseling.

Over the next few months, what had begun as a purely platonic friendship gradually slipped into romance. I was falling in love with this beautiful woman. It wasn't just her stunning good looks that drew me in, but rather a magnificence that was not visible to the naked eye. It was the depth of her character, her inner beauty that captured my respect and affection.

After a year of dating, we took what seemed to us to be the next logical step in our relationship: we bought a puppy together. He was a fine-looking Golden Retriever, and we named him Sedona after the town in Arizona, known famously as a place of spiritual healing. The next step was to move in together, and we bought a new home in Newport Beach.

After we had been living together for two years, we took a vacation in Yosemite National Park. One afternoon, we took a long hike culminating in a magnificent view of El Capitan. As Sally was gazing out at the remarkable edifice, I dropped to one knee, took her hand, and said, "I'm the happiest man alive. Would you make me even happier and be my wife?"

With tears in her eyes, she accepted.

Hiking back to the cabin, I asked her if she would like to pick the month for the wedding. "Sure," she said.

"And would you mind too much if I were to pick the year?"

She looked at me with a deep sense of uncertainty, then she started to laugh, and said, "Sure, that will be fine, but don't think for one moment about getting out of this commitment."

So I did—and it only took me ten years.

In 1998, we bought an older home in Laguna Beach that sat above Bluebird Canyon. We were enthralled with the beauty of the place, particularly the broad vista over the Pacific Ocean.

But as we would soon come to understand, we hadn't simply purchased a house; we'd bought a home with a great view, but in dire need of a total remodeling job.

We plunged into a massive renovation. As anyone who has experienced remodeling an older home can tell you, it puts a tremendous strain on any relationship, and Sally and I were no exception. It was the classic fixer-upper nightmare: the project took twice as long as anticipated and cost twice as much as we had planned. The stress of it all was absolutely tearing us apart.

Instead of enjoying an evening glass of wine on the patio as we had once been accustomed to doing, we would stand and argue about bathroom tile or crown molding. One of us always thought the other was being too extravagant, too stingy, too lackadaisical, or too driven. Meanwhile, behind us, the ocean view that had once taken away our breath away just hung there dully, like cheap wallpaper. The laughter stopped, which, as you'll recall, had always been my cue to get out of Dodge. Even our physical desire for each other had waned; where before I had felt euphoria in her embrace, now there was a bland ambivalence. I had lost that "want to reach out and touch her" feeling.

Then, as life would have it, on top of the remodeling project and the souring of our relationship came my personal crisis of turning sixty. I desperately needed a change of scenery, but could our relationship survive my absence? As soon as I had dreamed up the adventure of sailing around the world, I became so obsessed with its details that it was as if my absence had already begun. By making the choice to pursue the dream that I believed would preserve my sanity, I was putting our relationship in grave jeopardy. I knew it, and Sally knew it.

It would have been so much simpler if she had just agreed to go with me. What could have been better for our love than heading out to sea together? I pictured us poring over charts, enjoying morning coffee on deck while dolphins cavorted off the beam. But the reality was that she would have been an unwilling companion, barfing over the transom half the time and, no doubt, hating me for putting her through it all. The only way she would ever venture offshore was if I had a 200-foot mega-yacht with a crew of twenty, and even then, I'd have to do something about her seasickness.

Can your heart tell you one thing if your gut tells you something else? I had had enough of failed relationships and was committed to working things out with Sally. And yet, something told me that I could go out into the world like Ulysses, do my voyaging, come home, and patch things up with my Penelope . . . and, in the end, be a better person for it.

I had found my dream of a lifetime and was making up my mind to fulfill it, with or without Sally.

One night in early April I got up out of bed and walked down into the backyard. Before me sprawled the Pacific, stretching to the other side of the world, teeming with adventure and challenge. I stood there letting all my conflicting feelings wash over me. Then I took a deep breath, and said out loud: "I will sail around the world!"

The dream was on.

• • •

CHAPTER 2

Three Good Reasons to Just Say No

What lies behind us and what lies before us are tiny matters compared to what lies within us.

—Ralph Waldo Emerson

1. *"But you've never sailed past Catalina Island,"* Sally said.

That was an excellent point. My longest sail offshore was just twenty-six miles over to the island. Run a marathon and you've covered more mileage than I'd ever managed in a boat. I had, of course, spent years sailing up and down the coast. Up to Santa Barbara, Long Beach down to Dana Point, I had even harbor-hopped down to San Diego; but bluewater sailing—leaving land far behind and striking out for a different continent—is another animal altogether. I didn't need Sally to remind me of my inexperience, as there was already a voice in my head, plenty loud, saying at regular intervals, *"Boy, have you lost it? You have never sailed out of sight of land. How do you think you're going to sail around the world?"*

Something grand, I answered. Something grand.

• • •

When I was a young man, sailboats never interested me. I liked my watercraft loud, fast, and galloping with horsepower.

15

For a brief period in my—prime—Tryout Twenties, I made my living as a professional water-skier, performing in four shows a day, six days a week. Private yachts would anchor nearby to watch the show, and occasionally, some of the spectators would wave us over to their boats for a drink. My Texas friend world-champion skier Bob Nathey and I would scan the various boats to see which one had the prettiest young women on board. On one particular evening, after our last show of the day, a small group of spectators invited us onto their sailboat.

This was not your average beater. It was a sleek, 100-foot sloop with a dark blue hull, teak deck, and all the wood trim varnished to a high sheen. The mast loomed like the Chrysler Building, stretching so high you'd strain your neck gazing upward to find its top.

The owner pushed a Scotch and soda into my hand, asked for autographs, and barraged me with questions. "What's it like to ski barefoot? Isn't it dangerous to fly through the air on those kites?" I tried my best to answer his questions, but as we slowly motored out of the harbor into Lake Michigan, I was becoming more and more preoccupied with the boat.

Two crew members hoisted a mammoth mainsail, then a headsail up the towering mast. As the sails filled with wind, the yacht began to move differently through the water. I had expected moving under sail to feel just like motoring, but it didn't. Something utterly magical happens when a boat's sails are trimmed just right in a good wind: the boat heels over onto one side and slices through the water effortlessly, silently. It is the difference between pushing and being pulled. It is as if, unknown to you, the universe around you has always been just slightly out of whack, but now things have clicked into place and are humming along as intended. This sailboat had transported me to another world, where elegance, beauty, and grace replaced noise and speed. That night, under the stars out on Lake Michigan, I began my lifelong love affair with sailing. Well, to be fair, it was more of a love affair with coastal cruising.

Okay, yes, a love affair with day sailing.

2. *"You learned to sail on lakes. How are you going to handle the open ocean?"* my sister asked.

It's true that I learned to sail on Lake Lansing; but in my defense, it kicked up some decent breezes from time to time. As a junior at Michigan State University, I signed up for some sailing lessons. Before we were even allowed to step foot on any sailboat, we had to memorize pages and pages of nautical nomenclature and tie six different types of knots. I didn't give a hoot about the difference between a rudder and a keel, and learning six knots seemed excessive. What's wrong with one good knot? But it was the only way they'd teach me to sail, so I muddled through.

At last, one fine Saturday morning, I was given my first real sailing lesson. It was in a twelve-foot, two-person Snipe. The instructor walked me through a dizzying array of details, and I tried to listen, but I figured I really only needed to remember two things: keep wind in the sail and keep your hand on the tiller.

The next day I went back for my second lesson, but the instructor didn't show. Perhaps he'd forgotten about me. No matter. I felt sure that I could handle this little rig on my own. I pushed the boat into the water, ran up the sail, and there was really nothing to it. I was sailing all by myself! For the first half hour, the wind was very light and I had no trouble maneuvering the tippy little craft around Lake Lansing. But then as I approached the middle of the lake, the wind picked up and the boat began to behave erratically. The mainsheet—the line (on a sailboat, there are only *lines, sheets,* and *halyards*, no ropes) attached to the boom and used to control the mainsail—became taut and mercilessly heavy from the pressure of the wind on the sail. It was getting hard for me to hold on while keeping my other hand on the tiller. The line kept slipping through my fingers, chafing and burning the skin on my hand. I could feel blisters forming, but I hung on. The more pressure I felt on the line, the more I tightened my grip and the harder I pulled back, determined not to let the mainsheet get away. Finally, a bigger gust of wind came along and I hauled on the mainsheet with all my strength. In a split second, the Snipe tipped over and dropped me into the middle of the lake. I bobbed up to survey the damage and realized that I still held the mainsheet clenched firmly in my fist.

Ah, grasshopper. One cannot change the direction of the wind. But you can trim your damn sails.

3. *"You don't have anything to prove,"* my children said.

They were wrong about that.

If you've read firsthand accounts of solo sailors who have circumnavigated the globe, it's impossible not to be deeply impressed by their fortitude, stamina, and determination. My first, and still my favorite, is Joshua Slocum's *Sailing Alone Around the World*. Though published in 1899, it remains fascinating to this day, perhaps in part that the author wasn't aided along by GPS systems, high-tech navigation equipment, weather reports, or a radio. Slocum covered a distance of over 46,000 miles, relying exclusively on his own ingenuity and good common sense.

Another favorite of mine is Robert N. Manry's *Tinkerbell: The Story of the Smallest Boat Ever to Cross the Atlantic Nonstop*. Manry traversed the Atlantic Ocean in a thirteen-foot boat, or "miniature sloop," as he called it, which is like riding Niagara Falls in a barrel and calling it a rudimentary elevator. It must have been hell of an experience, yet Manry was able to write about the voyage in a way that made it seem romantic. A couple of lines in particular left an everlasting impression on me: "To me, nothing made by man is more beautiful than a sailboat under way in fine weather, and to be on that sailboat is to be as close to heaven as I expect to get. It is unalloyed happiness."

While I agreed wholeheartedly with this sentiment, I wasn't at all sure that I had what it took to accomplish something of that magnitude. My God, I'd been an insurance agent for the past twenty-five years. My two favorite leisure activities were walking the dog and putting golf balls. Was I in denial? Was I really more the type to slip quietly into my Serene Sixties?

No, no.

One man's serenity is another man's stagnation. The more everyone tried to talk me out of this "crazy" idea, the more I became committed to it. I reverted to my arguments until they were entrenched in my consciousness: I had spent my life fulfilling the constant expectations and demands put upon a husband and father of four, always working hard to earn enough money to support my family. I had spent my whole life building up my career with the hope that I could create a better life for my four daughters than I had growing up, which, as far as I know, is every father's dream. There's nothing wrong with that. It's how things are supposed to work. But after that usually comes freedom.

I thought a lot about the grandeur of the undertaking. It's true that something burned within me to make my family proud of the old man, whether they thought I had anything to prove or not. In the history of the world, only about 300 adventurers have ever completed a solo navigation of the globe. I wanted to join the ranks of the extraordinary, and I suppose in retrospect, that had something to do with my less-than-glamorous upbringing.

When I was a boy in Michigan, my parents both worked full-time jobs and still, they could barely make ends meet. My mother was a secretary at the Ford Motor Company and my father worked on the factory floor. If I wanted a new pair of shoes or a baseball glove, I had to earn the money myself. We weren't poor, but my upbringing would be considered austere, or thrifty at best.

During the summer, I would wake up at 6:00 AM, ride my bike three miles to the Washtenaw Country Club, and spend the day caddying for wealthy members. On a good day, I would carry two bags for eighteen holes, earning eight dollars, including tip. After caddying all day, I would ride my bike home and begin my second job, delivering the *Ann Arbor News*. At dusk, I would pedal home, eat some dinner, climb into bed, and start it all over again the next day. I suppose one of the things that I was looking forward to was touching the shore ground after my circumnavigation, and saying to myself, "you've come a long way from Michigan, kid." I also thought it would set a great example for my kids and grandkids: if I could get this far from my humble upbringing, think how far you can go, considering how much more you've been given.

My parents taught me the value of hard work and I never strayed from it a day in my life. That work ethic was no doubt fueling my desire to fulfill this dream as well. I wasn't ready to stop working hard yet . . . I had more work to do. But that was only part of it. I knew that sailing around the world, alone, would be a grueling task. It would afford me the opportunity to test myself, rely on myself, and answer to nobody but myself. That was both the best and worst part of it. In family life, we're constantly sharing, negotiating, compromising; particularly once you have children, your own wants and needs plummet and occasionally fall off the priority list. I don't begrudge this tendency; it's the way families generally function. But damn it, I was running out of time.

It was my turn to live the dream.

I was awash with enthusiasm and a sense of total freedom. I was ready for an adventure on my own terms. Just thinking about it made me start to feel younger.

CHAPTER 3

Desperately Seeking
Slip Appeal

Ships are the nearest things to dreams that hands have ever made.

—Robert N. Rose

O NCE I'D MADE MY DECISION to sail around the world, the next challenge was obvious: finding the right boat. I had purchased five sailboats before, my very first being a nineteen-foot Lightning class sloop, a family day sailor, used extensively (but exclusively) on Michigan lakes. It was the boat that my daughters grew up sailing on. I currently owned a thirty-foot Catalina sloop, moored in Newport Beach, California. It was perfect for day trips to Catalina Island, but was hardly sufficient for bluewater sailing. Unfortunately, she would have to go. I was lucky to sell her quickly for $24,000 to a person with no three-quarter-life crisis and no quixotic aspiration to sail farther than Catalina Island.

I spent hours researching boats on the Internet, slowly building up a list of criteria essential to any "offshore" vessel. First and foremost, the boat needed to be stable . . . very stable. Some boats rock and roll more violently than others; some can't handle dramatic wind gusts and breaking waves; some boats, when they're knocked down, won't come back upright. I wanted a smooth ride, a vessel that could take a few on the chin; one that could protect me from my inexperience.

In Southern California, the market is flooded with light, cheap, and fast sailboats, but these weren't in any way suitable for a long voyage. Besides, I was totally turned off by these plastic Tupperware-style boats. I wanted something with heft and dignity, worthy of my ambition to establish a lasting legacy. Oh, I wanted her to be swift, but in a let's-get-the-hell-out-of-this-storm way, not in a showy SoCal hey-babe-check-me-out style.

And then there was ease of handling, since I anticipated sailing alone much of the time. So the checklist went about like this:

- Stability
- Price
- Speed
- Ease of handling

Oh, and one more thing . . .

I'll admit that, even at the advanced age of sixty, I needed her to be pretty. It just wasn't in me to sail around the world with an ugly gal. She had to have "slip appeal."

Right away I was faced with a serious case of sticker shock. I gazed longingly at the new boats with all their bells and whistles, and then crashed back down to earth. If I bought a brand-new boat, I'd be making payments on it for the rest of my life. So I switched gears and began the hunt for an older boat in excellent condition. My price range spanned from $50,000 to $75,000.

And just like that, the thrill was gone. Most of the boats available for $50,000 are—how do I put this nicely—a mess. I started to call them the Dry-Rot Wonders. Everywhere I turned, it seemed like there was a fungus among us. I wasn't in the market for a fixer-upper, but nothing else was available in my price range. Something had to give, so I upped the ante to $100,000 . . . and then things got interesting.

When you get right down to it, I was dating a fleet of boats. I would find a good-looking girl online, get all dressed up to meet her, feel the butterflies as I hurried to our rendezvous. But again and again, the entire date would be dominated by her all-too-obvious flaws: dry rot, decay, too large, too small, too old. Suddenly, I'd get that sinking feeling in my gut, make a lame excuse (I've got to get up early in the morning . . .), and drag myself back home in a funk. Then I'd get back online in a day or two, check out another really good-looking girl, and get my hopes up all over again. Over the course of six weeks, I had kissed a lot of hulls, but nobody was good enough to bring home to meet the family.

I was getting so frustrated by not finding the right boat that I hired a yacht broker, and he called one evening to say they had just listed a boat that might be perfect for me. Reluctantly this time, I drove to San Diego, expecting more disappointment.

This was love at first sight. I saw her sitting in her slip and knew in an instant, that my search had come to an end. She was graceful, elegant; with a cropped stern and a narrow clipper bow. This Bayfield 40 was designed by Ted Gozzard, a devotee of L. Francis Herreshoff, the most famous naval architect of his time. The sun on the water reflected off her gorgeous black hull. Her topsides were white, with just the right amount of teak. She boasted a broad bowsprit (a forward extension for adding sails beyond the bow) with a five-foot teak platform stretching out over the water. As I walked into the cabin, I was drawn to the stately feel of its lush mahogany woodwork, hand-finished by Amish craftsmen. It felt more like a comfortable den than the cabin of a boat. With a full keel and an incredibly thick fiberglass hull, she was a no-nonsense ocean-going vessel with class and style.

Like so many love affairs, this one included a touch of serendipity. The boat had been built in Bayfield, Canada, on the shores of Lake Huron. I had spent many hours sailing on Lake Huron as a younger man, and this little detail mattered to me.

Built in 1986, she was thirteen years old, but seemed so much younger. In fact, I told myself, she was practically new. For starters, she was never used in Michigan winters, meaning that the boat was only in the water six months out of the year. So, you could knock off half her age right there; let's now call her six years old. Then there was the fact that she had only sailed in fresh water, never corrosive saltwater, which made her even younger; let's now call her three years old. Add to that the fact that her previous owners had taken exceptionally good care of her, using the boat as one might use a weekend cottage. Hell, once I counted all the ways she seemed younger than her actual years, I had practically convinced myself that this boat was brand-spanking-new. Give me enough time to think about it, and I could convince you (or, more importantly, convince myself) that for all practical purposes, she would be built sometime next year.

This sailboat could smell the ocean and was chomping at the bit for big water.

I made an offer, the owners counter-offered, and we agreed on a final sale price of $111,000. After completing the sea trial (where the potential buyer sails the boat with the yacht broker before making the final decision to purchase) and a short shake-down sail with the sales staff, we consummated the deal. It gave me great pleasure to realize I was now the owner of a yacht, a beautiful oceangoing sailboat. Not bad for a paperboy from Ypsilanti.

• • •

I've often heard it said that a boat is a hole in the water, surrounded by wood, into which one pours money. I had already blown my budget, and I knew that this was just the beginning. Heavy expenditures would be required to get her properly equipped to head offshore. Since her previous owners had sailed only seldom, on inland lakes, she needed a long list of expensive gear, installed by very expensive workers, before she would be ready for the kind of adventure I had in mind. I rationalized this problem by telling myself that all my equipment would be brand-new and I would have the luxury of customizing all the gear on board. Wasn't that a lot better than having a boat fully equipped with old, out-dated gear that would most likely malfunction or break while out at sea? At the time, I had no idea just how enormous the expense would be, nor how excruciatingly long it would take to equip my new boat. Love is blind, and I was naïve and in love.

The first night after I took ownership, I slept on board my new big boat with Sedona. Sally was conspicuously absent. She did not share my enthusiasm about this new addition to our family, which she correctly interpreted as a signal of the seriousness of my intentions. Oh, well. At least Sedona was excited.

The next morning, I had the urge to take this black beauty out for a sail. I was a bit intimidated by her size. She was easily the largest boat I had ever owned or sailed by myself. But hey, what kind of guy wins the fair bride and then chickens out on the wedding night?

As I stood at the helm, the boat seemed comically enormous, like an aircraft carrier or the *Queen Mary*. How in the world was I going to get this mammoth creature out of the harbor without looking like a damn fool? An irritating little voice in my head was saying, "*Old dude? You may be out of your league here.*" The thought occurred to me that I might want to find an experienced sailor to go with me, but it's just not my style to ask someone for help unless I really need it. There would be nobody to help me on my voyage, so why prolong the inevitable? I needed to learn how to handle this big mother all by myself.

The first challenge was to back her out of the slip and into a narrow passageway filled with other boats without hitting anything hard—like, you know, one of those other boats. Most large sailboats don't do well in reverse and are near impossible to back up in a straight line. This was most certainly true of my new baby; she tracked backward like a drunken elephant, sliding to the right, and then for no apparent reason, lurching in the opposite direction. I backed her up slowly, painstakingly, as though I were practicing docking a space shuttle to the International Space Station. I figured I still might hit something, but if I was moving slowly, the damage would be less catastrophic.

I was relieved that I had my trusty first mate, Sedona, on board. He was perfectly oblivious (or pretended to be, bless him) to the signs of humiliation I was giving off—flushed cheeks, cursing, and mumbling under my breath. He dashed over to his favorite position in the cockpit and stood bolt upright with his tail swishing back and forth, inhaling the salt air with gusto. He looked as proud as I had ever seen him. Here was a dog who knew how to focus on the important things in life. Sure, we were motoring around the marina like rank amateurs, but for him, all that side-to-side movement simply broadened the view and brought new scents in the air.

Once I finally (somewhat) figured out what I was doing, we forged ahead into San Diego Bay. It's a spectacular place for a sail, surrounded by luxury hotels, marinas, restaurants, and active naval bases. The liveliness of the Bay offers all kinds of visual distractions: there's always a steady stream of Navy aircraft taking off and landing at the North Island Naval Air Station, huge warships crisscross the water, and every imaginable private vessel both large and small contributes to a tableau of picturesque bustle. I had sailed in San Diego Bay before and always enjoyed the variety; but today, all these distractions seemed threatening rather than entertaining. I was a sitting duck, and every other vessel on the water was a missile headed my direction.

I took some deep breaths and looked over at Sedona for moral support. It was critical that I gain confidence in my ability to handle the boat alone. Time to hoist the sails. Running up the mainsail without a crew member to assist, without an autopilot to steer the boat, with sweaty hands, all while attempting to maintain a steady course in crowded waters, is quite complicated. The boat inevitably drifted off course during the process, so my job was to move about as quickly as humanly possible before getting into any trouble. After checking to be sure that no other boats were nearby, I positioned the mainsheet and the main halyard (lines used to trim and hoist the mainsail, respectively), then darted to the mast in fast-forward, like one of those guys in an old black-and-white slapstick movie. Using a winch, I cranked like mad to start lifting the mainsail up and into position. It was a humongous sail, much larger than any I'd ever handled before, and it seemed to take forever to reach the top of the forty-five-foot mast. I cranked and cranked, looking wildly around for boat traffic, as the sail inched up into place.

Once I had the mainsail secured, I scrambled back to the cockpit, trimmed in the mainsheet, grabbed the helm, and watched with satisfaction as the wind filled up the huge sail. We were sailing! I unfurled the first of two headsails from the cockpit, secured its sheet, put both hands on the helm, and stood in place for a moment to assess our position. Sedona had settled onto a boat cushion, enjoying the ride, and looked up at me with a big smile on his face (Yes, Golden Retrievers do smile). His expression said, "Good job. Way to go, man, I'm proud of you." All at once, the anxiety-fueled adrenaline rush gave way to a sense of exhilaration as I savored the feeling of my new boat cutting effortlessly across the bay. I was flooded with an enormous pride, like a poor student who's just aced a test. I wanted to shout at all the nearby boats, "Hey, look at me! I am sailing my new big boat all by myself!"

But my elation was short-lived, quickly replaced by panic when I realized we were mighty close to shore and rapidly running out of water to maneuver in. My beautiful new boat was making directly for the rocks in front of the Hilton hotel. I needed to come about (swing the front of the boat around to take the wind on the opposite side) immediately to avoid treating the Hilton guests to the spectacle of a hundred-thousand-dollar yacht disemboweling itself as they sipped their morning coffee. No matter. Coming about is the simplest maneuver in sailing. Summoning my jauntiest, most nautical tone of voice, I shouted the traditional commands to Sedona, "Prepare to come about. Coming about. Helms alee!"

Like I said, coming about is pretty much the first thing a sailor learns. You give a sharp turn to the helm so that the bow moves across and through the wind, release the sheets so the boom can swing to the opposite side of the boat, then trim the sheets to pick up wind and sail in the new direction. I had, quite literally, accomplished this simple feat thousands of times in my life. So, I laid the wheel over to leeward and released the sheets. The bow began to move across the wind just as God intended, but it somehow didn't make it all the way around. Instead, the boat stopped short, with its lovely teak bowsprit pointing directly into the wind.

Here's a fun fact for all you non-boaters out there: sailboats can't travel directly into the wind. They can travel *generally* in the direction of the wind, but not right into it, which is why, if you've ever sat and watched a boat beating to windward, you'll have noticed that it made its way via a relentlessly zigzagging course, called tacking. The idea is to sail as close to the wind as physics will allow; but it's useless to face the wind head-on.

Here's another nugget for you: a sailboat, by default, *wants* to point directly into the wind. If you're really observant and you've ever passed a marina on a windy day, you'll have noticed that all the moored boats (the ones attached to buoys and not docks), are pointing directly into the wind like so many weathervanes. So, a windward orientation is the boat's posture of greatest inertia. Getting stuck with your boat pointing into the wind is, therefore, something of a problem.

There's even a colorful nautical term for this little predicament. It's called being caught "in irons." You can't steer the boat out of the situation, because you've surrendered control of your vessel to the wind. When a sailboat gets caught in this position, it's a truly pathetic sight. The hitherto graceful boat becomes suddenly motionless, and then ungainly, drifting with the tide like a derelict as the sails begin flapping violently in the breeze, making a hellacious racket; the captain panics and feverishly attempts to extricate himself from this situation before *everyone* on shore starts to point and laugh.

I had been caught in the irons before while navigating my smaller boats, which wasn't a big deal. You'd just grab the boom (the cross-piece at the bottom of the mainsail), manually angle the sail out away from the boat until it grabs some wind and the boat gains some momentum, and then head off on your merry way. But this twenty-two-ton boat had her own ideas about being pushed around by hand. My attempts to strong-arm her into submission failed miserably . . . she wouldn't budge. My arms quickly grew exhausted by my attempts to backwind her enormous mainsail as we drew ever closer to the jumble of rocks in front of the hotel. "Oh, crap," I thought. "First time I take my boat for a sail and I'm going to crash her on the rocks." The next few minutes passed in a split second that took about a year. My heart was pumping so hard I could feel it slamming against the inside of my chest; my mouth was so dry that I couldn't have spat to save my life.

I reckoned that I must have been overlooking some long-forgotten technique, so I hastily scanned my mental inventory of sailing tricks, but came up completely empty-handed. "Christ," I thought. "How am I going to sail around the world if I can't even handle being in a peaceful bay?" I'd have to think about that one another day; right now, the rocks were closing in fast. So I did what all self-respecting sailors dread: I turned the key, fired up the diesel engine, and motored the hell out of there.

Running under the power of the engine, I recovered my composure and got us out far enough into the bay to confidently resume the sailing portion of the day's agenda. I cut the engine and turned to Sedona. "Take two," I said. He looked at me as if I were a champion, which was exactly what I needed.

We moved easily across the bay in a pleasant ten-knot blow from the west in the direction of North Island. I could see that we were once again fast approaching the shore line, so I prepared to come about sooner this time, leaving myself a much larger cushion of open water. I glanced over at Sedona. "Okay, big boy," I said, with too much tremor in my voice to be anticipating such a simple maneuver. "We're going to try this again. You'd better hang on." He looked up at me, cheerful as ever, and thumped his tail on the seat cushion.

I eased the big wheel to leeward, and the bow of the boat reacted nicely, cutting across the wind. I began to smile broadly, like the biggest idiot in the village, and all at once the boat stopped her shift in direction and came to a standstill, her nose pointing stubbornly into the wind. The sails began luffing thunderously, as if to alert everyone in the bay: *Hey! Over here! Check out the total dumbass at the helm. He's caught in irons . . . again!* I worked the sheets frantically, pulling one line after another, trying to capture some wind in the sails, and desperately hoping she would move off from center.

Not a chance.

I scanned the shore to estimate how much distance remained between us and the naval station and was relieved to see that we were in no immediate danger of running aground. But as I turned back to the boat, I was horrified to see the churning whitewater bow wake of the aircraft carrier USS *Ronald Reagan* bearing down on us with incredible speed. At that point, I mentally retracted any comparisons I'd made between my new boat and an aircraft carrier. She was a raindrop and it was a hurricane. This ship was 1,092 feet long . . . mine was forty. The *Reagan* weighed in at 97,000 tons . . . my boat weighed twenty-two. The carrier had 5,600 personnel on board . . . my crew was me and a Golden Retriever. The ship cost $4.5 billion . . . my boat had broken the bank at $111K. Was I by any chance outmatched?

The gunmetal gray hull bore down on us like an avalanche. Sedona's relaxed, supportive attitude had vanished; now he exuded fear from the pads of his paws to the roots of his fangs. Instead of congratulating me, he was saying, "Get us the fuck out of here, you madman!" There was no time for me to panic and no time for sailing lessons. I turned the key to the diesel engine, dropped the gearshift into forward, and got the hell out of that aircraft carrier's path.

For a half an hour afterward, my hands and knees wouldn't stop shaking. Drops of sweat slid down my forehead and into my eyes. My tongue felt like it was made out of peanut butter, and my ego was severely, severely bruised. Good God. I was a skier who boasts that he'll race down K2 but keeps falling down on the bunny hill. It felt like I'd let the boat down. Here she'd been tethered to a quiet existence on lakes her whole life; she finally gets an opportunity to sail with the big boys, and I can't even turn her around without throwing her into harm's way. As honeymoons go, this was a total dumpster fire.

Then, I had the feeling that she might be trying to communicate with me. Yes, I was her new owner, but that didn't mean I was in command. She was showing me that she needed to be treated with proper respect—which meant advanced sailing skills. In order to gain her good graces, I would have to dramatically improve my chops.

It was time to go home. I'd had enough excitement for one day and I wanted to quit while my boat was still in one piece. We made it back to the slip without further incident and Sedona bounded triumphantly onto the dock like we'd just won the America's Cup. Forgiveness . . . just like that. There's a reason for the expression "man's best friend."

As time passed, the day's events seemed less disastrous. After all, the boat sailed like a dream . . . when she was trimmed properly and she had wind in her sails. All of the problems were purely a result of operator error. She and I would get along just fine sailing around the world—*with a little work on my part.*

CHAPTER 4

. . .

King of Provisions

Whenever your preparations for the sea are poor, the sea worms in and finds the problems.

—Francis Stokes

I SET A DEPARTURE DATE of May 15 and began readying myself and my boat for the voyage of a lifetime. It was time to get us all dressed up, because we definitely had someplace to go. But before we set out, the first thing my boat needed was a new name.

At the time I made my purchase, the vessel was called *Black Knight*. She had a dramatic, pitch-black hull, but I couldn't see myself cruising around the world in a *Black Knight*. I challenged my daughters to a name-that-boat contest. Kerry suggested we name her *Sundance*, a motion that Katie seconded. She said she liked to imagine the boat dancing in the sun as it sailed over the ocean. For my part, I had always loved *Butch Cassidy and the Sundance Kid*; Butch was full of crazy ideas, and Sundance was always ready for action. So *Sundance* and I became the founding members of our own Hole-in-the-Water Gang.

Next, we needed a designated hailing port. A boat owner can select any hailing port he pleases within the United States; technically, it doesn't even have to be a port. It doesn't even have to be near the water, for that matter. The Coast Guard simply requires each owner to register a specific locale to assist in vessel identification, if it comes to that.

I chose Aspen, Colorado, and had those words emblazoned on my boat beneath its new name. For many years, my family had lived in a small town near Aspen, and the place eventually came to feel like home to us. Besides, I've always loved a good joke, and this choice of hailing port became a constant source of amusement for me. To strangers in new ports, we were "*Sundance*, out of Aspen, Colorado." I can't tell you how many times people would see the hailing port, think hard for a minute, and then ask, "How'd you get here from Aspen? Wasn't it a difficult sail?"

"Oh, yes," I'd answer. "Getting through the Rockies is a bear . . ."

The amount of gear required to get *Sundance* ready for blue-water passage was mind-boggling. Long gone were the days of navigation via sextants and dead reckoning; I loaded up on all the latest gadgetry and instrumentation. Here's but a small sampling of my new gear:

- Two autopilots
- Radar system
- Radar deflector (to help other boats' radar systems detect my presence)
- Single-side-band radio (to communicate with ship-to-shore radio stations)
- VHF radio (to summon rescue or communicate with harbors, marinas, and other vessels)
- Life raft (we all know what *that's* used for, and the less said the better)
- A 406 MH2 EPIRB (Emergency Positioning-Indicating Radio Beacon, so the rescue crew can locate me before I sink)
- Instruments that track vessel speed and water depth; masthead sensor (measures wind direction and speed)
- Anchor windlass (to raise and lower the anchor)
- Two large anchors with chain rode
- Running rigging (the lines needed to trim the sails)
- Eight new large batteries

- Five solar panels to charge the batteries
- High-output alternator
- GPS navigation system plus an additional four handheld units (to ensure I don't get lost)
- New IBM laptop connected to a modem
- Software to send and receive e-mail
- A weather fax

Believe me, this is just a *partial* list. Did I mention that every single piece of new equipment had to be installed by a professional at a rate of $75 to $125 per hour? Each of these shiny new toys also had its own lengthy instruction manual attached to it. My office was stacked high with heaps of documentation explaining how to use all of this hyper-technical gear. To put it mildly, I'm no technophile. My VCR still flashes at 12:00. The learning curve was slow and scattered. I scanned the manuals, mostly looking at the pictures, and reminded myself that all the equipment was brand-new. It's not going to break! Mostly I just wanted the expensive hourly workers to stop their endless installations and let me go sailing. May 15 was fast approaching, and right behind it was the dreaded hurricane season. It was critical to get out of San Diego as soon as possible, as I didn't want to be dodging hurricanes all the way to Tahiti.

There was also the little matter of figuring out how to sail my boat. Chastened by my inability to make her come about, I subjected myself to a rigorous Sailing 101 lesson, striving to re-learn all the basics, right down to "Red Right Returning," the mnemonic device by which sailors entering a harbor keep the red-colored buoys off the boat's right-hand side where they belong.

I solved the coming-about problem one day in late March. I took her back out on the bay on a perfect sailing day—just enough steady wind to have something to work with, but not so much as to cause any concern. I had been thinking about the problem for days. What was different about this boat from all the others I had owned? As I cut across the water on an easy beam reach, I thought about their keels, the cut of their sails, and the shapes of their rudders. And then, I had a thought that made me feel a bit ridiculous: *Well, hello. This boat is quite a bit **bigger** than those others, isn't it?* Of course it is! Lighter sailboats are more sensitive and respond to any changes in the helm quickly. *Sundance* is a twenty-two-ton ocean-going vessel with a full keel. A bigger boat would need more momentum to get through the wind. Could it be that simple?

I looked around to make sure the coast was clear, and gently eased her nose into the wind, being cautious not to lose speed. She needed lots of turning room; I tried to forget about turning on a dime like you would in an Aston Martin and instead pictured changing direction in a fully loaded Greyhound bus.

Next, I smoothly turned the helm to leeward. Once the wind was out of the mainsail, I held off on releasing the headsail until it was back-winded just a bit. This helped push the bow across the wind and into the new direction. It was working!

I repeated the maneuver again and again (not always successfully), discovering little twists to make the operation go more smoothly. I found, for example, that if I counter intuitively allowed her to slide off the wind, she could gain more speed before I brought her back up on the wind.

I returned to shore that day with a feeling of elation out of all proportion to the accomplishment. Yes, it was a simple thing I had learned to do; but because it was so simple, it was absolutely crucial, a show-stopper if I hadn't figured it out. Of course, even in the months to come, I was not successful in every attempt to come about, but at least I knew each time what was wrong . . . and in the rare case of finding myself in irons, good old FUJIMO came to my rescue.

When I wasn't doing practice sails, fuming about the rising cost of outfitting the boat, or studiously ignoring dozens of instruction manuals, I began to stock provisions. On land, they're called groceries. On a boat, they're *provisions*. This wasn't a matter of stashing some cold sandwiches and beer in the mini-fridge, as I'd done countless times before. No, we had to "stow provisions," a much more serious-sounding undertaking, one that apparently required more advice from a highly paid professional.

Enter George, King of all Provisions. Everyone on Shelter Island knows George. He's the guy walking down the sidewalk wearing his trademark Aussie sailing hat and old-fashioned Porsche sunglasses that look like something James Bond might have worn in the early eighties. He is short and fifty pounds overweight, with longish, unkempt, oily black hair. His nose is flat, pushed in against his cheekbones, making his green eyes seem to bulge like those of a little pug dog. George is just one of the many characters you see hanging around the docks.

It didn't seem like George wanted me to have a very good time on my trip. "Priorities change when you're on a sailboat out to sea," he said. "You'll need to save the juice in your batteries, so forget about cold beer from the fridge."

I wanted to have enough provisions on board to last six months, but it became painfully obvious that my boat was so cluttered by all the new equipment that there wasn't enough room for typical bagged or boxed pantry items. George had the annoying habit of over-emphasizing the seriousness of mundane situations by sprinkling the phrase "strongly recommend" throughout his speech. Well, he "strongly recommended" that I supplement my provisions with military MREs (meals, ready to eat). George had a highly developed theory about the value of MREs, based on his unwavering belief that America's military leaders would only serve the very best to their men and women. "The U.S. government wouldn't feed our soldiers anything less than the best—or they'd risk losing a war!" George said.

It just so happened that good old George had 300 MREs that he was willing to sell me at a steal of a price. I looked the packages over. They seemed harmless enough; they came in a number of choices: potatoes and ham, chicken à la king, beef stew, beans in tomato sauce, and omelet with ham. Sounded practically gourmet. Each MRE provided a self-contained nutritious meal and compact packaging designed to withstand parachute drops and total submersion. They were very compact, about six by twelve inches, packaged in sturdy Army green plastic; a six-month supply fit neatly into my cramped cabin space. There was no telling how old these things might be, as none of them had any expiration dates.

What the hell.

Swayed by George's patriotic faith in the Pentagon, I bought all 300 packages; and just like that, the provision issue was largely behind me. The next day I had lunch with my daughter, Kerry, who had recently returned home after serving four years in the Army.

"Hey, guess what?" I said. "My new boat is stocked with the United States military's finest chow. I bought 300 MREs!"

She looked across the table at me like I'd lost all my marbles.

"Dad," she said sadly, like she was talking to a foolish child. "Do you know what we called MREs whenever we were forced to eat them? Meals Rejected by Ethiopians."

So much for impressing my daughter. Later, I would learn a few more such monikers, each of them a testament to the creativity and wit of our enlisted men and women: *Meals, Rarely Edible. Morsels, Regurgitated, Eviscerated; Meals Requiring Enemas.*

George also fancied himself an expert on safety equipment. Another of his rather alarming sayings was, "Your life and your boat will depend upon X," with just about anything aboard the vessel serving for X. Anchor, strength of the chain rode, GPS system, etc. George could convince you that the strength of the toilet paper on board was critical to your safety. He could hold forth for an hour on the topic of why one particular life raft was better than another. And it just so happened that George always had whatever it was *strongly recommended*, upon which *my life and my boat would depend*, sitting in one of his many storage sheds in the marina, always available at a bargain-basement price. I think his heart was in the right place, but he was driving me crazy.

The 300 MREs would be the staple of my diet; but after Kerry's words of warning, I was not planning to eat an MRE three times a day . . . I needed more food on board. My meager budget was shot to hell and I was complaining to George that I still needed additional provisions. George said, "I know how you can supplement the MREs without spending a lot of money."

"Come on, George," I said. "Don't tell me you have a storage shed full of groceries. Have you been holding out on me?"

"No," George said with a wave of the hand. "I sold the last of my stale stuff to that dumb-ass from Canada last month. By the time he opens up the dried-up boxes of pasta, he'll be halfway to Vancouver."

I couldn't tell whether or not he was joking, which bothered me a little. Then he said, "I'll never see him or his fat wife again. He was a cheap son of a bitch anyway. Serves him right."

Okay, so he wasn't joking.

"All right, King of Provisions, what exactly do you have in mind?"

"Well, it so happens that I'm familiar with a huge grocery store down in Tijuana. It's called the 'Gigante Super Mercado,' in the Plaza Monarca. I used to buy stuff there all the time for my own personal use."

"You used to do your grocery shopping in Tijuana?"

"Oh, yeah. A few years ago, when I had a live-in girlfriend, my bella dama, sweet little Conchita, from Puerto Vallarta, she used to take me there all the time. Man, you should have seen that señorita; I hooked up with her when I was living on my boat down there for the winter."

"Don't get distracted, George. Tell me about the grocery store."

"Dude, they have all the same stuff you buy right here in San Diego at half the price. Same stuff, but with different labels on it."

"How can it be the same if it has different labels?"

"'Cause it's Mexico, man. All the stuff has to have Mexican labels so they can read it, but it tastes the same. And it's cheap."

The next morning we headed down the 5 Freeway to Tijuana, about twenty miles south, on what I would come to remember as the Great Grocery Expedition. Driving into Mexico is simple—no stopping for customs, no searching your car, just basically a big sign saying "Come on in!" Everything and everybody is welcome. However, when you want to cross back into the States, it's an entirely different story.

During the drive, George picked up right where he had left off telling me about his Mexican lover. "Her skin was the color of coffee with cream," he declared. "Her eyes were black as dirt, and she had a body to die for. She was a little thick, but I didn't care."

"You mean she was plump, don't you, George?"

"Well. You'd probably say she was a little heavy for her height."

"How tall was she?"

"She was almost five feet tall."

"And how did you meet this lovely *señorita*?"

"She was working at the marina."

For some reason, I was finding it impossible not to tease George. I said, "Oh, a marina worker. Nice. What did she do at the marina? Pump gas?"

"No, man. She didn't pump gas. She was a bottom cleaner!"

I burst out laughing. "She was a what?"

"You know. She was a diver. Made her living cleaning the bottoms of the visiting yachts."

"Is that how you met her, George? Did she clean your bottom?"

"No, man, she didn't clean my bottom," George said. "I was selling the gear to clean the boats. That's how we met."

Maybe I should have let up, but it had been a long time since I'd laughed so hard, and George seemed happy to entertain me. "George," I said. "If she was so fine, what the hell was she doing with you?"

"She loved me, dude. She thought I was hot. We used to make some awesome love up in the V berth of my little twenty-two. We were going after it hot and heavy one night, and we caused so much wave action coming off the bow that the Mexican Coast Guard posted a small craft warning in the harbor. I think they thought a tsunami was coming."

"Did you bother to take off your Aussie hat? And how about your James Bond sunglasses? Did you stow the shades or leave them on the whole time?"

"No, I was cool without them. But I will tell you this: I certainly left my foul-weather boots on just in case. You know, maybe the anchor would pull free with all the rocking and rolling."

I was laughing so hard that thick tears were streaming down my face. Just the thought of porky little George in his foul-weather boots making love to porky little Conchita the Bottom Cleaner was more than I could handle.

Driving in Tijuana is not for the timid. The town is crowded with 1.5 million people who drive like there are no rules. Stoplights are taken as suggestions. You have to be on your toes all the time. It helps not to be doubled over with laughter.

George was giving me directions, but he quickly became confused, then flustered. Within twenty minutes, we were thoroughly disoriented. I looked around. It did not appear to be a particularly nice place to be lost.

"George, I hope you remember all the Spanish Conchita taught you," I said.

"Oh, hell yeah, man. My Spanish is pretty damn good. Let's ask somebody where the hell the Plaza Monarca is."

He yelled out the window at a man standing at the corner selling flowers. The stranger had to be at least eighty years old, dressed in a Buffalo Bills T-shirt and a pair of jeans that had never seen the inside of a washing machine. He didn't seem to understand George's request, so he shuffled over to the car with a big toothless grin and held out his flowers.

George, the King of Provisions, seemed a little embarrassed. He nervously rattled off a string of Spanish words that even I could tell he was mangling. The old flower guy never stopped smiling, but he kept repeating "*Lo siento. No intiendo, amigo. No comprendo.*" He stuck his flowers further into George's face. "*Cinco dolares, amigo. Es mui barato.*" He held up five fingers.

George turned to me with a wild look in his eyes and explained, as if he'd just deciphered the Rosetta Stone, "Dude! The guy wants me to buy some of his flowers! He says they're only five dollars. He *insists* we buy them. Give me five dollars, quick! If we piss him off, he might call for some of his *amigos* and that won't be cool. We might never get out of here."

"That's pretty good, George. But I thought you said you could *speak* Spanish."

"I can, I can. But when I get nervous, I fuckin' get the words all mixed up."

"Well. You got us into this mess. I think you should pay him the five dollars."

"I can't. I don't have any money."

"My ass. Pay the guy the five bucks, you cheap son of a bitch."

"No, you have to believe me. I never carry any money when I come to Mexico—that way I can't get robbed."

I reluctantly gave him the five bucks, which George exchanged for the lovely flowers. "*Muchas gracias*," the vendor said. As I watched him walking away, it seemed to me that he was laughing. Suddenly he turned around and came back to the car, grinning wider than ever. "*Amigos*," he said. "Go through the next three lights. Turn left at Calle La Coahuila. There you will find the Gigante Super Mercado." He bowed slightly and walked away, still laughing.

George rolled up his window, fuming. "That bastard could speak English the whole time. Run that son of a bitch over."

I didn't run him over. Instead, I drove through the next three lights and made my left onto La Coahuila Street. After driving a few blocks, I couldn't see anything that resembled a grocery store. What I did see were strip clubs, one after another, and painted ladies of the night peddling their wares on every corner. Maybe I should have run over the old flower vendor after all; he had given us directions to the heart of the red light district.

George sat in the passenger seat with his window down, holding the large bouquet of flowers, uncertain whether he should be angry about where we'd ended up. When we had to stop at a red light, four hookers walked up to George's side of the car. The girls spotted the flowers and immediately assumed George had brought them as some kind of offering. They leaned through the window, laughing, giggling, and pecking George on his cheek.

He looked over at me with a shit-eating grin. "What do you think, man? They're all so beautiful. Should we take time to enjoy a nooner?"

"A nooner? It's 10:30 in the morning. And I thought you didn't have any money."

"This is what qualifies as a Nooner-But-Sooner. Okay? And I do have some money. I tucked a Ben Franklin in my shoe this morning for emergencies."

"And this is your idea of an emergency."

"It's just a matter of perspective, dude. And right now, my perspective is telling me that these ladies are looking pretty damn good. What do you say? Let's go for it."

"Sorry George, I don't have the time or the interest to participate in any extracurricular activities this morning. We came down here to buy some cheap groceries, not to get laid."

Teasing George had been one thing, but denying him the hookers was something else entirely. He looked like he was about to cry. He handed the flowers to one of the ladies and said gravely, "*No, gracias, amiga*. I am so sorry."

The painted lady bent forward to whisper something in his ear as we started to pull away.

"What did she say, George?" I asked after we had moved on.

She said, "*Vete a la chingada, gringo*," George said despondently.

"I understand the *gringo* part. What's the rest of it mean?"

"Go fuck yourself."

Poor George.

We drove aimlessly for a few more blocks until we saw a policeman walking across the street. Now, George miraculously remembered how to speak Spanish. "*Por favor, señor*," he said. "*Dónde está el mercado?*"

Fifteen minutes later, we rolled into the parking lot of the store. We walked up and down its aisles, loading canned goods into my cart, guided more by the pictures than the labels. "This looks good," George would say, turning a box over in his hands. "You'll probably want to take some along, whatever it is."

In the end, we loaded up eight bags of groceries, which I carried home and stowed aboard *Sundance*, wondering exactly what I'd purchased. But George had been right: the Tijuana goods were darned cheap. The Great Grocery Expedition had been worthwhile, both for its cost savings and for its comic relief. Reflecting on it later, it seemed like it had been ages since I'd had any fun. If provisioning the boat was any indication of what lay ahead, this voyage would be packed with laughter and adventure.

• • •

After five months of intensive work on the boat, I was almost ready to test out the deep ocean waters. The only problem was, I had become so preoccupied with making decisions, purchasing the necessary gear, managing workers, and making payments that the newly functional equipment still sat idly on board. In particular, I was daunted by the Furuno GP 31 Global Positioning System; the Simrad AP21/5300x autopilot; the Icom single-side-Band radio with the Inmarsat satellite communication to receive weather fax and e-mails; and the Furuno 841 Mk11 thirty-six-mile radar. Every time I opened a manual, it made me feel old and inadequate. It all seemed so newfangled and complicated, and my dyslexic brain revolted. The trip was already two weeks behind schedule, and hurricane season was looming. The longer I delayed, the greater the chance of encountering heavy weather. *There will be plenty of time to study these manuals at sea*, I decided. They would provide perfect reading material for the long, lazy days ahead out on the Pacific.

As the list of "must-have" gear mushroomed by the week, I began to wonder if the cost of labor and parts would exceed the price of the boat itself. It was a true test of my resolve. The endless decisions and purchases involved in outfitting the boat ramped up the financial pressure (along with my blood pressure) and forced me to ask again and again and again: *Are you sure you want to do this?*

In fact, I was not sure. Yes, I had committed to the trip and was moving forward with my plans, but there had been no magic moment in which all my doubts had vanished. I was still plagued by the most basic practical considerations:

> *Do I have enough sailing experience to complete a circumnavigation? Maybe I'm too old. Oh, crap, I've never sailed past Catalina Island. I don't know diddly-squat about navigation. I don't even know how to work a GPS. Hell, I've never sailed out of sight of land.*

But those thoughts weren't the worst of it. What really got me was waking up in the middle of the night torn by the existential dilemma my plans presented.

> *Is this simply a huge ego trip? A completely self-serving adventure? Is it okay to put so much importance on what I want to do? How can I justify spending so much of my hard-earned money to fulfill a damned dream?*

After a great deal of soul-searching, I came to some conclusions. Firstly, I accepted the fact that my doubts would ride with me all the way around the world. There was nothing to do about that. How could it be otherwise? You do something deliberately crazy, set yourself apart from the rest of the responsible world, part company with your old, responsible self, and of course you're going to wonder what the hell you're doing. I told myself, yes, this undertaking was completely selfish. I was not, after all, taking my $200,000 and using it to build schools in the slums of India; there was no getting around that. This was a decidedly personal pursuit. Of course, I saw it as an attempt to better myself, and in some small way perhaps that would better the world around me, but I was not going to fool myself about it either way. Still, I maintained, it was certainly true that if more people dared to follow their dreams, the mass of human beings would be the better for it.

I at least had Sally's reluctant blessing. She was in no way thrilled at the prospect of having me be gone for months at a stretch, but she had come to accept that this adventure carried a great deal of meaning for me. In retrospect, I can now sympathize with what she must have been struggling with at the time. What I took for nagging attempts to undermine my resolve were no doubt the very reasonable reactions of someone who sees a loved one begin to display obsessive, even dangerous, behavior. She tried to talk me back to reason, but the greater her efforts to save me from my folly, the deeper I dug in my heels. Finally, she said to me one night, "Michael, I just want you to know that I'm done trying to talk you out of this. For the record, I'll say one last time that I think it's a bad idea. But it's become the most important thing in your life right now, so I'm going to do my best to support you in it."

"Baby," I said. "You're the most important thing in my life. But I just have to do this thing right now."

"Go and do it. I'll be here."

Damn it, my time has come. I have earned the right to chase a dream by working at least two jobs since I was fourteen years old. I worked my way through seven years of college and hold a Masters Degree to show for my persistence. Over the past twenty years, I have worked diligently to build a successful insurance agency and have helped my four daughters earn college degrees. I've paid for four weddings and three divorces. (The divorces were all mine, of course).

Yes, it is my turn. I will chase my dream.

People at the marina were starting to ask almost every day: *When are you leaving?* At first, I enjoyed being asked about my plans, but this daily question soon became an annoyance. I now understood how a pregnant woman feels when a never-ending stream of well-meaning friends and strangers ask, "When are you going to have that baby?" Out of frustration, I developed this stock response: "When you look in our slip and you don't see *Sundance* there anymore, that will be a pretty good indication that we've left."

Ernest Gann describes the so-called "Dock Committee" that watches sailors prepare to head out to sea. He writes:

> The hour of the day has little effect on the magnetic power of the sea. It makes no difference if you bring a vessel into port at three o'clock in the afternoon or three o'clock in the morning. It matters not if the sun is shining or if it is pouring rain. *Someone,* at least *one* human being, will appear and take your heaving line or just stand watching while the vessel is secured alongside the dock. Weather and time influence only the number of people so compelled, and the same silent supervision applies to any vessel departing, whether previous notice had been given or not.
>
> . . . . The people who engage themselves in this activity are of every race and environment. They appear from nowhere and are known collectively as the "Dock Committee" though their numbers may vary from one to a thousand.
>
> . . . . There are women who stand as transfixed as any man; there are well-dressed businessmen, entire families, lovers, and the lonely. . . . All watch in a kind of reverent silence, seldom moving, and when either the arrival or sailing has been completed they continue to hold their positions. Only their eyes move, hungrily, as if they fear missing the slightest detail of a vessel or her rig. They stare at those on board, observing every activity in a manner which becomes infuriating until you meet their eyes and understand they are not really seeing you but themselves. For their eyes are glazed with the faraway and they are totally unconscious of their rudeness.
>
> . . . . To Dock Committees and to others who linger on a lonely beach, the sea horizon has forever been limitless. Beyond it is adventure and romance, mystery, the swirling kingdoms of every man's imagination. These are essentials beyond the ocean horizon not to be found in daily life, neither in books or in music, nor art of any form; and as modern existence becomes more and more protected, those essentials become increasingly more difficult to enjoy. So, it could be that the members of the Dock Committees

are starving. Only by coming down to the sea can they suck up morsels of adventure, which is essential to a full life.

So much of my life had been spent among the ranks of the Dock Committee. Not by choice, of course. I was either without a boat, or the boat I owned was much too small to go offshore, or most likely, I was too bogged down in family and work concerns to break free of the workaday orbit that kept me on land. It was a thrill to realize that I was now the owner of a forty-foot yacht capable of sailing anywhere in the world. When the Dock Committee came to stare at my boat and inquire about my departure, I relished the feeling that, for once in my life, I was a man of adventure and romance, mystery and imagination.

• • •

CHAPTER 5

Single White Male

Take in laundry before you take in partners.

—Proverb

THE STACK OF TECHNICAL MANUALS towered in my office, untouched for weeks. As my new departure date of June 15 grew near, the urgency of planning and preparations instilled in me a stronger sense of reality about my situation. I admitted to myself that I couldn't very well sit back and read the manuals while sailing alone. The vision of lazy days on calm seas was no doubt an empty fantasy. What I needed was a crew member, another set of eyes on this first leg from San Diego to Tahiti. Someone who knew how to work all that equipment, or at the very least, could manage the boat while I learned. Unfortunately, I had waited so long to admit this to myself that I now had only two weeks to find someone.

With so little notice, there was no time to play the dating game. *Bachelor Number One, do you prefer long days and nights of endless rocking and rolling or the daring thrill ride of gale-force winds?* One evening, while flipping through a sailing magazine called *Latitude 38*, I came across an ad for a guy from Chicago looking to join a crew crossing the Pacific. He was fifty-five years old and said he had years of open-ocean sailing experience. We talked on the phone and, while he didn't come across as Mr. Personality, he seemed like an all-right guy. It was understood that he wouldn't be paid—just a bunk, passage to Tahiti, and all the MREs he could eat.

DH wasn't going to be the life of the party, I could plainly see that. He was entirely too serious on the phone, he tended to mutter under his breath, and he was overly sarcastic. He gave the names of three people in Chicago to check for references, but I have a disdain for references. Who in their right mind would ever provide a reference for someone who might say something negative? References are crap and a waste of time. But what can I say? He was the only game in town, he claimed to have extensive ocean-passage experience, and I had thousands of other things to think about. I go with my gut on big decisions and it usually works out.

Not all the time.

Much of the time.

Sometimes, anyway.

By early June, *Sundance* was fully loaded and ready to run across the Pacific. I called DH and told him he had the crew job and he should fly to Orange County as soon as he could.

A week later, I went to the airport to meet DH, I was taken aback by his size. He was six-foot-three and must have weighed two hundred fifty pounds. *I guess he'll provide some decent ballast*, I thought to myself. His chest was broad, his shoulders so huge that he might have to turn sideways to fit through the cabin door. His head was roughly the size of a late-summer watermelon, topped by gray, closely clipped hair. He wore a pair of shorts that were so tight on his big ass that I thought they would split up the middle at any moment.

Sally organized a "bon voyage" party at our home in Laguna Beach for some of our closest friends and family. Three of my daughters, Kelly, Kasey, and Kerry, were there with six of my grandchildren.

DH was a little strange; he rarely smiled, although his attitude seemed pleasant enough once the party was under way. He helped himself to a few beers. And then a few more.

Late that afternoon, we were all sitting on the patio looking out to sea—me, Sally, Kasey, Kelly, and my new first mate—when

DH leaned forward toward the women and broke the silence with a sudden hiss of words: "How do you know your father will be safe with me? We have only just met. He doesn't know me and I don't know him. I could very easily hit him over the head with a winch handle, drop him overboard, and sail off with his new boat."

We were, to put it mildly, stunned. Sally and my daughters gaped silently at one another, aware that this man had just spoken aloud their greatest fear. *Dad is in danger. Dad could die out there. Dad isn't coming back.* DH waited a beat and then let out a howl of laughter in that you-should-see-the-look-on-your-faces way that doesn't really dispel the underlying fears. Sally and my daughters tried to laugh, though it sounded more like choking. We whispered together later, "He's had too much to drink. What a ridiculous thing to say." But none of us forgot. Oh, my, this was the first red flag.

The previous weeks had been a blur of sails and rigging, navigation and electronics, supplies and crew, and I was exhausted. Maybe I dove into the preparation with such gusto in order to push aside thoughts of what I couldn't bring on this trip. About whom I'd be leaving behind. Still, she was never far from my mind.

Sally.

True to her word, she was supporting my dream as best she could. "Go," she said repeatedly. "You need to do this." On my final night on shore, Sally and Sedona drove from Laguna Beach to send me off. We knew this would be our last night together for a long time. We rented a hotel room on Shelter Island, directly across the street from the marina. My beautiful boat, *Sundance*, bobbed gently in her slip, waiting to explore the deep blue waters on the other side of the horizon.

We spent the evening talking about my adventure and how Sally should handle things while I was away. Hours passed like minutes. All too quickly, the sun came up—and with it, the time for Sally and Sedona to head back home . . . alone. I was torn apart inside. I've always hated the gut-wrenching feeling that comes with goodbyes. We stood together in the bright sunlight, hugging, and within seconds, the tears were sliding down the slopes of her cheeks. After a long, strong embrace, we kissed like it was our first, and then like it would be our last. I fought with all I had not to break down. After months of preparation and anticipation, the boat was finally ready to go. Even so, my gut told me I wasn't ready to leave. But this was no time to chicken out. I had to go.

I knew I couldn't ask Sally and Sedona to stand on shore and watch, helplessly, as I sailed off toward the horizon. They had to leave first. I helped load her car, moving as if in slow motion. We had one more hug. It felt so good to hold her in my arms, to feel her warm body so close to mine. I never wanted that last hug to end. Sedona gazed at me sadly with those big brown eyes, sensing that something was out of sorts, and was hesitant to get in the car. He wasn't willing to leave my side, so I lifted him in and scratched behind his ears, his favorite spot. "You be a good boy. Take care of Sally for me, okay?"

As Sally drove away, I could see tears streaming down her beautiful face. Sedona pressed his large, black nose against the back window. He kept his eyes on me as long as he could, and then the car moved out of sight. At that moment, I felt like the world's biggest, most selfish bastard, as if I had betrayed them both. My heart rose into my throat and the tears began running down my face. I wanted to chase after Sally, tell her I couldn't do this without her, but it was much too late for that. There was no way I could turn my back on this dream. I had to suck it up and regain control of my emotions. It was time for me to go. When I think back on that morning, I can truthfully say it was one of the most difficult moments of my entire journey.

I have come to the conclusion that a journey begun under such a spell of gloom is destined for disaster. Oh, boy, was I in for it.

CHAPTER 6

• • •

Rock and Roll

Twenty years from now you will be more disappointed by the things you didn't do than by the ones you did do. So throw off the bowlines. Sail away from the safe harbor. Catch the trade winds in your sails. Explore. Dream.
        —Frequently (and probably incorrectly) attributed to Mark Twain

JUST AFTER NOON ON JUNE 15, 2000, I took the above piece of advice and applied it directly—and quite literally—to my life.

Sailing out of San Diego harbor, I could see the hotel where Sally and I had spent our last night together. My stomach tightened, the lump rose in my throat again, and my jaw started to quiver. I glanced over at DH, instantly resentful that it was he and not my beloved Sally playing the role of first mate. I forced back the tears and tried to put myself in the moment.

Off to my right loomed two of the Navy's ominous-looking nuclear submarines, sitting peacefully at the dock, belying the vast destruction of which they are capable. To my left stood the North Island Navy Air Station, where just now an F/A-18 Hornet was lifting off. I thought about my close friend, Colonel Jeffery Devlin, call sign "Jungle," a Marine fighter pilot. Recently he had sailed through here with me and shared his perspective as someone who usually covered these distances strapped into a forty-million-dollar jet moving at more than 400 knots. Whoever was in that Hornet above me was seeing me as part of the

tableau that Jungle had described: even with thousands of in-
stantaneous technical decisions to make (maintain proper vector,
descend to 3,000 feet, ensure correct position relative to wingman, etc.), that pilot is no doubt glancing down and marveling
at the sight of my pretty little boat slicing across the blue water,
Catalina Island approaching in the distance hard green against
hard blue, the land falling away in infinity in one direction, the
sea in the other. Once, Jungle happened to look down and see a
pod of gray whales, the water over their bodies as blue as wiper
fluid. He couldn't help himself; he dropped down to 500 feet,
mesmerized by the natural beauty as he circled the animals in
his thunderous killing machine. I forced myself to smile. Hey,
I would probably see whales up-close. Not the best consola-
tion at having left half my heart behind, but it would have to do
for now.

As I sailed away, I watched Point Loma and the California
coast grow smaller and smaller. It was a strange feeling to know
that this would be the last bit of dry land I would see for Lord
knew how many days. On top of the energy-sapping loneliness,
two conflicting emotions waged war inside my chest: the thrill of
total freedom and the anxiety of total unpredictability.

When we were out of sight of land, I picked up the cell
phone and dialed Sally. The reception was already poor, and I
wondered if I'd even get through. I knew this would be our last
conversation for a very long time; I'd better make it good.

She picked up on the second ring. "Michael. Is everything
okay?"

It hurt my throat to force sound through it. "Yes, baby. Did
you and Sedona make it home all right?"

"Yes. We had an easy drive. No traffic to speak of. We're here."

"Baby . . . I miss you already. I love you so much." There was
an awful stillness on the line. "Baby?"

The call had failed. How much had she heard? I tried to
redial, but I had completely lost the signal. I stood there for a
moment, staring down at the phone like it was a totem that had
lost its medicine. The boat was pulling me farther away from her

with each passing moment. I was so upset that I threw the phone into the ocean and watched it disappear beneath the frothy waves.

DH sat off by himself, oblivious to my turmoil, whistling a tuneless song that seemed to my ears as an anthem to heartlessness and detachment from the world. I went down below to check the weather forecast and pull myself together.

Spooked by the possibility of severe storms, I had contracted with Walter the Weather Guy, a New Jersey–based meteorologist, who would send me updates via single-side radio e-mails. I didn't have enough equipment or experience to predict the weather myself, and Walter's service provided forecasts to shipping companies and private yachtsmen alike. It gave me a small measure of comfort to know that this guy had my back.

The weather had never been much of a factor in my previous experiences as a sailor. I'd wake up in the morning and, if it was sunny and breezy, well, time to pick a destination and pack some sandwiches; we're going for a sail! In Southern California, weather-related troubles usually come in the form of too little wind. Some days it was like sailing in a bathtub: flat, glassy, smooth, and boring . . . this would be a bit different.

We had been under way for less than eight hours when what would prove to be one of the voyage's great recurring nuisances manifested itself for the first time: the business of voiding the bladder while at sea. In my life back on land, I had gamely accepted that it was my rightful plight, as an aging male, to be the owner of a weather-beaten prostate gland, but frequent trips to the office bathroom are a trifling inconvenience compared to urinating every two hours on a constantly rollicking boat. In case you didn't know, the deterioration of the prostate not only makes you go more often, it also plays hell with the once-simple act of releasing the necessary muscles and getting a good flow going. Even standing on dry land, it becomes a challenge to relax the myriad interrelated muscles in the legs, the abdomen, the lower back—all the levers and pulleys that might affect the operation. So, imagine attempting that while balancing on a sailboat in a heavy swell. It's like trying to relax while standing on a couple of wild Mustangs.

I was not looking forward to my first try, but the moment was fast approaching, whether I liked it or not. "DH," I said, once it seemed that I couldn't hold out any longer. "Take the helm. I've got to take a piss."

DH looked up at me and deepened his perpetual scowl. Evidently I had interrupted his pleasant reverie. He had been sitting forward in the cockpit, glaring across the deck out at the empty sea, grumbling to himself or perhaps to someone who had wronged him in the past. He slumped off his bench and took the wheel without a word. My suspicion that something was not right with him was deepening. And, by the way he clumsily steered the boat, I had the first inkling that his sailing experience was perhaps not as extensive as he had suggested.

With regard to the task at hand, I had two choices: go below to the head and make an awful mess down there or attempt to dangle it over the rail, an awkward and truly dangerous method which, as sea lore has it, has taken the life of more sailors than any other single maneuver. I opted for the awkward and truly dangerous choice.

Of course, I had bundled into a whole catalogue's worth of watch clothes: shorts, pants, bib overalls, T-shirt, sweatshirt, foul-weather coat, and foul-weather boots. Also, I had waited too long to begin this process. Mr. Happy, as I jauntily to refer to it, was in an agitated state. I danced in place, all too conscious that the sullen DH had nothing better to look at as he steered than my contortions as I fought my way through my layers of clothes in search of the elusive Mr. Happy. With one hand clinging to the rails, I opened the zipper of the coat. The bib overalls that served as my foul-weather pants were a top-of-the-line product, with one glaring oversight: they had no fly opening, only a useless zipper beneath my chin. Once I had gotten past that barrier, the search was on in earnest. There he was, nestled deep inside the pants (another zipper) and my underwear (a flap). I wrestled him free. "Welcome to the elements, little man," I said at last. "All right, have your way."

Nothing. Mr. Happy was having none of it. What, out here? In this clammy, salty damp?

Come on, Mr. Happy. We've come all this way together.

I waited and waited, closing my eyes, visualizing all the muscles relaxing. Levers and pulleys, levers and pulleys. Waterfalls, spigots. More than once it seemed to be coming, and then it retreated. A seabird wheeled above me, and I experienced a bizarre surge of envy at its ability to let loose whenever and wherever fancy struck it. Wait, now it felt like it was coming . . . yes, it was coming. And then, *boom!* The boat shuddered as wind caught the sail and I grasped at the rail with both hands to keep from pitching penis-first into the waves. *Shit!* DH had come too far off the wind and then sloppily corrected course. Goddamn fucking DH. He had ruined any chance he might have had to regain my good graces. It sounds funny to say it now, but you just don't mess with certain things, even through ignorance or incompetence. Some things are sacred.

Utterly disconsolate, I packed Mr. Happy away, re-flapping all the flaps, re-zipping all the zippers, all the while holding the boat with one hand. I scrambled back to the cockpit, avoiding DH's eye. He couldn't keep it to himself, though. "Took you long enough," he said. "Forget how it was done?"

I ignored him and went below, still dying to piss. I looked wildly around in the galley for a solution. My eye fell on a stack of Sprite sodas. I seized one, twisted off the cap, and emptied it down the sink. From my pocket I pulled my rigging knife and sliced off the neck of the bottle. I held the base up to the light. Good enough. I raced back up through the hatch and told the leering DH to go back to what he had been doing. In the cockpit, I could brace myself better, and after battling my way back through my clothes, found that Mr. Happy was much more content when housed within green plastic. "Do it, man," I murmured.

And after a minute or two, Mr. Happy obliged. Oh, what a wonderful feeling. Such sweet release! Caught up in the everyday, it is far too easy to overlook the small pleasures of life. Try to imagine a greater joy than being able to take a leak when you feel the urge.

The green-bottle solution was workable, but the urination problem would plague me for the rest of my journey. The pattern was always the same: just a few minutes into a watch, the urge would come sneaking in like an unwanted visitor, and no matter how hard I fought back, I would find myself fighting my way through the layers of clothing, probing around for Mr. Happy, trying too hard to relax, enduring false starts and delays, sometimes having to abort the whole process and stow both Mr. Happy and the green bottle because the wind had changed direction or the sails needed trimming.

I dumped the pee over the stern and rinsed the bottle in seawater. DH was grinning smugly, sitting with his arms spread wide against the windward rail like a mafia don on a leather sofa. I could tell he was struggling for just the right insult, which apparently never came to him, because he remained silent (I don't give him credit for holding his tongue out of judiciousness). After a few moments, he resumed his infernal whistling.

Maybe, I thought, *I'll be the one bludgeoning somebody with a winch handle on this trip.*

During that first night at sea, I spent much of my time thinking about Sally and our last night together. We had opened up about how we had been drifting apart and how we had been taking each other for granted, how we were both unhappy and anxious to find some answers to put the love back into our lives. We reflected honestly on the past year and the way we had allowed our feelings for each other to slip far down on the list of priorities. We used to have so much fun just being together. What the hell had happened to us? Why did the laughter die?

We'd spent most of the night searching for answers, finally simply agreeing that our behavior toward each other had been despicable and irresponsible, and resolving to let the impending absence make our hearts grow fonder. Yes, we cried and we made love, but somehow, we also found ourselves laughing that night—surely a good sign, given all our troubles and the months of separation to come. After she fell asleep, I sat there staring into the dark with an idiot's grin on my face, turning a single thought over in my mind like it was a pretty stone I had found: *I do love Sally.*

The first day or two at sea, the sailing conditions were exactly the kind I'd grown used to off the coast of Southern California: light winds, smooth water, and slow progress. I tried not to be lulled by the easy conditions—this wasn't a shakedown cruise or a practice run; this was the real deal. We were setting out on a great adventure.

On our third day out, Walter the Weather Guy mentioned a hurricane forming off the coast of Mexico. "It might be headed your way," he wrote in an e-mail. "You don't have to change course immediately, but it might be necessary. I'll watch the storm's path and keep you posted." A ripple of panic pulsed through my body. *My God. Three days out, and we're talking hurricanes . . . so much for the honeymoon.*

With that e-mail, the honeymoon was truly finished. That same afternoon, the seas changed. The winds remained light, but *Sundance* started bouncing around like a rubber duck in a Jacuzzi. For the next several days, we continued moving slowly; on a good day, we covered 100 miles, but, on a bad day, it would be more like sixty. The hurricane scuttled off harmlessly to other precincts, but in the days to come, I would find myself almost wishing for something like it to put an end to my misery. We encountered lumpy seas day and night, constant swells that would slap us on the beam (the side of the boat), and wave action that would smack us in the bow. This slapping and smacking caused the boat to rock side to side as well as up and down. It was constant and relentless. Slap (whoa!), smack (yikes!), slap (whoa!), smack (yikes!). Repeat for days, no breaks for sleeping or eating or seeing to bodily functions.

Once we hit rocky water, the boat began to make noises I'd never heard at sea before, noises that took some getting used to. She moaned and groaned, creaked and cracked, and the sounds intensified with stronger winds. Every now and then a noise would be so sharp and cutting, that it felt like something deep inside the boat was ripping apart. It was all quite unsettling. I had to train myself not to think about the vast depths of cold water beneath us every time it sounded like my boat was twisting apart.

I also had to develop a new and improved set of sea legs...and fast. Movement on and around the boat became an advanced balancing act. Occasionally, I could get away with holding onto the boat with one hand, but most of the time I had to cling on with both, hunched and crab-like. Simply moving from Point A to Point B on the boat was a dangerous and labor-intensive endeavor. I began rather foolishly to curse my previous ingratitude at never having truly appreciated how easy it is to move around on dry land. This felt like I was riding (living, really) on a mechanical bull in a country and western bar, but without the pretty ladies and stiff drinks.

No, instead of pretty ladies, I had DH. We were getting very light winds from aft, requiring us to sail on what is called a broad reach. Because you're traveling roughly the same direction the wind is blowing, there's little need to tack (or zigzag); you simply ease the sails out toward perpendicular to catch as much of that wind coming from behind you as possible. The headsails act like a parachute in front of the boat, pulling it across the water.

As I maneuvered the sails into position, DH, who had been nearly silent till now (but for his dreadful whistling) muttered, "You know, if we trim the sails in, it might help us to actually reach Tahiti."

Now, I'm no world-class sailor, but trimming the sails in is precisely the opposite of what one does to maximize the effect of the wind when sailing on a broad reach. I gave a little laugh, and then realized that DH wasn't one to joke around or attempt to lighten the mood. Still, I looked over my shoulder to see if he could be serious. He was staring at me with disdain. Which could only mean one thing: this asshole *had* lied about his sailing experience.

And yet, I desperately needed for DH to take the helm. I hadn't gone off watch for the first forty-eight hours at sea, so preoccupied was I with setting our course and learning the new equipment. We were sailing on a tight starboard reach in light, five- to eight-knot winds, and I went down below to get some rest. After an hour of sleep, I heard DH yelling like his hair had caught fire, and I raced up to the cockpit terrified that something had gone seriously wrong.

"This fucking boat!" DH bellowed.

"What the hell, man?" I shouted. "What's happening?"

"The fucking boat has moved off the wind and won't come back when I turn the wheel."

I looked up at the sails. They were back-winded (the wind was hitting the sails from the wrong side, the back side), and the boat had moved off course by at least forty-five degrees.

DH had let go of the helm. He was standing with both hands on his hips, his face beet red, like a toddler in the throes of a temper tantrum. I didn't even want to know how long he had been standing there like that, screaming like a baby while the boat drifted off course. He continued shouting (goddamn boat, shifting fucking winds, etc.), while I trimmed the sails and pulled us back on course, exhausted and running on fumes myself.

Oh, boy. What I had here was not a mate but a passenger—and a surly, mentally unstable one at that. How could I ever trust this guy to sail the boat? He wasn't knowledgeable enough to handle it without my supervision, and that was whole purpose of having a first mate: one guy sleeps, eats, whatever, while the other guy sails. How could I ever go off watch and leave him alone in the cockpit, totally in control of the boat? I had kept a keen eye on DH his first day or two on board, still shaken by his winch-handle remark, but now I had a whole new set of safety concerns.

I lay in my bunk the next afternoon, and instead of sleeping, inventoried DH's despicable traits: Liar. Sarcastic. Mean-spirited. Inexperienced sailor. Whistler. Goddamned motherfucking son-of-a-bitching whistler. For you on dry land reading this, that probably seems funny. Ha ha, the one sailor has a quirky personal habit that really gets under the skin of the other sailor! But I tell you, on a boat where there's no escape, a thing like that can drive you crazy. And DH's incessant whistling really had begun to drive me insane.

All day . . . he whistled. All night . . . he whistled. He was just one of those guys who had to be whistling all the time and it invaded my personal space. I couldn't get away from it, any more than I could get away from the constant rollicking of the boat. I turned over in my bunk, fuming about being trapped with that SOB for God only knew how many more weeks, and then I noticed a distinctly queasy feeling. A clammy, cold sweat. Mild dizziness.

Oh, for Christ's sake. What was *this*? The symptoms worsened. Increased flow of saliva. Nausea.

Now, I had been sailing for over thirty years, and I'd never been seasick a day in my life. When others looked queasy on board, they received no pity from me. Wimps! Buck up! It just didn't seem possible that I could be stricken with such a thing. We weren't even in particularly heavy weather. The boat was bobbing and weaving, yes, but the winds were light and we were sure to encounter far worse conditions in the upcoming weeks. Yet, I couldn't deny that with each movement of the boat, my stomach lurched with it. Wonderful. Our noble captain was suffering from a case of seasickness.

And oh, man, it was bad. I felt as if I were throwing up cheeseburgers I'd eaten in the sixth grade. It zapped all my strength, crushing my attempts to handle even the smallest jobs around the boat—and this at a time when I had lost all confidence in DH's sailing abilities. To make matters worse, going belowdecks was now out of the question (that only exacerbates the condition), so I had no place of refuge from DH's volatile behavior or, of course, his goddamned whistling. I felt like death warmed over as I sat chewing soda crackers and concentrating on keeping them down. How in the fuck had it all come to this?

One of the best descriptions of what it's like to experience seasickness comes from Abigail Adams, the wife of President John Adams. She was accompanying her husband on a voyage to Europe in 1773. She wrote:

> To be seasick is the most disheartening malady . . . No person, who is a stranger to the sea, can form an adequate idea of the

debility occasioned by seasickness. Imagine being extremely drunk and hung over all at once, and you have some idea: whirling, reeling, nauseous and lassitude.

Well said, Abigail!

The boat began to feel like a prison . . . no, that sounds too metaphorical. The boat *was* a prison; a torture chamber, even. I was being endlessly subjected to physical and psychological stresses over which I had no control over and no freedom to walk away. The effects of the sickness, physical exhaustion, frustration with DH, and sleep deprivation were all steadily accumulating. The wonderful irony of the situation, given my background, was that in contemplating this sailing adventure, I had given severely short shrift to its psychological demands, leaving me completely unprepared to deal with them. I had, of course, read several books by authors who had sailed around the world. Most of them make no bones about describing, in detail, how the hardest part is mental, and yet, I'd either forgotten about their psychological anguish or blown it off as inconsequential. *Hell, I have a graduate degree in psychology. My psyche is rock-solid.*

I quickly came to the realization that I didn't know jack shit about what was in store for me out there on the high seas. When we're living on dry land, we're in control of our environment (unless, of course, we're in prison, I hasten to point out), and it's hard to imagine otherwise. If we're too warm, we crank the air conditioning. If we're hungry, we raid the fridge. If we're tired, we shuffle off to bed. It's not often that we can't change what's making us uncomfortable at any given moment in our lives. It's hard to overstate the psychological comfort that comes with the power to control our lives. But once you step on board, set sail, and find yourself hundreds or thousands of miles from dry land, all of that power evaporates into the sea spray. Stripped of the capacity to control your environment, you've entered a foreign world. Without question, this had become my greatest challenge of all.

Before the voyage, I had at least taken the opportunity to speak with Dr. Jerry Linenger, an astronaut who once carried the distinction of having spent more time in outer space than any other American man. I asked him how he'd handled this problem of losing control over his environment, and he stressed the importance of establishing and adhering to a daily routine.

On shore, I had enjoyed a predictable routine. Wake up at 6:00 AM, take the dog for a run, eat breakfast, drive to the health club for a workout (and on that drive, it bears mentioning, I could move as fast as I needed and always in the *right direction*). After the workout, stop for a cup of coffee, and then head to the office. Around 3:00 PM, knock off work and stop at the golf course to hit a few balls. Once back at home, run the dog, have dinner at 6:30 PM, watch the evening news and whatever else looked good on TV, go to bed whenever I felt sleepy, usually around ten or so, and sleep, undisturbed, through the night. That's what I call a routine.

God knows, I tried to take Dr. Linenger's advice and establish a routine at sea, but it was damn near impossible when the circumstances of the day, the hour, and the moment were always changing. And yet, somehow, at the same time, it felt like nothing at all changed from one day to the next. That became painfully obvious as I tried to videotape my adventure. On the first day, as we left San Diego harbor, we'd had a Navy submarine off our stern and it was a thrill to see this vessel on a similar course to ours. But by the fifth day of going on deck with my camera, I realized that we wouldn't be seeing submarines or anything else photogenic. The scenery looked exactly the same on day five as it had on day four and as it would on day six: water, waves, and a cloudy sky. We saw no other boats or ships. Occasionally, we'd see a shark, and I was surprised to see birds so far from land. Rarely did a day go by without seeing at least one flying overhead. I am not big on species of birds, but I think they were terns, boobies, and petrels. Sometimes, they would circle the mast a few times as if surveying their prospects of finding anything on board to eat. There was no land, of course. No trees for miles. *Where do these birds live?* I should have taken comfort in their presence, but in my anguished state, their sudden appearance nagged at me.

There were plenty of flying fish, which are fun to see once, maybe twice. Seemingly out of nowhere, one would burst out of the water with its wings flapping a hundred miles an hour, skim across the surface of the water, and then crash, totally out of control, back into the ocean. Most mornings, I would find two or three flying fish spread across the deck (probably after they had hurtled blindly into the sail during the night), and I would toss them back into the ocean. I suppose that became a part of my "routine"—slinging fish in the AM.

Still, I dutifully reported to the deck with my fancy video camera and shot the blank horizon. It finally dawned on me that this stultifying video would be death to anyone who bothered to put it into a VCR. If the weather was calm enough for me to shoot a video, that usually meant that there was nothing to see but miles of steely gray water. If the weather picked up, my hands were too occupied in hanging on for dear life to shoot any video. By the end of the first week, the video camera was stowed away for good.

The endless expanse of water and clouds started getting to me. It was cloudy every single day, lending an extra feeling of gloom to the already gloomy expedition. So much with navigating by the stars; there were no stars . . . and no contrails from jets to use as a guide.

Some years ago, I had read about an adventurous kayaker who'd had the bright idea of paddling from San Diego to Hawaii without any navigational aids whatsoever. He never reached Hawaii, and no one ever saw him again. Now I had a good idea why; I was happy to be packing five—yes, five—GPS units on board.

As soon as the sun dropped into the ocean the temperature also dropped until it became very cold.

The nights were cold, very cold. During the "dog watch" (midnight to 4:00 AM), I'd put on layers of clothes, trying to stay warm. I was basically dressed for skiing, not sailing. Someone had warned me that the salt air deposits miniscule particles in your pores, so when cooler air comes into contact with the skin, it intensifies the chill. A fresh-water shower takes care of the problem, but that wasn't practical. *Sundance did* have a shower stall in the bow, but she only carried 100 gallons of fresh water in the bilge, which was not enough for a decent wash. I used the on-board facilities more like what my mother used to call a "bird bath," rinsing myself off from time to time with a washcloth. It was a far cry from the long, hot high-pressure showers I'd known all my life as a landlubber.

On the eighth day, I began to feel the wind picking up from the northeast. Could it be? Yes! I felt like cracking open a bottle of champagne. We had reached the trade winds! These breezes have pushed sailboats around the oceans for centuries. They teased us at first, blowing only eight to ten knots, but they eventually picked up to a steady fifteen knots, making for some really nice sailing. We covered more than 100 miles just about every day. On our best day, we moved 110 nautical miles in twenty-four hours. This lifted my spirits, but unfortunately, not for long.

DH was becoming more unstable by the hour. I tried to remind myself that he was subject to most of the same stresses I was—maybe swapping out my agony over his whistling for the inadequacy he must surely have felt about his sailing skills. Or, hey, it was just as possible that I had some annoying quirks that I wasn't even aware of. But there was no question I was doing a better job holding it together. What started as peevish grumblings soon graduated into a series of cutting remarks, which in turn blossomed into violent outbursts and outright delusion. He was seriously unbalanced, in need of professional help, but I hardly had the energy to stand upright at the helm without tossing my cookies, let alone offer any kind of substantive counseling. At the same time, I began to feel that my very safety depended on how well I could convince him to abandon his delusional thinking.

Oh, how I wished I'd packed a gun on board! The question had certainly come up during the months of preparation, but I had been envisioning attacks from pirates who would surely have more guns, and bigger guns. It had never once occurred to me that I'd require protection from my own crew. All I had to defend myself with were a baseball bat and my years of training as a psychologist.

Both felt entirely inadequate, as driven home to me one night when I was on the deck, cruising along in the trade winds, and heard yelling and crashing sounds coming from the cabin. Wild man DH was down there slamming a frying pan into the stainless steel sink with such force that it left a permanent indentation the size of a piece of pie.

Another evening, after his habitual two glasses of rum, DH started muttering and growling under his breath. I could barely hear him, but the tone was unmistakable, like something issuing from the throat of a cornered wolverine. He stood up, placed himself within my personal space, thrust his shoulders back, pushed his chest out, and raised his chin. He leaned forward until I could smell his putrid breath. "This boat should be mine," he snarled.

A jolt of adrenaline powered through my body. "I'm not sure what you mean," I said.

"What I mean is you don't deserve this boat. It should be mine." He emphasized each word as though speaking to a kindergartener.

Under other circumstances, I might have laughed in his face and waved him away. But DH had a nervous energy about him that made me incredibly uneasy. We were a thousand miles away from civilization, and if he wanted to own this boat there was an easy solution. It took all my willpower not to rush over to the winch handle and hurl it overboard.

I reviewed the facts of this guy's life as they had emerged during our earlier conversations and realized they represented a series of devastating failures. He had no job. His first and second wives had both left him. His third was filing for divorce. His two children wanted nothing to do with him. Now he was drifting across the Pacific Ocean with a total stranger, reviewing these painful life events and seeking reparations.

He had ranted about how much he'd accomplished in his life, foiled always by superiors who had overlooked his contributions time and again. Women had always done him wrong, despite his sacrifices to make them happy. He was forever running out of money, through no fault of his own, which always brought the conversation back to my boat. He wanted my boat. He needed my boat. He *deserved* my boat.

I was alone at sea with an extremely troubled and very large man. I was beginning to feel like a wounded deer trying to escape a 500-pound grizzly that had locked onto my scent and was salivating at the thought of dining on me. I had about as much chance of defeating DH in hand-to-hand combat as I would going up against a grizzly; he outweighed me by more than 100 pounds. There was no place to run, no place to hide, no 911 to call for help. My only means of survival was to outsmart him. I approached the problem in three ways. First, I kept a small but very sharp dive knife in my pocket at all times. Second, I took a flare gun out of its waterproof container and hid it in a tiny storage space in the cockpit. It might not fire bullets, but a white-hot flare to the midsection carried some stopping power, if Hollywood movies had taught me anything. And finally, I put DH on the couch, as it were. Twenty years ago, I had made a living helping people save their own lives by working through their suicidal feelings. Now, I would use those same skills to save my own life. I immediately started searching my brain for what I had learned (and forgotten) in graduate school. The undertaking was not only outside my therapeutic limits, but also light-years beyond my skill set, and virtually doomed by circumstance, since my antagonism for the man only grew with each passing hour.

With a severely limited bag of psychological tools, I developed a theory of his condition as showing signs of pathological denial, or definitely some sort of thought disorder approaching psychosis. (A severe mental disorder in which thought and emotions are so impaired that contact with external reality is lost.)

I attempted to assure him that killing me and taking my boat would not solve his problems. We spent hours imagining a life for DH as a delivery boat captain. He could pass his days on the water, earning a nice living, saving up to buy his own boat. I encouraged him to *see* himself as a delivery boat captain standing at the helm, to picture, in detail, the boat he would buy. I asked him to plan out his first ocean voyage. I particularly emphasized the reward of *earning* his own boat through hard work as opposed to the guilt that would haunt him if he obtained a vessel through treachery. We never quite confronted the elephant in the room—that he wanted to kill me and take my boat—but we danced around it. It was tough going to say the least. My daily therapeutic sessions with DH felt like clinical calisthenics that left me feeling even more drained, something I hadn't thought was possible.

Meanwhile, I was furious at myself for not having vetted the bastard before ever agreeing to board a boat with him. The excuse that I had been pressed for time now seemed flimsy. Talk about stupid: we talked on the phone, he claimed vast bluewater sailing experience, and, just like that, I gave him the keys to the kingdom. What a fool! It wasn't until we were well offshore that I had even begun the process of separating the chicken shit from the chicken salad where DH was concerned. Okay, so I had screwed up royally. But I knew one thing now: I had to get this psychopath off my boat, and I would not be going about that blindly.

Was I apprehensive? No, friend, I was scared for my life. DH literally wanted to kill me and sail away with my boat. I had never in all my life felt a homicidal impulse. But as the nightmare with DH went on, I indeed began to experience such fantasies. I could see it all happening in my mind. While I was on the dog watch, DH would haul his big ass up from the cabin to take his nightly piss, balancing precariously there on the leeward rail, one hand pawing around for his pecker and the other lightly holding onto a shroud. All it would require was a subtle push in the middle of the back. I could almost hear the satisfying splash. The sharks would thank me for such a lovely dinner. No more DH. I would be safe from (and clear of) the sick bastard. For God's sake, it was self-defense, although I wouldn't explain it that way to the authorities. No, keep it simple: high seas, rogue waves, all attempts to rescue him failed, never saw him again, etc. I had no obvious motive that might raise suspicions. His family surely wouldn't cause a fuss . . . but, unfortunately, it wasn't really in me. I could never have lived with the guilt.

• • •

On the twelfth day at sea, I lost it. The monotony, the sea-sickness, and the stress of managing DH's delusions had all been holding steady at a slow burn. But when I discovered that we had made a navigational error and sailed 148 miles in the wrong direction, I wanted nothing more than to get off this boat, and now. I wanted to go home. The whole endeavor had been a colossal mistake. To hell with my $200,000.

It was only then that the true gravity of my situation hit me like a blanket of dread was suddenly dropped over my head, kick in the balls. So what if I really decided to quit? It wasn't like I could click my ruby slippers together and find myself transported home to Sally's arms. The fact was simple: I couldn't go anywhere. If it took me twelve days to get this far riding the trade winds, it would take me at least as long to get home.

I went into an absolute state of shock, panic consuming every inch of my body. I was truly overcome with a feeling of utter despondency, to an extent that I had never before experienced. I am without the power of choice! Helpless as a baby. There is no Plan B; there are no options.

I feel like I am losing control of my mind and my bodily functions all at the same time. Am I having a mental break? What's happening to me? This was supposed to be a dream of sailing around the world. Instead it has turned into the worst nightmare of my life. I am a prisoner trapped with a crazy man who wants to kill me.

There was nothing to do but dig deep, get a grip, and suck it up. I had to sail on.

It took twenty-four hours just to get back to where we had gone off course. I frantically searched my brain for something, anything that could get me out of this situation. *I'll call the Coast Guard. They'll rescue me.*

Oh, sure. Get a grip, dude. I was much too far offshore for any dramatic rescue operation (It's called the "Coast" Guard for a reason). Besides, even if I did call, their first question would be: "Is anyone's life in danger?" I imagined a frantic conversation in which I described my fragile mental health, the crazed crew member, the three-quarter-life crisis that had led me into this precise moment of miserable and crushing remorse. All the while, some kindly Coast Guard dispatcher would be nodding in sympathy, and then he'd offer these compassionate words of wisdom: "Sorry, dumb-ass, but you got yourself into this situation and only you can get yourself out of it."

My imaginary Coast Guardsman had a point. I alone was responsible for constructing this personal nightmare. Turning back was not an option. That left one thing: I had to suck it up and go forward; force out the bad thoughts and work hard to replace them with something that could provide peace of mind. *We can't control the environment, but we can control our thoughts.* Seemed like I had heard that somewhere before, but I couldn't think of where. I thought about Sally, my daughters, and my grandchildren. I thought about Sedona, my constant companion, my boy. But these thoughts were bittersweet. I had to keep reminding myself: *They'll be there when I get home. They're still there, waiting for me. Nothing has changed. It won't be long now.*

The boat was rocking and rolling, and I started to dream of land the way a starving man dreams of food. Dry land. *Terra firma.* What a beautiful phrase. Almost poetry: *Terra firma.* Solid land. A land where DH no longer existed. The dream of sailing to the South Pacific had completely lost its allure. It now appeared utterly stupid, selfish, and sophomoric. More importantly, it required thirty-two to thirty-six days of life aboard this boat, an intolerable proposition.

That night, while I stood watch, every fragment of my being screamed, *Get off this fucking boat!* I went below and asked the GPS to show me to the nearest body of land. There it was: Hilo, Hawaii, 1,000 miles off to the west. I felt a rush of excitement as I calculated out the course. If we made for Hilo, we could reach land in twelve days instead of twenty-three.

Screw Tahiti. Screw the entire South Pacific. Screw any piece of the too-watery planet except Hilo, Hawaii, and Bluebird Canyon. I frantically adjusted the sails, laid the helm over, steered the boat to the new course, and breathed a huge sigh of relief.

CHAPTER 7

• • •

Hilo Hawaii Ho

When you come to the end of your rope, tie a knot and hang on.

—Franklin D. Roosevelt

D H WENT BERSERK WHEN I told him I'd changed course. My decision did not suit him one bit. "You can't do this! What am I going to do in Hawaii? How am I going to get to Tahiti?" But I was not about to budge, no matter how much he cursed and screamed. We were going to land on those tiny little dots in the middle of the Pacific Ocean, and we would just have to figure out the details later.

After the furious battery of abuse subsided, DH went silent . . . stone silent. For the next two days, he stood stock-still in the bow of the boat refusing to speak. No talking. No eye contact. Even the whistling ceased. Hallelujah for that small miracle! If I'd known this would shut him up, I'd have threatened him with heading to land days ago.

We still had to take turns on watch, but it was done wordlessly on his part. My biggest fear was no longer that he'd clobber me with a winch handle (though God knows he may still have been contemplating such a thing behind his stony visage); rather, I couldn't sleep for fear that he would change our course back to Tahiti. Every day I calculated the remaining distance to Hawaii, ticking off each and every mile like an imprisoned man counting the days until his release. If I had to cover even one mile beyond those I had already calculated, I'd fall to pieces. This passage had whipped me mentally as well as physically. Game, set, match!

The trade winds continued to blow at a steady twelve to fifteen knots out of the northeast, and the seas were six to eight feet with a constant swell on the beam. The occasional rogue wave would jump the rail and soak my lap or the back of my neck, as if the sea were not quite done fucking with me. It was a bit like the end of a football game when the winning players dump Gatorade over their coach's head. He knows to expect it, at one level, but he still recoils from the physical shock of ice-cold liquid crashing over his limbs. As often as it happened, I never did get used to getting drenched. Thankfully, the effects of the dreaded seasickness had mercifully subsided to a manageable degree (although I would never be completely clear of it).

With DH transformed into an ornate carving on the boat's prow (more gargoyle than sexy figurehead, to be sure), I could pour all my energy into sailing with utter precision. We all learned in tenth-grade geometry class that the shortest distance between two points is a straight line, and I pulled out all my sailing tricks to coax *Sundance* to follow this simple mathematical truism. Unfortunately, it was extremely difficult to steer on a layline course. Much of the time, the wind was dead aft (coming from straight behind the boat), which meant we needed to sail directly downwind. I know that this sounds great to a non-sailor: *Hey, wind at your back!* In fact, sailing directly downwind is rather tricky and a little bit dangerous. It's not so much a problem for boats equipped with a spinnaker, a lightweight sail that balloons out in front of the boat and pulls it along. Unfortunately, *Sundance* wasn't rigged to carry one.

I tried sailing wing-and-wing with the headsail and the mainsail placed opposite each other, both let out at almost ninety degrees (picture standing with your back to the wind and both arms held straight out parallel to the ground). But, this point of sail requires constant vigilance. If both sails aren't kept full of wind, it could lead to an accidental jibe (in which the mainsail swings violently from one side of the boat to the other, sweeping its way across the deck). Such an error could damage the rigging or capsize the boat. After several wing-and-wing failures, I gave up and was forced to tack downwind, zigzagging off course by as much as thirty degrees, with an average speed of four point two knots . . . it was torture.

Harness Old Dobbin to a buggy, and you'll do four point two knots if he takes it easy. Go for a brisk walk around the block, and you're clocking in at four point two knots. If you'd been out there taking a walk on the Pacific Ocean that afternoon, you would have passed us with a smile and a wave, leaving us a dot on the eastern horizon, because, in your infinite wisdom, you would have chosen to walk in a straight line.

· · ·

It was critical that I get some sleep. To sleep the sweet sleep of the innocent was not possible on *Sundance*. And let me tell you, I love to sleep. Night is one of my favorite times: the cool sheets, soft pillow, slowly drifting off to dreamland. On board *Sundance*, sleep was a torment. Think of the worst turbulence you've ever had on an airplane, in a booming thunderstorm with rain spraying in through the windows . . . and imagine that lasting for days on end.

The boat rocks from side to side *and* up and down . . . all at once, physically hurling you off your bunk. The sheets are sticky from the salt air, the boat makes those constant creaking and thudding noises, and just when you've grown accustomed to them, a large wave comes along and the boat climbs up so high that it crashes down the other side with a thunderous boom. The mast shudders and shrieks like it's going to collapse and pierce the keel.

Then there are times when the world's finest crew member engages the autopilot, falls asleep at the wheel, and lets the sails get back-winded so badly that they begin to flutter wildly, causing their own kind of thunder. Then, once the wind changes direction or another swell pushes the boat around, the wind snatches the mainsail and yanks the boat sideways with such a horrific racket that the bleary-eyed captain leaps from his bunk with a sudden conviction that his vessel has just capsized.

Sleep deprivation is a bitch. I needed some help on the helm, so DH and I agreed on a watch schedule. The first watch would be from 8:00 PM until midnight. Dog watch is midnight until 4:00 AM. Third watch is 4:00 AM until 8:00 AM. I was allotted a maximum of four hours' sleep at a stretch, but it always amounted to much less. Given DH's helplessness at the wheel, I was always on call if we experienced a change in weather, wind speed, or direction. I would haul my tired ass out of the bunk and try to handle whatever came up, but the sleep deprivation rendered me slow, inefficient, and prone to despair.

On the fourteenth day I began sleeping in the cockpit. I always wore my safety harness, secured to a rock-solid cleat on the boat. That way, if I were to be thrown overboard, the harness would keep me close enough to the boat that I could be hauled back onto the deck should anyone care to do so. It's a great idea, much better than falling overboard and watching your boat sail away without you. Going overboard was one of my constant fears, and this harness gave me the confidence to sleep without worrying about being swept out to sea, but its use was somewhat complicated.

I would lie down on the bench and use one of the seat cushions for a pillow. The bench was short, so my legs hung off the end. If I tried to lie on my side, my arm would wedge itself into the little storage space where I had stashed the unwrapped flare gun. It so happened that the winch handle was stored in this little space as well, and I'd work myself around so that the clunky device wasn't prodding my arm. The bench was so narrow that I was forced to stuff my other arm into my foul-weather jacket pocket to keep it from dangling off the edge.

The first night of this new arrangement, during dog watch, it felt pretty darn good to stretch out. I could see some of the mainsail and hear the slapping of the waves against the hull; the harness was attached to a cleat; the radar alarm was set. *Why haven't I been doing this all along?* I wondered. *This is great!* I fell asleep with a big grin on my face. Minutes later, an enormous swell rocked the boat so violently that I was tossed onto the cockpit floor with a giant thud. Not a pleasant awakening.

I studied the situation and jury-rigged a way to stay put. I wrapped the safety harness around one of the winches three or four times so it had much less slack. When the boat rocked in a swell, I would start to fall off the bench, but the tether would go taut and hold me in place. Once I got over the whole "Whoa! I'm falling!" sensation, the movement became almost pleasant. I was back in the cradle, being rocked to sleep.

The harness kept me secured to the boat, but I still worried about the possibility of encountering another ship out there. We hadn't seen another vessel since our third day out of San Diego, but I had read somewhere that 46,000 merchant ships ply their trade on the world's oceans. We definitely weren't alone. My boat was equipped with a radar alarm that could detect vessels within a twenty-mile radius. If a ship came within range, an alarm would sound to wake me up and I could change course, if necessary. Since most big ships cruise at twenty-two to twenty-five knots, I estimated having approximately fifteen minutes to change course once the alarm sounded. As long as I woke up immediately, that would be just enough time, which shouldn't be a problem, given the conditions.

Some nights, my "bed" felt less like a cradle and more like a casket; and I was the living dead. Although the boat maintained a steady course while the autopilot was engaged, it still required endless manual adjustments depending on changes in the weather, wind direction, wind intensity, and so forth. I could immediately feel when the wind shifted. The sails started luffing and I'd pull myself out of an all-too-brief sleep to make the tiny adjustments necessary. This scenario repeated itself every twenty to thirty minutes throughout the night. "No job too small"— that could have been my motto.

On nights when it rained, I might haul myself under the shelter of the dodger (a cover made of canvas). Most nights, I'd just say to hell with it. Let it rain. I hadn't been dry to begin with.

In this new reality I was facing, my mind fell into the pattern of drifting back and forth between two worlds: the immediate future and the long-ago past. Sometimes I'd lie awake and dream of putting a For Sale sign on the boat in Hawaii; or better yet, I would catch the first plane back home and have the boat delivered to San Diego, and then sell it. It was already fully equipped for bluewater passage. Hell, I'd throw in all my unused MREs for free. A steal of a deal, as George might say.

Other times, I'd look up toward the sky and dream of the past. One night, trying to sleep in the midst of a light sprinkle, I recalled an evening long, long ago, playing catch in the front yard with my then-six-year-old daughter, Kasey. The third of my four daughters, Kasey always woke each morning with a sweet smile on her face that warmed my heart. I was teaching her how to catch a softball, but the ball slipped through her outstretched hands and bounced off her nose. Tears welled up in her eyes, but she didn't want to cry. She wanted to be brave for her dad. I rushed over to make sure she wasn't bleeding and to give her a hug, and as I checked her nose, she started laughing at herself. I laughed with her, and we tumbled to the ground. As we laid in the grass on that warm summer evening, a light rain began to fall. We both looked up at the sky, feeling the soft patter of the droplets on our faces, neither of us wanting to go inside and break the spell. Lying there aboard *Sundance*, I could still feel Kasey lying next to me, hear her laughter, and feel that rain from decades ago on my face. I missed my girls terribly. Just about every evening, I asked myself: *What the hell am I doing out here?*

After two full days of complete silence, DH opened his big mouth.

"Do you know why I chose you and this boat to cross the Pacific?"

I immediately missed his silence, but there was nothing for it. Press on.

"No, I sure don't. Tell me why you picked this boat."

I had a pretty good idea where he was going with this, and I felt myself getting anxious. We exchanged contemptuous looks, and I felt my antagonism toward him once again ratcheting up.

"Because you had the perfect boat for me, a good ocean boat, and you were going alone. It would just be the two of us. I had some other boats that needed crew but there were too many people on board. I wanted to sail with just one other person."

As he said it, he stood up, towering over me, staring directly into my eyes for an uncomfortable minute. Then he slithered down below like some prehistoric creature. He hadn't quite come out and said it, but he had come close enough. And his declaration of doom shook molecules in my body I didn't even know I had. I had to fight the urge to slip the flare gun out of its cache and follow him below . . .

Minutes later, my murderous urge gave way to its complete opposite. I was just so exhausted from lack of sleep, suffused with such a sense of defeat, and wrenched with such utter regret about this whole miserable voyage that I felt like handing him the winch handle and saying, "Just get it over with."

The next morning, DH came up from the cabin, whistling. The deep freeze was over, and now I could look forward to lots and lots of jaunty whistling.

On quieter days, I passed the time by studying the charts to make certain we were on course to the islands or listening to music and books on tape. This eased my crushing boredom and gave me an excuse to wear headphones, thereby blocking out any unwelcome noise emanating from DH. I had brought hardcopy books, and of course, I had all those manuals lying about, but seasickness prevented me from reading a word. Whenever the seasickness did subside for a brief spell, I would go down below and fire up the laptop to read e-mails from my family. It was my only form of non-DH communication, and I clung to it like a lifeline. When you're in the middle of the ocean, the isolation is so devastating that it's easy to begin to feel like you're the last person left on the planet. Even though my loved ones didn't know half of the adversity I was facing, it helped to read their keep-your-chin-up messages. Sally's expressions of love and support, in particular, kept me sane. Lord, I missed her so much that it ached all over. My feelings for her had actually surprised me. Considering my personal history, I had come to doubt that I could ever again love someone with complete abandon; but now I found myself balancing in the cabin, using one finger to stab out this message: "One positive aspect of this experience, the realization of how much I love you and need to be together for me to be happy. I always knew that but not to this extent. Even if I sail on to paradise, it would not be paradise without you there! I want to be with the one I love."

As we drew closer to Hilo, my patience with the wind grew thin. We didn't hit any big storms and the weather was reasonably good for sailing, but the winds were consistently inconsistent. On days when the winds were so light as to be approaching non-existent, I called upon FUJIMO, my little fifty-five-horsepower diesel engine. It pushed us along at a steady five knots, consuming half a gallon of fuel every hour. Unfortunately, since I only had fifty gallons of fuel on board (with another twenty gallons in jerry jugs lashed to the lifelines), I had to exercise restraint. Even though *Sundance* carried six solar panels to help charge the battery bank, we needed to conserve fuel to charge the batteries every few days. It was also critical to conserve enough fuel so I could enter the unfamiliar port in Hawaii under power.

I came up with the name FUJIMO during my years racing sailboats. The rules in sailboat racing are explicit: under no circumstances do you engage the engine, except to save a drowning man. Consequently, if the wind stops, the boat stops. And the entire crew must sit and wait for the wind to return. One year, as a member of the crew on a forty-foot sloop in the Chicago-to-Mackinac yacht race; we surfed all the way to Mackinac Island in record time, blasted along by steady twelve- to twenty-two-knot winds. The very next year, I joined the same race and we had so little wind that the entire fleet set a record for slowest elapsed time. It took twice as many days to reach the island.

When I bought my first boat, I took it out for a sail with

some of my racing buddies. We lost all wind and were sitting dead in the water. "Time to crank up FUJIMO," I said.

One of my friends said, "Oh, you named your engine for a mountain in Japan?"

"Hell, no, it's not a mountain in Japan," I said. "It's an acronym: Fuck You, Jack, I'm Moving On!"

CHAPTER 8

Dry Land

If at first you don't succeed, try, try again. Then quit. There's no use being a damn fool about it.

—W.C. Fields

KEEPING A SHARP EYE ON the primary GPS as well as the back-up handheld units, I watched as the hours left till our estimated arrival in Hilo harbor ticked down. Shortly after noon on the twenty-second day, I saw what looked like a large cloud bank on the horizon. I squinted at it for a while, canting my head, wondering. The cluster of cloud wasn't moving, and it appeared to be growing. Could it be? As we inched closer, a great rush of excitement swept over me. Yes! This was not a cloud bank; it was land! Land—the most beautiful concept in the world. I grabbed a pair of binoculars, ran forward and stood on the bow pulpit, my heart pounding like a jackhammer. I balanced myself on the top rail to get a better look, lifted the binoculars to my eyes and brought the scene into focus. "Land ho!" I screamed as loud as I could. "Land ho!"

My cloud bank was actually the earth's most massive volcano, the 500,000-year-old Mauna Loa, rising from sea level to over 13,000 feet. No wonder it was visible to me from over fifty miles offshore. I imagined the volcano was welcoming us to Hawaii, just as it had welcomed Captain James Cook and his sailing vessel HMS *Endeavor* a few years before *Sundance* poked her nose into these exotic waters. I stood grinning up at the mountain. I could almost hear it saying, "Welcome to Hawaii, young fella. Come on! You're almost here."

Whew and Hallelujah, time to break out the Mai Tais! It's hard to convey the excitement that I felt; I guess you could compare it to Christmas morning when you were a kid—*combined* with the excitement of your birthday, all rolled up into one overwhelming feeling of pure joy. I will never forget the thrill, the elation, the excitement to which I completely abandoned myself. I laughed; I cried; I danced a jig on the cabin top. Hosanna! Glory be! My dream-turned-nightmare, my sail from hell, my torture and imprisonment, would soon be over. And I was still alive. It seemed a miracle.

DH had an entirely different reaction to seeing land. He stood silently, watching the volcano come into view, not uttering a word . . . and then he started to cry. But he was not shedding tears of joy like I was; his were tears of sorrow and disappointment. He did not want the passage to come to an end. Being isolated at sea was his most comfortable place in life. He was able to avoid all the conflicts and issues he had to face on land. I began to feel the stirrings of sympathy; how badly must he have wrecked his life that he preferred the hell of a cramped, pitching sailboat on gray seas under steely skies? But it would have been foolish to feel sorry for him. Now more than ever, I had to be on my guard. For the next twelve hours, I would not so much as turn my back on him. This close to reaching landfall, I wasn't about to let him fulfill his fantasy of taking my boat without pesky old me on board.

Eleven hours, thirty-five minutes to reach the entrance of the harbor, according to the GPS. That would put us there in the middle of the night. Crap. That presented a bit of a problem. Actually, it presented a pretty big problem. One of the most basic precepts of coastal cruising is that you should never attempt to enter an unfamiliar harbor at night. DH insisted that it was too dangerous to try entering in the dark.

"We'd best just sail circles outside the harbor until daylight," he said.

Oh, I hated him so, especially when he was right. Circling outside the harbor is exactly what the cruising manual would suggest we do. But this was not a normal circumstance. After twenty-two days at sea and 2,300 nautical miles under the hull, this captain was taking his ship ashore, no matter how dark it happened to be. End of discussion.

I spent the rest of the day preparing myself for a night entrance into Hilo's Radio Bay. Glancing up only enough to make sure DH wasn't coming at me with a winch handle, I pored over the charts and cruising guide, studying each of the hazards involved in entering the harbor. As badly as I wanted to reach dry land, I certainly had no desire to swim ashore after putting *Sundance* on a reef or smashing her into some rocks. The radar was a crucial part of this procedure, and would serve as my eyes in the dark. The chart showed a number of lighted navigational buoys, which would be my visual targets. "Red Right Returning," I mumbled to myself: I must keep the red navigational lights to starboard and the green ones to port.

It was 1:00 AM when I spotted the first navigational light in the distance. I swallowed hard. *Push on, boy*, I said to myself. *You can do this.* Minutes later, I breathed a sigh of relief at the appearance of the range markers that would guide me into Radio Bay. These markers function a bit like peep sights on a gun: they consist of two lights positioned near each other. When viewed from offshore, the two beacons only become aligned vertically when your vessel is positioned on the correct bearing to enter the harbor opening.

The radar showed a break wall off to the port side that wasn't visible by eye but was very clear on the radar screen. The depth finder provided the other key piece of data for my approach. *Sundance* always required at least six feet of water under her hull. If it became too shallow, my plan was to put FUJIMO in reverse and head back out to sea. As we crept toward land, the water depth dropped steadily: two hundred feet, one hundred, fifty, now steady at twenty-two feet. One more thing worried me: What was the tide doing? Under the best-case scenario, we'd enjoy a high tide, which would give us the greatest amount of water depth to work with. But without an up-to-date tide table, there was just no way to be sure what to expect. The chart indicated there was enough water to accommodate *Sundance's* six-foot draft, so I pushed on. The water depth held steady at twenty feet or higher, but watching the depth finder made my stomach churn.

The navigation lights appeared one after another until the harbor's red and green entrance lights were just off the bow. I had DH go forward with a powerful flashlight, hoping he would see any obstacles and avoid collision with anything hard. The radar showed that I needed to make a sharp turn to port just outside the first set of harbor lights; once past the lights, I laid the helm over and easily made the turn. We were close, only a mile or so to go. We had cleared the break wall off to the port side, which stops the surf from crashing into the harbor. Smooth water, at last! What a strange and comforting sensation to be on flat water. In the distance, I could see a pier jutting out on the starboard side, leaving what looked like a small entrance into Radio Bay. *Okay, just heave to*—and then the depth finder alarm started screaming. I had set it to ten feet, and it was now showing that the ten-foot mark had come and gone. The water level was dropping; now there were less than nine feet under the hull. I had to make an immediate decision: Continue on and hope we don't run aground, or put her in reverse and try to back out of a very tight spot.

Hell with it. I had come too far to hit reverse. I could almost taste the act of dropping the anchor. Push on. The water got down to eight feet. It had to be low tide! I tried not to picture the thin two feet of water left between the unforgiving bottom and Sundance's keel (*bathtub, kiddie pool, throw a coin into the fountain*). Just when it looked like we were going to hit bottom, the depth alarm stopped yelling at me and the water started to get deeper. A moment later we were floating on a comfortable twenty feet of water, then thirty. With an abundance of water under the hull, the danger of running aground had thankfully passed. Thirty feet of wonderful, flat, water with no more danger of us running aground. Dodged another bullet!

• • •

It was now two-thirty in the morning. My painstaking progress into the harbor had taken more than two very nerve-racking hours. What a magnificent feeling. I had not been at all confident I could do it, I had been scared, but in my determination to get off the ocean that night, I had done it; I had managed to get *Sundance* inside the harbor without hitting anything or running aground. I motored on, looking for an anchorage.

On July 9, 2000, at 4:32 AM, I dropped the anchor in twenty-five feet of calm water in Radio Bay, next to the little town of Hilo, Hawaii. I listened to the anchor's little splash, and then savored the satisfying tug as it set on the bottom. I stood there in the dark for a moment, just breathing. I had never felt such triumph or such a colossal feeling of pure relief. My God. I was safe after twenty-three excruciating days and 2,175 miles of bottomless Pacific Ocean.

I took a step. Hey! Someone had mercifully unplugged the mechanical bull. I could stand up and walk around the boat without the fear of being tossed overboard. Imagine getting such joy from the simple act of standing up without holding on for dear life—probably the last time I'd felt this way was when I was ten months old.

Next order of business: sleeping in a stationary bunk! I hurried below and wasted no time crawling into the warm sheets, resting my head on a real pillow and drifting off into a deep, slumbered state. Seldom do I dream, but this night my overspent brain must have been firing off all kinds of random signals. In the morning, I couldn't remember a single specific of any of these dreams, only that they were constant, and that they were strange, wild visions, about things that made no sense . . . the dreams of a madman.

I woke up about five-thirty, feeling like I had put in a good night's sleep rather than simply an hour. I crawled out of the bunk and climbed the four steps of the companionway ladder leading outside to the cockpit. Dawn was just breaking, a lavender

smear out over the Pacific. Once again, I was struck by the overwhelming feeling of pure relief. As the sky brightened, I looked
hungrily around at my surroundings. Up on shore, I could see
the familiar sights I had always taken for granted back home.
Look . . . trees! To see a tree made me as giddy as a groupie spot-
ting a rock star. Oh, yes, there were plenty of trees. And you
know what else? Green grass! And what were those—people?
Yes, people, walking out on the breakwater!

And the smells . . . land, grass, leaves, soil. But what I enjoyed most of all were the sounds. Listen there: That's a dog bark-
ing. Hark! Birds singing, a plane taking off, cars grinding along
through the street. Nothing, of course, was unique about these
sounds. They are what we hear all day every day as landlubbers,
and in fact, they are what we often wish to escape. We seldom
ever stop to listen to the birds singing or enjoy the roar of airplanes taking off. But when you haven't had the pleasure of hearing these sounds for almost a month, all of a sudden they sound
very special, and they remind you that, wander as you might, you
are by your nature a part of the human family and your place is
in its bosom. This passage had taken twenty-three days. That is
a long time to not see a tree or hear a dog bark, to be all alone
except for a person who is your antagonist. Now I was back
among my species, in its habitat. I stood there for the longest
time, drinking in every smell, every sound, every sight, smiling
the biggest smile that came from deep in my gut. I was safe.

Hilo Harbor is located in a commercial shipping area, some
three miles from the town of Hilo. There are limited pleasure
boat facilities, no yacht clubs, and no marinas. It's very industrial-
looking, hardly the vision of the Hawaiian harbor I had been
treasuring, which had involved pretty dancing natives in grass
skirts leaning forward to drape flowery leis around my neck. But
I couldn't have cared less. This was a safe harbor and I was happy
as hell to be here. Check that: I was *overjoyed* as hell to be here.

I went up to the bow to pull the anchor so we could motor over to a stone wall with a ladder that would be our access
to land. Big boats like *Sundance* use an electric-powered winch,

called a windlass, to raise the anchor. It is connected to a battery for which powering the windlass was its only purpose in life, the better to ensure that there would always be plenty of juice. I stepped on the switch and nothing happened. What? I tried it again. Nothing.

The windlass is an essential piece of equipment on a cruising sailboat. Without a powerful windlass, one must hoist up the anchor by hand. *Sundance* actually had two anchors, each weighing forty-five pounds, attached to three-eighths-inch chain that is called the anchor rode. I had purchased the brand new Lofrans Kobra windlass at a price of $2,975 in San Diego. The professional installation had cost over $1,000. And now, the first time I asked this expensive windlass to go to work, it didn't do jack shit. It wouldn't budge, zip, whir, hum—nada, nothing. Shit.

I opened the anchor locker and crawled inside to see if anything caught my untrained eye. I immediately saw a thick white coating of corrosion covering everything in the locker. During the passage, salt air and saltwater had accumulated, slathering the whole works in crusty white goo. The corrosion had completely eaten away the small electrical wires that provide power to the windlass. The windlass itself sits on top of the deck encased in plastic and canvas to keep it dry, but I'd had no idea that seawater could get into the anchor locker and do so much damage.

That meant that the forty-five-pound anchor was going to have to be pulled up by brute strength. human power—*my* human power! I stretched and flexed a little in preparation for the task, not wishing to force out any hernias. Then I sat on the bow, braced both feet out in front of me to try to get some leverage, and with both hands began to pull. Holy hell. It took every ounce of my strength to move the chain, mere inches at a time. The weight was just tremendous. I stopped for a break, shaking from the exertion, and then pulled on the anchor line.

Someday, perhaps, I will draw up a list of all the dumb things I am guilty of doing on my boat, and when I do, I'll probably use this anecdote to kick off the list. There I sat on the bow, straining and trembling, sweating bullets, pulling with all my might to get that anchor up. I had decided I must have gotten the anchor about three quarters of the way up when I experienced a strange sensation of movement, followed by a crushing realization. *Oh, for Christ's sake. Oh . . .* For all my effort, I had not budged the anchor, which was no doubt still set stubbornly on the bottom. No, what I had been doing was taking all the slack out of the anchor line by *pulling this twenty-ton boat through the goddamned water* toward the anchor. What a non-idiot would have done to get the slack out was, you know, start the engine and motor over to above where the anchor was laying on the seabed. I can be such a dumb-ass sometimes that I amaze even myself.

Once the boat was sitting over the anchor, all I had to do was pull the damn thing up, which went quite easily. Before, as I had been laboring to pull the boat through the water, I'd been savoring a self-righteous resentment toward DH for lying asleep in his bunk while I did all the work. Once I'd realized my howler of a mistake, though, it suddenly seemed just as well that he catch up on his shut-eye.

With the anchor secured on deck, it was time to work the boat over to the stone wall where we could climb up built-in steel ladders and onto the land. I went below and stood over DH. "Come on," I said, like a little boy waking up his brother on Christmas morning. "Let's go on land!"

He rolled toward me and scowled and sighed. "Now?" he said.

"Yes, man. Now."

The procedure was to first drop and secure the anchor off the bow, then back the boat up toward the wall and get close enough to tie a couple of stern lines to a cleat located near the top of the wall. Once the boat was tied in place, I inflated the dinghy and we dropped it into the water and lowered ourselves into it. We puttered the few feet over to the ladder, and I almost jumped onto the first rung. I actually counted the eight ladder rungs, so significant did the moment feel. Neil Armstrong in reverse. And just like that, at long last, I was standing on dry land.

At that moment, if a ten-year-old had walked up to me and offered me his lunch money in exchange for *Sundance*, I am sure I would have sold her there on the spot. I was so happy to get off that damn boat that I was certain I would never step foot on another one in my lifetime. I couldn't even bring myself to look over my shoulder at *Sundance*. *That's it*, I thought, as I took my first few steps on shore. *This dream has come to an end. Stick a fork in me, 'cause I'm done. I want to go home, hug Sally, play with my grandchildren, sit in my leather recliner watching football, and pet my wonderful dog.*

Once on land, I needed to locate a pay phone, since I had tossed my cell phone into the ocean (which I regretted at this point). I needed to call Sally to let her know that the foolishness was over; I was off the dangerous ocean and standing on solid ground—although the solid ground did not *feel* very solid. It was moving, rocking back and forth, as if a 9.7 earthquake were happening right under my feet. I staggered and caught myself against the trunk of a tree. *Phew. Must have left my equilibrium back in San Diego.* I had forgotten how to balance on a surface that wasn't moving, and here on terra firma, I was nearly incapacitated. My leg muscles had turned into pasta *al dente*, and vertigo was wreaking terrible havoc on my coordination. It was next to impossible to walk the walk of a sober man. Anyone observing the way I was staggering about would assume I was just another drunken sailor.

God, it was good to hear Sally's voice on the phone. I wanted to crawl through the line and give her the biggest hug and kiss. "Are you really safe?" she said.

"Yes, baby. I'm on shore . . . on land!"

"And you're safe?"

"Of course. Yes."

"Then you should come home. Come home right this minute!"

"Oh, you have no idea how bad I want to come home. If I could be there in a minute, I would. I will be home just soon as humanly possible."

I staggered away from the phone with a big lover-boy grin on my face. Thankfully, despite my wobbling, I no longer felt nauseous. The seasickness had subsided as soon as I'd placed my feet on solid ground. That meant that I could eat, and I wasn't fucking around when it came to that order of business. I asked a local for directions to the closest restaurant, and he told us it was about two miles down the road toward town. DH and I started the long walk. Even though it was a little hard to walk a steady course, I welcomed the opportunity to stretch my legs, and relished the sublime act of walking.

It was still morning when we found the restaurant, and I pigged out on the largest breakfast of my life: eggs over easy, hash brown potatoes, crispy bacon well done, sourdough toast, and a hot coffee. Yes, that was a nice first course. Then I ordered up some pancakes with strawberries and whipped cream on top. As I stuffed them down my gullet, I pondered a third round that would involve waffles with chocolate syrup, but I discovered there *was* an end to my greed, and I spared the waffles for another day.

After breakfast, DH headed back to the boat to sulk and I walked alone into town. I marched straight into the first travel agency I found and bought two one-way tickets—one for me to get home, the other for DH to return to the Windy City on the first flight out the next morning. I would not waste another moment getting that SOB out of my life, and was more than happy to buy the ticket, since that had always been our agreement. My flight to LAX was scheduled to leave Hilo in three days—just enough time, I hoped, to sort out the mess on *Sundance*. My next goal was to find the closest motel.

Once in the room, I stood there under the blast of the shower until the hot water was gone. I then laid down on the bed and within five minutes, I was ten toes up, dead to the world. Sometime during the night, I awoke suddenly on my back with my arms out to either side with a death grip on the edges of the bed. In my sleep, I had dreamed vividly that I was falling off the bench seat where I'd attempted to sleep on the boat for the last twelve nights. I was clinging to the bed as tightly as I could, desperate not to fall. It felt so real. I would wake up confused, not knowing where I was for the first few seconds. Once I realized that it was only a dream, it was easy to fall back to sleep, but not for long. Again and again I woke with the terrible sensation of falling, with the cold ocean water hitting me in the face. Finally, I took a pillow and the blanket and lay on the floor. At last I drifted into a peaceful sleep, luxuriating in the feeling that I was safe and dry.

• • •

The next morning I had an appointment with a large plate of waffles, which I dispatched with gusto. I then strolled to a car rental place, still getting my land legs, and rented a red compact Ford, which I drove back to where *Sundance* was anchored. I found DH sitting in the cockpit with his back to the land, staring out at what appeared to me to be a featureless sea.

"DH," I said. "You should get your stuff packed. You're scheduled to fly out of Hilo in two hours."

He gave me a wounded look, as if I'd said something uncalled-for, and then his face went dark and he mumbled something under his breath.

I was about to ask him what he'd said, but he got up and went below to pack, and I thought it best to hold my tongue. A few minutes later he emerged into the cockpit with his paltry duffel bag, and we walked silently up to the car. We drove to the airport without exchanging one word. I was thankful for the silence.

I pulled up to the curb of the small terminal, left the car running, yanked on the emergency brake, and got out and opened the trunk. He lifted his bag out and I and handed him his ticket. To my own surprise, I heard myself say, "Thank you for all your help."

He lifted his eyes to meet my gaze, and I read emotional confusion there; he was nearly wincing with the effort to sort out his feelings. At last he said, "Yeah. That was interesting."

He shouldered his bag and walked into the terminal. I leaned against the car, watching through the large glass doors as he lumbered up to the ticket counter, and I lingered until he headed through security. I got back in the car and drove a couple hundred feet over to where I could see the tarmac through a chain-link fence. I stayed there until I saw him galumphing over to his plane amid a gaggle of passengers, looking as dangerous and outsized as a bull walking among schoolchildren. I watched him climb the metal stairs and stoop through the door of the plane. Still, I sat in the car. I didn't take my eyes off of the plane until the door was closed and secured shut and the portable stairs were pulled away. Then, I waited until the aircraft slowly lifted off the ground. The massive wheels receded into the belly of that beautiful aluminum bird that was carrying my adversary away over the endless ocean. Dexter Higginbotham was gone, and I was truly safe at last.

When I got back to the boat, I was surprised at how peaceful it felt without DH on board. I felt like I had been living with my fists clenched for weeks, and now I was finally able to relax and focus on cleaning up the boat. Of the five other sailboats tied up to the wall, only one had made a crossing from California. Its skipper, Rob Denner, had just completed his third crossing, along with his wife, Susan. In stark contrast to my frazzled state, Rob and Susan were calm and cool about the crossing. To them, it seemed like sailing from California to Hawaii was no big deal at all, rather like a jaunt out to Catalina Island. It's amazing what a good crew and a big spinnaker can do to make a long-distance passage seem like a walk in the park.

"Well," I said. "I wish it had been that easy for me, but it wasn't. I'm going home just as soon as I can."

"Sure," Rob said. "You've had a tough crossing. We'll be tied up here for a month, and we'd be happy to keep an eye on *Sundance* for you until you come back to finish your trip."

"I'd love it if you'd look after the boat," I said. "But I won't be finishing this trip."

Rob and Susan looked at each other and smiled. "Don't be so sure," Rob said. "Anyway, go home and unwind. *Sundance* will be fine."

Well, they could think whatever they wanted to. But I would rather be blind, crippled, crazy, and pushing up daisies than get back on that damn boat. Two days later, I boarded my flight to LAX.

* * *

CHAPTER 9

Home School

Pain is temporary. It may last a minute, or an hour, or a day, or a year, but eventually it will subside and something else will take its place. But if I quit, however, it lasts forever.
—Lance Armstrong

THE FLIGHT TO LAX TOOK a total of five hours in maximum comfort. I leaned back in my seat, looking down toward the endless pan of ocean speeding away beneath me; five luxurious hours to zip across the monstrous expanse that had taken me a total of twenty-three days to struggle over in constant discomfort.

Sally and Sedona were waiting for me in the parking area of the airport. The sight of them standing there made my heart jump into my throat and the tears started to roll down my cheeks. I ran to Sally; we hugged, we kissed, we hugged some more. I didn't want to let her go. She felt so good, she looked so beautiful, and she smelled so good. I was right up bumping heaven. Sally drove us home to Irvine. Sedona lolled happily on my lap, all 100 pounds of him. My face hurt from smiling.

* * *

Home, home at last. "The sailor has returned from the sea." I had learned my lesson, and was more than content now to slide into the Serene Sixties. All I wanted to do was to hug Sally, walk Sedona, play with my grandchildren, eat, and sleep—forever. I was emaciated, gaunt, my hair was longer than it had ever been, a razor had not touched my face since I left San Diego, and I felt like my teeth must have be green. When I stepped onto the scale at my health club, I saw that I had lost a total of sixteen pounds on the twenty-three-day passage. Before setting sail, I had weighed 178 pounds and was in pretty good shape for a sixty-year-old man, thanks to my routine of working out five or six days a week. Now the scale showed that I weighed 162 pounds, and I wasn't particularly surprised. It's not difficult to lose weight when your caloric intake is minimal and you throw up most of what you have consumed.

My equilibrium quickly returned, and it was now possible to walk a straight line. The only time I felt the effects of being at sea anymore was when I stood in the shower, which rocked and rolled for about another week. Altogether, my physical recovery was amazingly rapid, within ten days, I was back to normal.

Sally hung on to me all night long, and when she occasionally let go, I found her in the dark and pulled her against me and went on sleeping. On the second morning after my return, she made me a lovely breakfast, and we sat beaming at each other over our coffee. "So," she said. "Have you decided what to do about your boat?"

"Makes the most sense for me to sell it, don't you think?"

"Yes. Oh, I'm glad to hear you say that."

My plan was to find a delivery boat captain and pay the $8,000 fee to have him sail the boat back to San Diego, where I would put a For Sale sign on her. I just knew that I didn't want to continue the torturous experience of sailing across the Pacific Ocean. I did not want to leave Sally again, and I didn't want to leave my comfortable home. I knew that I would not be able to deal with being tired, cold, wet, and hungry for days at a time ever again. I was sure that I wanted nothing more to do with *Sundance*. I was willing to admit that my dream had been a huge mistake. *Abort the dream*, I told myself.

But, as the days went on, I realized there was some tiny part of me that was not quite keen with that decision. Part of it had to do with how quickly things around home were returning to the way they had been. At first, everything around me had seemed vivid and new, but it didn't take long at all before I realized that nothing here at home had changed. Everything was just the same as when I'd left. The people, the traffic, the office, and the radio stations I listened to—they were all exactly the same.

As my newfound domestic contentment began to erode, so did my resolve to sell *Sundance*. I was conflicted, and more than a little confused, by my qualms about aborting the dream. Something was wrong inside me. Somehow I had climbed aboard the vacillation roller coaster and it was picking up speed.

When it came down to it, my growing sense of dread about selling the boat could be captured in one word: *quitter*. That's what was eating away at me: a concept that, for my whole life, had been completely anathema to me. If I abandoned the dream of sailing around the world at this point, I would be a *quitter*. Can I live with the knowledge that I am a quitter? The very thought of *being a quitter* made my intestines cramp like a clenched fist. A decision to quit would hound me—would define me—for the rest of my life.

Humans have the wonderful ability to repress painful experiences; to force them deep into our subconscious. Without this ability to bury the memories of things that have hurt us, women most certainly would never have more than one baby. And, I believe, many men would only get married once.

As I sat in the comfort of my big brown leather recliner, surrounded by my loving family and my wonderful dog, or drifting cozily off to sleep in Sally's arms each night, or enjoying good food each day, the natural process of psychological repression was fast at work. How hard had it been out there on the boat? Not so bad, surely. Hadn't it actually been bracing?

One morning after a particularly restless night, I found a legal pad and grabbed some pencils, and with a hot cup of coffee, I went outside to sit in the sun and begin an intensive period of self-analysis. I put myself on the therapist's couch. This was a process of self-exploration, of reality therapy; searching for an answer from within. Refusing to allow anything but the truth from myself, I spent the next several days taking an in-depth look at why I had reacted with such great negativity to the ordeal at sea. During the process, I decided to call on a good friend of mine who was a psychologist, hoping he could help me find some answers.

"Well," he said right off. "Have you read Stadler's book?"

Apparently I had not, because I had no idea who Stadler was.

"I've got a copy right here," he said. "Come by and pick it up. *Psychology of Sailing: The Sea's Effects on Mind and Body*. By Michael Stadler."

The next day I devoured the book, my jaw hanging open the whole time.

We grow up and develop in a world on land. When we go to sea we are forced to go through the process of socialization for a second time. Onboard a boat for long periods of time in extremely cramped conditions with no personal privacy and no possibility of escape, we become part of a group with a fixed formal structure that does not necessarily coincide with its psychological structure.

Social density on a sailboat is extremely high. Elsewhere, similar spatial conditions are only to be found in overcrowded prisons.

Aha!

Everyone needs their own space and even private space. Their own area of responsibility, the chance to withdraw from others. On board, the invasion of one's personal space has to be accepted for a considerable length of time. The bunk becomes your nest of private space and acquires almost symbolic significance. Prolonged conditions of stress can and will make life unbearable.

Well . . . I'll be damned. My reaction to the situation at sea had been predictable and completely within reason. I cursed myself for not having read this book before going offshore. It would undoubtedly have helped me keep perspective on what was happening, or at the least given me some warning about what to expect.

Sally was on to me, I could tell. More than two weeks had passed and I hadn't done a thing about selling the boat. And I was obviously in the kind of agitated state that had led to my original decision to put to sea. Her eyes began to shrink away from me, like someone who stumbles upon a leper. It hurt me to think of causing her more pain.

Still, I continued my self-analysis, well aware that I was running out of time. The nice people watching my boat in Hilo were going to be moving on in another ten days. I needed to make a decision to either sell the boat or go back and continue sailing.

I wrote the following conclusion to my self-therapy:

You have the opportunity of a lifetime to sail on to Tahiti and beyond. You are uniquely privileged with the adventure of sailing the high seas and accomplishing something meaningful in your life. The chance to experience who you are . . . to get to really know yourself.

Yes, you will be away from those you love so dearly. And yes, that is a hard pill to swallow. It is difficult to leave family behind, especially your Sally. But you won't be gone that long—three or four years at the most. You will be able to experience a lifetime of adventures.

Sure, sailing is hard. Everything is inconvenient and it can be very dangerous, but falling asleep in front of the TV in your leather recliner every night is not an acceptable alternative.

You have made one bluewater passage. Twenty-three days at sea. It was hard, you were miserable, and on the verge of losing your marbles. But you did it, damn it.

Think about how fast you recovered from this misadventure. In just three weeks, you were fully recovered, with no long-lasting adverse effects (except for what may remain in your head—your mental state is going to require some more work).

I wrote much more. About how one's attitude is the key to happiness in life, and how my attitude during the passage had been unacceptable. *If you can't change your attitude, you should not return to sailing, or you will continue to be one miserable SOB.*

Of course passage-making is hard, I reminded myself; it requires a lot of work under difficult conditions. But just wait a minute, boy. This is nothing—nothing!—compared to what many people face every day. Hell, forget about serious adversity and just look at the great mass of people all around you, driving on packed freeways on their way to mundane jobs with very little reward and certainly no excitement. You have to put this situation into a much better perspective. All around you, people are living their own private hell: subsisting as wage slaves, pursuing meaningless careers in hopes they can keep paying the mortgage, and you have the audacity to complain about a life of *sailing*? Why, you dumb-ass, you great big wimp. You had better realize just how good you have it. Stop your bitching; stop all the complaining. Compared to ninety-nine percent of the people out there working their asses off every day, you are one lucky son of a bitch.

But I get so lonely and miss everyone I love.

Get a grip. Everything here at home will be the same as when you left. It's not like you are going away for any great length of time. You can come home during the three-month cyclone season when you can't sail anyway. Do you really want to piss away the opportunity of a lifetime? Do you really want to walk away from your dream? Do you want to kiss off what will be a meaningful accomplishment?

On and on I lectured myself: you'd better remember that you came into this life alone and you're going to leave it alone. If you depend on others for your happiness, you will be miserable most of your life. It's entirely up to you to determine how happy you choose to be. Will you work to be happy or indulge yourself in a life of self-pity?

It was all pretty basic stuff, the kind of thing you can read in any self-help book or hear from any motivational speaker. *Am I working on being happy or am I accepting the negative crap in my life?* I knew how important it was to carry a dream in life. Just letting a dream guide and motivate you can vastly improve the substance of your life, even if the end-goal eludes you. When I was a kid, my dream was to play football for the Detroit Lions. This goal served as my motivation all through high school and college. Obviously I never made the Lions, but the desire to do so helped me become a much better athlete than I would otherwise have become. Life without a dream can be sadly empty.

What happens to a dream deferred—especially when you're sixty? I remembered a conversation I'd had with the owner of the shipyard on Shelter Island where *Sundance* was outfitted for sea.

"You think you'll really do it?" he said. "Think you'll really sail across the Pacific?"

"Well, hell yes, I will," I said. It seemed obvious to me—I was here getting all this work done on my boat; didn't that signal the seriousness of my intent?

"No offense," he said. "It's just that in the past thirty years, I've probably worked on a few thousand boats for people who were dead set on making a bluewater passage. You know how many of them actually put in any time or distance?"

"I don't know," I said. "Half?"

He grinned sadly and shook his head. "No," he said. "I'd say it's about two percent. Two percent of them put to sea and really give it a try. Most folks have grandiose dreams of sailing to faraway islands in paradise. But year after year, their boats just sit here in their slips."

"Why don't they ever go?"

"Lots of reasons. I've heard 'em all. We're waiting for the kids to graduate. We're waiting for Uncle Joe to die and leave us the inheritance. Best one I think I ever heard: we're waiting for our cats to pass away before we head out."

So many reasons to not realize their dreams. Think of it: ninety-eight percent of those with dreams of bluewater sailing never make it past the entrance buoy to the harbor. His words resonated with me; I found it to be true in any marina, whether it was Newport Beach, San Diego, or even Hawaii; everyone talks the talk, but few of them actually walk the walk. When I look at a marina with hundreds of boats sitting in their slips with no people on board, I can't help but think, here is another "Marina of Broken Dreams." It sickens me to think that *Sundance* and I might become members of this disappointing group that lives as testimony to the fallibility of the human spirit.

I hated the prospect of regret. I pictured myself at eighty years old, sitting in my wheelchair with oatmeal spilled all over my chin, staring off into space, thinking, "Damn, I wish I would have gone on sailing off to the South Pacific . . . I should have pushed on."

Here was another scenario to consider. I am not feeling well. I go visit my doctor; he discovers I have an advanced stage of pancreatic cancer (exactly like my mother had when she was seventy-eight years old). "You have six months to live," he says. Now what would my attitude be when confronted with a *real* problem? Imagining that scene underscored to me the difference between an inconvenience and a real problem. What I experienced out there sailing was nothing more than a temporary inconvenience. I alone had been responsible for turning an adventurous sailing trip into a terrible inconvenience. That was cause for shame. I should be thankful for this wonderful opportunity to sail across oceans on my yacht.

I will not quit on myself. I will sail across the ocean.

With my newfound sense of optimism, I felt rejuvenated. It was time to start getting organized for the next leg of the adventure. But this time I would do it right.

I thought about what changes I might make sailing across oceans more acceptable, more enjoyable, less stressful, and maybe even a little bit more comfortable. I flipped through my notebook to zero in on my weaknesses, and the first item that leapt from the page was this: "For one to endure an ocean passage, he must be schooled to adapt to the inner contemplative life. This will help a man in solitary confinement from going mad."

And so my list began:

A. Have a better crew. Consider taking two guys for the next leg to Tahiti.
B. Seasickness. Find an effective medicine.
C. Work on having a better understanding of:

   1. The GPS and the charts to improve navigation.
   2. The diesel engine. Read a fix-it manual.
   3. Heavy weather techniques of sail trim and survival.
   4. Improve downwind sailing. Purchase a downwind reaching-type sail.
   5. The single-side-band radio. Get on a radio schedule. Talk to other cruisers.
   6. Eat more enjoyable food.
   7. Learn how to get more sleep.
   8. Improve anchoring skills. Repair the windlass.
   9. Learn how to "heave to" more effectively.
   10. Conquer your fears at sea.

I was confident I could accomplish everything on this list. It would take some time, a lot of studying, and a great deal of practice, but I was determined to get it done before I put out to sea again.

The next step was to break the news to Sally. When I sat her down to have our talk, she laughed sadly. "I know," she said before I began. "You're going back out there."

"Yes," I said. "How did you know?"

She laughed again. "It's been pretty obvious you haven't quite gotten it out of your system. You don't hide your emotions well, you know that?"

I laughed nervously. I felt a little like a man who's been caught having an affair, asking his wife for just one last hurrah with his mistress. "So how do you feel about it?"

She looked at me like I wasn't very bright. *Duh, Mr. Psychologist. How do you think she feels?* "Well," she said. "I'm not exactly looking forward to it. But I survived last time, and I guess I can survive again."

"Listen," I said. "This time I want you to come with me to Hawaii. We'll sail around a little bit, just some coastal cruising, nothing hard-core. That'll be a better way of sending me off, don't you think? What do you say?"

Her beautiful face brightened. "You'd want me along for that?"

"Baby, I'd want you along for the whole damn trip if I could have it that way."

"Well," she said. "I accept your invitation to Hawaii. Thank you."

Just like that, it was settled. *Sundance* and I had scheduled our re-match with what I had come to think of as "The Sleeping Giant."

CHAPTER 10

. . .

Heaven Helps the Man

You're burning, yearning for somebody to tell you that life ain't passing you by.
I'm trying to tell you it will if you don't even try.

—Kenny Loggins

SALLY AND I FLEW TO Hilo and headed straight to the boat. *Sundance* was sitting there tied up to the wall where I'd left her. She looked fine; I don't think she missed me at all. We thanked Rob and Susie for keeping an eye on her, and that evening we took them out to dinner and talked about ocean passage-making. As we spoke, it became clear that they had years and years of open-water sailing experience, which no doubt explained how they could somehow enjoy passage-making. *Maybe there is hope for me yet*, I thought.

Our plan was to sail from the "Big Island" to Maui, then over to Molokai and on to Oahu. Honolulu would serve as the staging area for my next passage, to French Polynesia. First, though, I thought it would be a good idea to take Sally for a short sail to the other side of the Big Island to Kona.

I asked around among the locals and learned that the sail to Kona was not a difficult trip at all, and should be an uneventful eight-hour sail on the leeward side of the island. Sailing on the leeward side of an island means that the winds will be quite light and one doesn't have to worry about encountering any heavy weather conditions. "Your wife won't even spill her glass of wine," one old guy told me. That was encouraging. I was secretly hoping Sally would enjoy this sail so much that she would decide to join me more often on longer passages. That, of course, was the worst kind of wishful thinking; Sally has gotten seasick while sitting perfectly still with the boat tied to a slip and could never handle weeks of constant rocking. Hoping for a miracle, though, I had her apply a seasickness patch before we pushed off in the morning.

We said goodbye to our new friends and started out of the harbor around seven in the morning with the hope of arriving in Kona late that afternoon. As FUJIMO pushed us along our way out of the harbor, a large motor yacht passed us heading in the opposite direction. When we hit its wake, a coffee cup jumped off the table down below and crashed to the floor, breaking into several pieces. Sally went down to clean up the mess just as we reached the opening of the harbor. There was a swell running and some small wave action which caused the boat to start rocking and rolling while Sally was on her hands and knees picking up the pieces of the broken cup. She was doomed; she never had a chance. Within less than a mile after leaving the harbor, she was feeling the first effects of seasickness. It had taken her less than thirty minutes to get sick. At first, it wasn't so bad; she just felt a little out of sorts. But we were heading offshore, and so the wave action increased and the swells caused the boat to rock back and forth ceaselessly. About an hour out, Sally said she felt like she was going to throw up.

"All right, baby. Can you please go to the rail and feed the fish?"

She staggered to the rail and knelt there, the very picture of abjection. Damn it. This little cruise around the island was going to be a miserable experience for her after all.

When she had finished her business, she returned to the cockpit, covered up in a blanket and drifted off to sleep in the leeward seat. But, unfortunately for her, that didn't last very long. Suddenly, she sat up and looked at me, her face wrenched with dread. "I have to go to the bathroom," she said.

This presented a bit of a problem. If she went down below to the rocking and rolling head, she was sure to get sick before she had time to complete her business. The alternative was to stay up in the fresh air of the cockpit and pee into a bucket, which is a pretty common maneuver on any sailboat. I explained all this to Sally, and, while I would not have thought it possible, her face grew even darker. She couldn't even hold my gaze. Looking down at the deck, she said, horrified, "It's more serious than that, Michael."

Oh, Lord. She needed to go number two!

"Okay," I said, trying to sound cheerful and casual. "Let me get you a bigger bucket and some toilet paper."

I went below to gather the necessities, and when I returned I called her forward to the mizzenmast. "Okay," I said. "Here's what you'll want to do." Like a coach, I walked her through the whole exercise, modeling it for her: "You'll set the bucket here, just forward of the mast, right? Then you want to straddle the bucket as you're facing aft, and lower yourself down the mast like a stripper crouching around a pole. See? Go all the way down and set your buttocks right inside the bucket. Wrap your arms right around the mast so you don't fall over. You see?"

She flicked her wrist and waved me away, both to hurry me off and to convey that she was not an idiot. "Okay," I said, trying again to sound nonchalant. "Good luck with everything."

She pulled down her swimsuit and slowly eased herself down as I had shown her, grasping the mizzenmast firmly. I was busy at the helm keeping the boat on course, and had nowhere to look except pretty much directly at her. My poor beautiful Sally looked up at me with those pretty blue eyes and said, "We have a problem. I'm going to get sick." Ho, jeez. I did not want her to puke on the cockpit floor and on my feet. One of my concerns was that if I smelled it, I would also be puking my guts out. We couldn't both be sick.

"Baby, can you move to the rail and give the fish another breakfast?" I said.

Without even pulling up her swimsuit, she lurched over to the rail, placed both feet on the seat, leaned over and let it fly. Oh, what an awful scene, and it was all my fault. Poor Sally, with her swimsuit down around her ankles, her bare butt pointed skyward, windblown puke streaking into her long blonde hair as she retched and retched. I was torn between keeping an eye on her to make sure she was okay and looking away out of respect. I felt terrible for getting her into such an embarrassing position. You should know that Sally is not the outdoorsy type; she would prefer to be shopping at Fashion Island in Newport Beach. She's not what you'd call high-maintenance—not by any stretch of the imagination—but she does enjoy a manicure, a pedicure, and a massage on a regular basis. She is an absolutely beautiful woman, much too beautiful to be with a dork like me.

• • •

With Sally back in her spot on the leeward seat, again sound asleep, we sailed along in the lee of Mona Loa. Late in the afternoon, I saw what looked like a large plume of smoke rising a thousand feet into the sky against the horizon. *Wildfire?* I wondered. I watched for a few minutes as the churning vertical line broke and dissipated. Moments later, it was replaced by a new column of smoke, in the same place and shape as the previous one. This pattern repeated itself every few minutes. As we drew closer, I realized that the smoke was coming from just offshore.

I nudged Sally awake. "Look at this, baby," I said. "The island is growing."

It was not smoke; it was steam. Molten lava was flowing down the mountain from the volcano and spilling into the ocean, sending up vast bursts of vapor as it met the water. What a magnificent sight. Bobbing along in our little boat, we were bearing witness to a continuation of the very process by which these islands had been formed millions of years ago.

The sun set beautifully that evening, and as the sky grew dark, we saw more stars than either of us had ever imagined existed. The Milky Way appeared so close that we could almost reach up and touch it. Sally was feeling much better and had not lost it since early in the afternoon. She wasn't up and moving about the boat, but she was comfortable. The nice breeze we were sailing on had died and we had to call on FUJIMO to push us toward Kona at the standard average of just over four knots. It was going on twelve hours and we were only halfway to our destination, which meant we were in for a very long night.

While there was little wave action, the water was serene and the stars were beautiful. We had just witnessed one of nature's most astonishing sights. I felt thrilled and content, happy as anything to be on the boat with Sally sailing along in Hawaiian waters. I could definitely get used to this.

The next morning at first light I checked the chart to see about putting ashore so that Sally and I could have a little breakfast. A small bay not far from our position appeared to be the ideal spot, well sheltered and not terribly deep. Within the hour, we were anchored in Kealakekua Bay in twenty-five feet of pristine blue water, and paddled ashore in the dinghy. It was good to be off the boat and walking on a sandy beach. Unfortunately, there was no restaurant within walking distance. After enjoying the short stroll, we climbed back in the dinghy and returned to the boat. I opened up my cruising guide and read about the little bay where we were anchored.

> In 1779, two ships were also anchored in this very bay. They were the HMS *Resolution* and the HMS *Discovery*. Their captain? Legendary explorer James Cook. This was his third visit to the islands and it would be his last. On February 14, 1779, he was stabbed to death here in this bay by Hawaiian natives during a skirmish involving the theft of one of his small shore boats by an islander. A young lieutenant serving as Captain Cook's sailing master was none other than William Bligh, who shortly thereafter was appointed captain of HMS *Bounty*. I think we all know the rest of his story.

As we were motoring out of the bay, we saw a small monument paying homage to Captain Cook. It made me shiver a little to think that we were in the same small bay where those historic events had unfolded 221 years before.

• • •

It was another four hours to reach Kona and then another hour to a marina in Honokohau. I used the VHF radio to call the harbormaster to see if he might have a transient slip for the next three days.

"Well," he said. "I do have one, but I'm not sure you'll want it."

"Why not?"

"Well," he said slowly, as if not quite sure how to answer. "It's, uh, on the fuel dock."

It was the one spot left in the marina that would accommodate our boat's size, and it was a stern-to-the-wall tie, not a slip. I had never seen the marina at Honokohau and wasn't sure what to expect. But I wasn't feeling too particular; I just knew I needed someplace to tie up *Sundance* so I could get poor Sally off the boat.

I radioed back. "That's no problem. I'll take it."

We found the entrance to the harbor and motored straight up to the marina, where it was easy to find the spot the harbormaster had reserved for us on the wall in front of his office. The maneuver to secure *Sundance* to the wall would be tricky, however. We first had to grab a mooring ball, attach the tether line to the bow, and then back up between two other boats to reach the wall. This doesn't sound like it should be too difficult to accomplish . . . but *Sundance* still hadn't learned to back up like a lady. We secured a bow line to the mooring ball easily enough. But backing up into a tight spot without hitting one of the other boats (as a hearty contingent of dock people stood watching) was another story. I floundered my way in until we got close enough to toss a line to someone on the dock, and then we manually pulled ourselves in the remainder of the way. I was embarrassed and lost a lot of "slip face" due to my incompetence.

Once we were securely tied up to the fuel dock, I set about my standard drill of cleaning up the boat in preparation for going ashore. After a few minutes, I noticed that Sally had climbed off the boat and was nowhere in sight. I kept working. And then I discovered why the harbormaster had been so hesitant to give me the tie-in.

As it turns out, the marina at Honokohau was the Hawaiian Mecca for deep-sea fishing, and almost all of the boats around me were the big vessels dedicated to the sport. The fishermen's favorite game fish are the really big whoppers like the blue marlin that can weigh up to 1,000 pounds. Sport fishermen do not have an appreciation for "yachties," who travel under sail. We tend to get in their way when they are out chasing the blue marlin. And so, when I looked up from my task of tidying my sailboat, I saw that *Sundance* was surrounded by macho fishermen giving me dirty looks. I ignored them and went back to work. A few minutes later, I was down in the galley when I heard a dripping sound coming from up in the cockpit. I peeked my head up through the companionway and saw that the seats and floor were all speckled in blood. Marlin blood.

Well, that *really* explained the harbormaster's reluctance, didn't it? When these fishing boats would return from their hunting grounds, they would back up to the wall beside me in one swift, smooth motion. Then they would offload their catch via a hand-operated overhead rail system running along the water side of the dock. The marlins were secured by attaching a line around their tails just below the fin. They were then hoisted up onto the rail system, tail first, with their enormous beaks pointing toward the water. Most of them weighed over 500 pounds. Once strung up on the overhead rail, they were pulled to the far end of the dock, where they were lowered into crates and then carried off to be processed or prepared so they could be mounted on some great fisherman's living room wall. And as they were being moved down the rail, they were usually bleeding, the blood streaming off their long, sword-like beaks.

The rail system hung out over the water, and also over the once-clean cockpit of my boat. Within an hour, my poor *Sundance* was a bloody, smelly mess.

Sally reappeared, standing there on the dock with her hands on her hips and a stern look on her face. The fishermen who had looked at me so rudely were all smiles for her. Go figure. She glared down at me like I was a fool. "I've reserved a room at the Four Seasons," she said. "You are welcome to join me or you can stay on your stinking damn boat." The fishermen laughed.

This was a no-brainer; I was going to the hotel with Sally. I collected my dignity, walked over and put my arm around her, but I couldn't completely surrender my pride. After a few steps, I reached down and gave her a squeeze. Those horny fishermen, who I knew were still watching, could eat their lonely hearts out; this beauty was mine.

We spent three lovely days enjoying the comforts of the hotel: sleeping in late, eating big breakfasts, and taking long walks on the beach. But it was impossible for me not to think about my next big challenge: sailing across the infamous Alenuihaha Channel to Maui. I tried to gather as much local knowledge about the crossing as I could by talking to anyone who might have some experience navigating this treacherous channel. I was lucky to find a charter boat captain who had made the crossing a number of times. He was a great guy and shared a wealth of knowledge with me. He explained that crossing the Alenuihaha is considered a rite of passage for anyone who sails on the Hawaiian Islands. You are not considered a serious or competent sailor until you have this dangerous channel under your belt.

The charter captain said he knew a young man who might like to make the trip with me.

"Name is Crosby Loggins," the captain said. "He lives on the island when he isn't in school. He sails a lot . . . and I mean, *a lot.*"

I ended up talking with Crosby on the phone. He sounded young, but seemed to have a good head on his shoulders, and he was clearly excited to join me in two days' time. Based on the captain's recommendation and my own good first impression, I told Crosby I'd be happy to have him make the crossing with me, and we arranged a meeting time and place.

The Alenuihaha Channel—the water between Maui and the Big Island—has the reputation of being the most dangerous channel in the world. It is only thirty miles across, but its unique geographic position makes it vulnerable to wild conditions: the northeast trade winds, which start to build off Alaska, travel unobstructed over thousands of miles of open ocean until they reach what amounts to a funnel between the islands. With Mauna Kea on the Big Island side and Haleakala on the Maui side, this funnel effect is even more pronounced, further boosting the velocity of the wind gusts. Inside the funnel, the winds are often up to five times stronger than those out on the surrounding water. It is not uncommon to experience sustained winds of fifty miles an hour, with forty being just a normal day. The maximum depth in the channel is 6,100 feet, a little more than a mile deep. It is critical that any skipper who considers making this crossing should first check with the National Weather Service to obtain the daily forecast . . . and *gale* is one word you don't want to hear. It is without question a daunting undertaking, and I was more than a little apprehensive. Did I have the skill to accomplish such an awe-inspiring task? Sailing over to Catalina Island was kid stuff compared to this. Yes, I had sailed to Hawaii from the mainland, but the winds had been benign compared to what lay ahead of me.

The charter boat captain had said I should sail north to tiny Nishimura Bay, the northernmost bay on the island. By starting out from a more northerly position, we would be able to take advantage of a much better course to Maui, sailing on a reach most of the way. My plan was to spend the night anchored at Nishimura and get an early start at 4:00 AM. This way, I could get some miles behind me before the winds reached their greatest velocity. I was glad I'd have Crosby along.

• • •

It was time for Sally to fly back to California. It had been wonderful to share some of the adventure with her, and it was remarkable how much more enjoyable it was when she was on board. I worried a little bit that she might never step foot on *Sundance* again, but it had almost been worth it. I drove her to the airport in a rental car—the same airport where I had dropped off my deranged crew member, DH. What a completely opposite feeling this was, saying goodbye to Sally. We stood there hugging forever; it didn't seem I could let her go. Finally she pulled away a little bit so she could look me in the eye.

"We'll be there, you know, waiting for you at home," she said. "We'll always be right there when you're ready . . ."

I nodded and blinked, struggling again not to lose control of my emotions.

"And we're all proud of you and we're all pulling for you," she said.

Then she walked away. My Sally.

That afternoon, I washed all the marlin blood off *Sundance* and headed back out to sea. This was the first time in a long time that I had been on board by myself, and was rather surprised at how good it felt. I missed Sally, of course, but it was nice not to have to worry about her or feel guilty for her discomfort. For the first time, I felt competent and secure on the water alone.

There was not enough wind on the leeward side of the island to sail, so I had FUJIMO moving me along at his maximum speed of five knots. I knew this was the calm before the storm; tomorrow the conditions would not be so comfortable. That evening, I found the little bay and dropped the anchor on a less-than-desirable coral bottom. I would always prefer not to anchor in coral; I know the coral doesn't like it and the anchor doesn't hold well. But there were no other places to anchor; this spot was going to have to do for the night.

I had expected the bay to be small, but was nevertheless surprised at just how tiny it was—there was barely enough room to hold three boats. The VHF radio had good reception and I was able to listen to the marine forecast. (I had terminated my contract with Walter the Weather Guy, as he was a bit too expensive.) To my relief, the word *gale* did not make it into the forecast. The outlook for tomorrow was good, with no high wind warnings. Sleep was next to impossible, though. The anchor was slipping over the coral bottom, making loud unpleasant sounds, and I was anxious to get on with the task at hand.

At 4:00 AM sharp, I saw a person with a flashlight moving down the hill from above the bay. Must be Crosby; who else would be walking around out here at this ungodly hour of the night? I yelled hello and he responded in kind. I launched the dinghy, paddled to shore and met my new crew face to face for the first time.

I liked him instantly. Firm handshake, good eye contact, and boundless enthusiasm for the adventure we were undertaking together. We chatted like old friends as we paddled back out to the boat, and then I pulled up the anchor. The moment had come: time to conquer the great, the treacherous, the notorious, Alenuihaha Channel. A stunning sliver of a moon just off the bow guided us out of the bay and into the channel. It was game time, and I was thinking: *Let's get it on. Come on and give me your best shot. I'm going to kick this mighty channel's ass today.*

Out in the channel, the wind was coming out of the northeast at about fifteen to twenty knots, and the sea action was six to eight feet with just a small swell running. We set the sails to carry us on a broad reach. Our speed was five and a half knots. Not wishing to be overcome by any surprise increases in wind speed, we had reefed the headsail by a quarter (meaning that we reduced its size, kind of like rolling up your pant legs), and put one reef in the mainsail to be on the safe side. That meant that, for the moment, we were underpowered—not enough sail out for this amount of wind. But I fully expected the winds to fill in and strengthen as the day went along. I would much rather be underpowered than get hit with strong winds and find myself with too much sail out. That's when things start to break, and I don't like it when stuff starts to break on my boat.

Crosby was a wonderful crewmate. His sailing skills were sharp, especially considering that he was still a teenager, and he was also good company. In the light winds of mid-morning, we chatted about our lives at home.

"What do you do for fun besides sail?" I said.

"Oh, I play guitar in a band."

"Yeah? Are you good?"

"Pretty good," he said. "My dad taught me how to play guitar and sing."

"Oh, your dad's a singer too?"

"Yeah. You've probably heard his music."

"Think so? What's his name?"

"Kenny Loggins."

"Hmm," I said. "No. I don't know who that is."

Crosby's eyes widened. "Really? You sure?"

"Yeah. Why? Is he famous or something?"

"He's pretty famous. Have you heard of Loggins and Messina?"

"Can't say that I have," I said. "But try me with a song or two."

"Ever hear of *Danny's Song*?" He sang a little bit for me: "Even though we ain't got money/I'm so in love with you, honey . . ."

"No," I said. "But that's nice. Sounds like a real nice song. Your father wrote that?"

Crosby was squinting at me like he'd encountered a space alien, and it was all I could do not to burst out laughing.

"What about *Footloose*? Have you ever heard that song?"

"Foot what, now?"

"*Footloose*. It was a pretty famous song, for a pretty popular movie," he said a little sadly. "Did you ever see a movie called *Top Gun*?"

"I think so," I said. "Isn't that the Western with Lee Marvin and Glenn Ford?"

"No," he said. "It had Tom Cruise in it. It's about fighter

jets."

I told him I'd never heard of it.

He tried me with a few more of his greatest hits, and I feigned ignorance of all of them. After a while, I said, "Take the helm for a minute, and will you, Crosby? I've got to go down below for something."

In the cabin, I rummaged around for a while until I found what I was looking for: a Kenny Loggins CD. I popped it in the player, cranked up the volume, and just about ran up the companionway stairs so I could see the reaction on Crosby's face when he heard his father's voice come over the speakers. It was worth it. Poor Crosby looked wildly around for a moment, cognitive dissonance written all over his face, and then when he saw he'd been had, he clutched his sides and laughed so hard he steered us off course. I went down and lowered the volume.

"Your father is one of my favorite singers," I told him, when I could speak without laughing. "I'm thrilled to have Kenny Loggins's son as my crew."

As the day progressed, the wind whistled down through the big, bad, Alenuihaha Channel, building to thirty knots, with ten- to twelve-foot seas. Now the channel was starting to live up to its reputation. I further shortened the headsail to reduce the strain on the helm. Too much sail out in high wind makes it very difficult to steer a good course; the boat will act like a runaway stallion, poking her nose up into the wind and champing at the bit. That's called a weather helm. Too much wind, too much sail, too much strain on the helm and also the helmsman. Under those circumstances, a strong gust can make it almost impossible to hold the wheel steady. If the sail area isn't reduced, something is going to break.

When a serious accident happens, it's usually not the result of one single failure, but rather a combination of several small failures building into one massive nightmare with disastrous consequences. I try to avoid such consequences by being attentive to the smallest details—especially when it's blowing thirty knots with the possibility of building up into the fifties. We were in a lot of wind, yet the present conditions were manageable; we were sailing on a tight reach, the sails were trimmed nicely, and Crosby and I were dry and comfortable. The GPS indicated we only had two hours to go to reach the island of Maui. I was getting a little cocky now that it looked like we were going to make this run across the channel without any serious problems. Standing at the helm, I shouted out, "Is that all you've got? We kicked your ass, Mr. Alenuihaha. You gave us your best shot and we kicked your big channel ass!"

Crosby was looking at me like I'd just taken a dump on the altar of a church. "We aren't all the way across yet," he said quietly. "You shouldn't piss off the channel gods until we're safely on shore."

Superstition be damned: in another two hours we were sailing in the wind-protected lee of Maui. We had made it across the channel without encountering any fifty-mile-an-hour winds or twenty-five foot seas. I was very proud of myself; to have sailed across this feared body of water significantly bolstered my confidence. It was a sailor's accomplishment, giving me bona fide bragging rights. I would lean on this new sense of confidence to get through some difficult situations in the near future.

We dropped the hook in a bay off the town of Makena, and I took Crosby ashore in the dinghy. We gave each other a quick hug, shook hands, and then he was off to catch a flight back to the Big Island. The next morning, I sailed on to Lahaina.

The Lahaina Yacht Club had a number of moorings available for visiting yachts. I located one of the empty mooring balls, tied up *Sundance*, put the dinghy in the water, and went in to town to find a good breakfast. To my dismay, I discovered that the town of Lahaina is tourist central, which was not for me. I'd been feeling lean and tough and independent after my successful crossing, and now I felt a bit deflated to be walking among the lily-white "tourons" with their newly purchased Hawaiian shirts, trying to look like they belonged on the island. (Yes, "touron" is equal parts *tourist* and *moron*.) I am not very fond of tourons; they typically insult my intelligence. I admit to a general feeling of superiority toward them, and I usually try to steer clear of them. But it was impossible to do in Lahaina, and that at a time when I was feeling *particularly* superior because of the badass crossing I'd just made.

It was nice to be secured to a mooring ball, since the windlass was still on strike and it wasn't much fun having to use the anchor without it. It also meant I didn't have to worry about the anchor dragging. Even so, I found it impossible to sleep because of the huge swell that violently rocked the boat all night. Ugh. This was unacceptable; I had to get the hell out of Lahaina. At first light, I set sail to the Island of Molokai. I looked back at Lahaina and muttered my good riddance.

Getting to Molokai would require sailing across another channel, named Pailolo. The winds in the Pailolo Channel can be awfully strong, but the good news is that it's only fifteen miles to reach the lee of Molokai. I enjoyed an uneventful sail across the Pailolo: a lot of wind, but nothing I couldn't deal with. Once securely in the lee of Molokai, I dropped the sails, fired up FUJIMO, and puttered around looking for a small bay near Kaunakakai. I found the entrance and motored in, searching for an acceptable spot to drop the anchor. But I had my doubts about being any more comfortable tonight than I'd been in Lahaina; the wind was blowing harder in this bay than it had been out on the ocean. It had to be blowing at twenty-five to thirty knots inside the bay.

At least from my windblown anchorage, the Island of Molokai appeared to be the exact opposite of Maui . . . there was nothing there. Not only were there no tourons, there were no people, no boats, nothing except for an old dilapidated wharf. Surprisingly, however, I did see a phone booth on the wharf. I was feeling rather desperate to get to that phone booth to call Sally, but the winds made it impossible to paddle the dinghy to the wharf. Damn it. No phone call today. This is what one would refer to as a vile anchorage.

The winds were much too strong for me to attempt to pull the anchor up by hand. Thanks to my broken windlass, I was stuck for three days and three nights until the wind subsided. I spent the time pacing around the boat like a leopard at the zoo. I tried to distract myself with books and music, but mostly, I just looked at that wretched wharf and cursed at the wind. Finally when conditions improved, I hauled the anchor on deck and got the hell out of Molokai forever.

Next destination: Oahu, which meant I had one more channel to cross . . . the Kaiwi Channel. If all went well, *Sundance* would sleep tonight in Honolulu's famous Hawaii Yacht Club next to the beautiful beaches of Waikiki. Entering the Kaiwi Channel, I was relieved to find favorable wind, and we glided over the deep blue water with full main and headsail on a nice broad reach. Off in the distance, I could see the volcanic cone of Diamond Head, recognizable the world over—Hawaii's Eiffel Tower or Mount Rushmore. This was pretty cool; I was really doing it. I was cruising off the island of Oahu on my way to the Hawaii Yacht Club.

I kept just offshore, maintaining a comfortable depth of one hundred feet. Now I spotted the next landmark, the pink hotel with the rainbow painted on the side. The cruising guide's instructions were to "set a course keeping the pink hotel off the bow. This will lead you directly to the mouth of Waikiki's Ala Wai yacht harbor." Well, this was not too complicated. Just find the pink hotel and sail on into the harbor. That's the kind of sailing I was accustomed to. I was back in my comfort zone, like I was sailing in the bay back home in San Diego.

I eased *Sundance* up to the "Aloha Dock" (reserved for visitors to the yacht club) with a huge grin on my face. I was enjoying a profound sense of accomplishment, which had eluded me up to this point. I suppose it was the sense that I had *arrived*. I was able to say, I *sailed* all the way from California. I didn't fly to Hawaii on a comfortable jet with a glass of wine in one hand and a warm chocolate chip cookie in the other. I *sailed* here, over 2,300 miles! Not many in these islands could make that statement. And then I had crossed one of the world's most treacherous channels. Finally, I could truly say that I was proud of myself!

It was a good time to reflect on the bigger picture, as well. One of my reasons for doing this trip had been to honor my younger self, the poor kid living in a rented house at 34 Water Street in Ypsilanti, Michigan, with the polluted Huron River running through my backyard and a set of railroad tracks just off the front porch. Okay, I told myself, just savor this: I am sitting on my forty-foot, cutter-rigged, staysail ketch sailboat, tied up to the Aloha Dock of the Hawaii Yacht Club, having sailed here from my lovely home in Laguna Beach. Pretty damn good for a sixty-year-old dyslexic kid from Ypsilanti.

• • •

The folks at the Hawaii Yacht Club were the epitome of the Aloha spirit. They welcomed me with open arms and made me feel more like a friend than a visitor. And this was no Harbor of Broken Dreams: many of the club's members were experienced sailors with a lot of respect for bluewater passage-making.

I rented a transient slip, and *Sundance* had a wonderful temporary home. The passage had been hard on her, though; there was a lot of work to do before she would be ready for the next leg of our journey, to Tahiti. We spent a good productive month at the yacht club getting her in shape, but cyclone season was coming and she would need a more permanent slip to sit out the winter. I found a good home for her at the brand-new Ko Olina Marina, on the grounds of a beautiful Marriott resort about twenty miles west of Honolulu. I was pleased to find such a first-class facility; it would give me peace of mind during my absence.

Yes, I would be absent for the next few months. Cyclone season in this part of the world runs from October to April. I had done well this time at bat, but I had no business sailing around in the South Pacific during the height of the storm season. It was a good time for me to return home and reunite with the ones I loved.

CHAPTER 11

. . .

Bail Like Hell

When you're safe at home you wish you were having an adventure; when you're having an adventure you wish you were safe at home.

—Thornton Wilder

ONE OF MY PRIMARY MISSIONS at home was to perform serious due diligence on a crew to sail with me on the next leg of my trip. After the miserable experience with DH, I was determined not to make the same mistake again. There are a number of sailing websites that match boat owners up with crew members. I reviewed more than a hundred possibilities before I located a young man by the name of Chas. Chas was twenty-six years old, with a college degree and extensive sailing experience, including six years as an officer in the U.S. Navy. He was perfect! After an initial e-mail, we began talking regularly by phone, and over the next two months I was able to get to know him. He was well spoken, he was well mannered, he knew how to sail big boats in heavy weather. I was truly impressed; I had found an officer and a gentleman. It was great news when he agreed to "come aboard" as my first mate.

Contemplating the long southerly passage between Hawaii and Tahiti—which would be roughly the same distance I'd sailed with DH—I thought it would be a good idea to hire someone in addition to Chas . . . so the search continued. In looking at a website out of Hawaii, I found a twenty-one-year-old Frenchman who was temporarily living in Honolulu. In his ad, he said that he had sailed to Hawaii from Tahiti and was looking for a crew position to sail back to Tahiti. I thought it might be good to take this kid with us as well. For one thing, he could teach me a little French, and since I was going to be spending time in French Polynesia, I figured it would be helpful to speak the language. Another bonus was when he mentioned that he loved to cook! I could just picture it: private French lessons and our own French chef to prepare the evening meals. We agreed to meet in person when I returned to Hawaii.

My next objective was to find something to help with my seasickness. After considerable research online, I found that most seasickness remedies have undesirable side effects. Scalopamine: not approved for human consumption; now, that doesn't sound like a very good idea, does it?

Companzine: may cause involuntary muscle spasms and twitches in the face and body; hmm, I wouldn't be seasick *and* I could entertain the crew with the contortions of my face and my flailing limbs.

Antihistamines: cause drowsiness; talk about being asleep at the wheel . . .

I found three acceptable options. There was "the patch," which was a sticker that you place behind the ear, which I had tried before; but it's only effective for forty-eight hours and a doctor needs to write a prescription for it. There was ginger, which reportedly helps in any form and has been used by sailors forever. And then there were elastic acupressure bracelets worn on the wrist. Some said the simplest solution is to take the helm and stare at the horizon while steering the boat. An airline pilot told me to look at the horizon while keeping one eye shut. Seems like everyone I talked to was a firm believer in their own favorite solution.

One thing was certain: I was determined not to get seasick again. When I returned to the boat, I would be armed with patches, wristbands, Ginger Snap cookies, and a firm resolution to look at the horizon with one eye closed. (Maybe I should have asked the pilot which eye.) I hoped that one of those remedies would work. I pictured myself standing at the helm, steering the boat in a huge storm with a patch behind one ear, wearing my new wristbands, munching on damp Ginger Snap cookies, peering at the mounting waves through one eye. But I would not be seasick!

The cozy winter months sped by. Sally and I made the most of our time together, seizing every opportunity to take weekend trips, go on long walks, and have deep conversations about our relationship and the future. She had finished the renovation of the house during my absence. (Advice to couples struggling through a remodeling project: one of you should just disappear for six months.) We joked about what a good palliative my adventure was proving to be for our relationship, how the ideal love affair was six months on, six months off, but we didn't mean it. I knew Sally wanted me home for good, and there was a part of me that felt that my urge to return to sea was little more than stubbornness. Yet, at the same time, I believed that if I did this thing right—carried my mission out to its real completion— then the beauty of my home, the thrill of being with Sally, the pure joy of spending time with my grandkids and with Sedona, would not flash so quickly in the pan. I could already see this effect: instead of the fevered ecstasy I had felt after my nightmare passage with DH, this time I had met my old surroundings with a more sober, more mature and sustained sense of gratitude and appreciation, which lasted much longer than ten days. I chalked that up to my feelings of accomplishment. I figured if I had the whole feat of sailing around the world under my belt, then I could truly come home from the sea and live contentedly for the rest of my life, which gave me a sense of urgency to get back out on the ocean. On the first of March, I kissed everyone goodbye and flew back to Hawaii.

· · ·

As I walked down the dock at the Ko Olina marina, I felt a thrill of excitement at the sight of *Sundance* waiting for me, and

I recalled how, on first making landfall in Hawaii, I had been unable to so much as look at her. Now she appeared as beautiful as ever sitting in her slip. It was hard not to believe she was impatient to put to sea. First, I had to go meet my new crew members; then on to Tahiti.

The Frenchman was not quite what I had expected. France has produced many world-class sailors, explorers, and adventurers, but my new crew member looked more like one of the teenagers who waits tables at the outdoor cafes in Paris. He said he was twenty-two, but he didn't look a day over seventeen. He stood about five feet nine inches, on the thin side, with long dark hair pulled back in a ponytail and a rather startlingly fair complexion. He showed up for our meeting wearing a green sleeveless muscle shirt and white shorts with flip flops, which I guess wouldn't have been so bad except that his arms were so skinny. The whole point of a muscle shirt, I'd thought, was to display your enormous "guns." He seemed eager to advertise his frailty: *Yes, ladies, they really are that bony . . .* His English was pretty rough, although I could understand him most of the time.

Having learned from my blunder with DH, I checked the Frenchman's character references in Hawaii, and they all spoke highly of him. I wasn't able to check his sailing references, though, as they were all in France. Another red flag ignored, although in my defense, I reasoned that since his character references portrayed him as an honest person, what he told me about sailing was likely true. And he was hardly boastful: he readily admitted that his sailing experience was limited, and that his trip up to Hawaii from Tahiti six months ago had been the pinnacle of his sailing career thus far. *Well. You don't sail from Tahiti to Hawaii without at least learning the basics,* I figured . . . big mistake. I should have learned my lesson with DH. Never assume anything, especially where people are concerned.

He asked me if it would be okay if he brought along his guitar. Oh, Jesus, what kind of leisurely cruise did he think we were undertaking? I didn't want a damn guitar on my boat for several reasons, not least of which was that there wasn't room enough for one. I didn't want to hurt his feelings so early on, and against my better judgment, I gave in and told him he could bring his guitar.

Chas was another story. He arrived by plane from the East Coast of the mainland wearing a blue Oxford shirt with the sleeves rolled neatly, pressed khaki pants, and brown top-siders. He was just less than six feet tall, with no excess weight. I particularly liked his "high and tight" haircut, which enhanced his air of directness and competence. Chas appeared just like you would expect a naval officer to look—self-confident, strong, and respectful. This is the kind of guy I would have wanted my daughters to date.

We spent ten days coastal sailing, helping the crew get familiar with the equipment and the idiosyncrasies of *Sundance*. My goal was to have them both be efficient and completely comfortable with their new surroundings. This was no problem for Chas, who was a natural. He moved about the boat like a cat. The Frenchman, on the other hand, was never comfortable aboard. He was unsure of himself and a slow learner. I had some serious and growing doubts about his sailing experience. But it was too close to our departure date to replace him.

March 29, 2001 –1:00 PM, Ko Olina Marina, Honolulu, Hawaii.

The sailing vessel *Sundance* departed for Papeete, Tahiti, French Polynesia. Estimated days of passage: eighteen to twenty-five. Navigation note: make a course well east before reaching the Equator.

The boat, the crew, and its captain (that would be me) were ready to leave on March twenty-eighth. But March twenty-eighth was a Friday! According to a centuries-old tradition, a ship must never start a passage on a Friday. As I am not one to go against tradition, and figured I could use all the help I could get to ensure a safe passage, *Sundance* sat patiently in her slip, waiting for Saturday.

There's another great tradition according to which, when a boat leaves a marina for an extended passage with no plans to ever return to that marina in the future, every boat owner docked there will sound their boat's horn. As we motored out of our slip and prepared to leave Ko Olina, more than a hundred boats blasted their horns and our friends the boat owners rushed to stand along the sea wall to wave us off, wishing us safe sailing. A new aspect of this tradition has evolved in the past few years. Along with throwing kisses, everyone has a supply of water balloons. As *Sundance* picked her way out of the marina, water balloons rained down upon her decks like blessings. I felt honored for the send-off and a little sad to be leaving so many new friends behind. *Hopefully we will meet again in a distant harbor*, I thought.

• • •

The GPS called for a course of south by southeast with an estimated distance of 2,380 miles.

My attitude leaving Ko Olina was much different from I had experienced sailing out of San Diego. I was happy with the new crew, happy with *Sundance*, and happy with my new sense of confidence. I felt positive, secure, and excited to be sailing to Tahiti.

Only four hours from land, I had an encounter that I will never forget. We were sailing on a tight reach, with a full main and headsail. The wind was strong at twenty knots, pushing *Sundance* along at a steady five knots. I had sent the crew down below to get some rest before they would have to take their turn on watch. Standing at the helm, hand-steering (without the autopilot), I was reveling in the feeling of my boat racing through the waves toward an exotic new destination. I heard a strange sound just off the starboard aft quarter and realized it was a whale releasing air out of its blowhole. I twisted around and there before me was the massive head of a killer whale, slowly lifting out of the water, its enormous left eye looking straight at me. We stared at each other, eye to eye, for what seemed like forever. Slowly, the beautiful creature slipped back into the water and I stood there at the helm panting from the intensity of the encounter. The orca had been not more than ten feet away from me. It was almost like the whale had peeked its head up to wish us a safe passage.

Unfortunately, my warm-and-fuzzy feeling was short-lived. A few hours later, I heard the Frenchman start yelling from down below. I canted my head, straining to understand what he was saying through his thick French accent. What was he so excited about? He yelled again, much louder this time, and I understood every word: "Water is coming in the boat! We have a leak!" Then Chas poked his head out of the cabin and, in a calm voice, said, "Yes, captain. We're taking on seawater." Oh, man. That was one of the last things I wanted to hear. *Okay, time to follow your own instructions and remain calm, cool and collected. Assess damage, locate leak, and stop the water from entering to prevent our goddamn boat from sinking.*

We were on a port tack, in strong winds with the starboard rail crashing through the waves (the intense wind was causing the boat to heel over on its right side). I eased off on the sheets, which helped set *Sundance* squarely back on the water. Chas took the helm, and I went reluctantly below, expecting to find the cabin flooded with water. To my great relief, it wasn't nearly as bad as the Frenchman had made it sound. The water was ankle deep in front of his bunk. He was terrified, sitting up there cross-legged as if the water were acid, clutching his orange life jacket close to his chest, a look of sheer panic on his face. He was ready to abandon ship.

It became quickly obvious that the leak was in the area of a chain plate (a piece of stainless steel secured to the hull used to support the mast). Under the circumstances, though, I could not find the exact location of the leak. Best guess was that it was between the hull and the inter-fiberglass liner of the boat, which wasn't accessible from the cabin. This meant that it would be impossible to repair while we were at sea. We appeared to be taking on about a gallon of water every hour. We broke out the towels, large sponges, and buckets, which allowed us to keep the boat fairly dry. But we had to face a difficult question: should we continue to sail on and hope the leak didn't get any worse, or should we head to a safe harbor?

Chas was a seasoned sailor, so I valued his opinion. We discussed the advantages and disadvantages of sailing on and concluded that if we continued toward Tahiti and the leak became unmanageable, there was the real possibility that the boat might actually sink . . . and nobody wanted that. In the end, it was a no-brainer; we needed to change course and get *Sundance* to a marina as fast as possible.

According to the GPS, the closest harbor was . . . Honokohau on the Big Island. Yes, reader, you are correct: the very same sport fishing harbor where Sally and I had taken refuge, the one with all the bloody marlin and surly fishermen. Well, now I was coming to appreciate the adage, "Any port in a storm."

After looking at the chart, I determined it would take us damn near twenty-four hours to reach Honokohau under the existing conditions. The wind speed was twenty-five knots with eight-foot seas and the boat heeled over with the rail still in the water. I backed off on the sheets once more to level out the boat, hoping that would reduce the amount of water coming aboard; but slacking off on the sails also meant we would lose speed. Oh, well . . . I figured a dry boat was more important than a fast boat.

About the time the sun went down, so did the wind speed— and with it went the boat speed . . . time to wake up FUJIMO. I cranked it up to 1200 RPM and the boat speed "skyrocketed" from two to four knots. The leak persisted, but we were able to keep things dry with constant mopping. With no wind and under power, *Sundance* sat level on the water and eventually the leak slowed to just a dribble. This was great news: it meant the leak had to be above the water line. I'll take that any day over having a hole in the bottom of the boat. At least we wouldn't be going down like a submarine.

The next morning when the wind filled in, the sails went back up and FUJIMO came off watch. Once the wind was blowing above twenty knots, while on a port tack (with the starboard rail back in the water), the leak returned. I tried to keep the rail out of the water and still maintain a course to the

Big Island with decent headway . . . and of course, the faster we went, the greater the leak. We limped along all day, trying to minimize the amount of water filling up the boat. Once again, when the day grew late, the wind died, and FUJIMO went back to work. We could just barely see the volcano on the Big Island on the horizon. Fifteen miles to the harbor, which should take us about three and a half hours? We should be able to make it before dark.

Just as it appeared I had the situation under control, FUJIMO started to complain like an ex-wife. It sounded like he was having difficulty breathing, actually. The RPMs would surge and then drop, surge and drop. Hand-pumping the fuel line helped a little, but not for long. It was around eight-thirty that night when FUJIMO took its last gasp of air and then stopped running.

Okay. It's dark. We have no wind, so sailing is impossible. We have no engine, so motoring to the harbor is impossible. We are dead in the water with no way to cover the five measly miles to Honokohua. I was biting my lip, trying to figure out how to get us out of this situation, when the Frenchman quipped, "Captain, have you any paddles on this boat?"

That was the first time I wanted to toss his ass into the ocean.

I put out a call to the Coast Guard in Honolulu. They responded with their usual question: "Is this a life-threatening situation?" Well, no. Our lives were not in danger, at the moment, so I responded in the negative. Their next questions were how many POB (people on board), and do they all have their PFDs (personal floatation devices) on? I answered: Three people, yes to the PFDs. I gave them our GPS location and a brief explanation of the circumstances and waited for their instructions. They said they would make contact with the Kona Coast Guard Auxiliary Group and to stand by. Within ten minutes we received a radio call from the CGA in Kona. Their boat's call sign was Kona7. I repeated the story to them, and they came back with a quick verdict: "If you're not in danger, we would like to wait until morning to provide assistance."

"No problem," I replied. "We can wait till morning." CG Honolulu came back to establish a radio schedule; they would call us every hour to check our status, until Kona7 had a visual on us in the morning.

"Roger that, Coast Guard Honolulu."

So there it was. No help tonight, but it was good to know we weren't alone and that help was on the way in the morning. When CG Honolulu called back after the first hour, I reported our coordinates and was surprised to see that our position had changed. It would continue to change all night long: A strong current was pushing us in a northwesterly direction, away from the island. Well, that would mean some inconvenience in the morning, but it was much better than having the current take us *toward* shore and possibly dash us into the rocks.

At 7:00 AM sharp, we were contacted by Kona7. They were preparing to launch their boat and proceed to help. At nine o'clock, I saw a boat on the horizon: Kona7, a small fishing boat, maybe twenty feet in length, with four men on board, all dressed in their Coast Guard blue shirts, light blue shorts and PFDs. They came alongside and tossed us a line, which I tied to our bow.

There. We were now under tow to Honokohau with an ETA of seven hours! We had drifted twelve miles offshore overnight. The crew of Kona7 consisted entirely of Coast Guard volunteers who were spending their Sunday helping the disabled *Sundance* get safely to harbor. We pulled in at four o'clock that afternoon. I was, to say the least, very grateful. I thanked them over and over again for their help.

The following morning, I had two missions to accomplish: locate and repair the source of the leak, and find someone qualified to resurrect poor FUJIMO. Finding a diesel mechanic was easy. Finding the source of the leak was not. In fact, it proved impossible. *Sundance* had spent two months sitting in the hot Hawaiian sun, which had probably caused the caulking to dry up and contract, leaving small holes. When the starboard side of the boat was under water from the pressure of the wind in the sails, it experienced enormous pressure, allowing water in through any small opening. Rather than taking forever to look for a needle in a haystack, I used a shotgun approach, expending seven tubes of caulking material to cover every possible source of leakage. The advantage to that approach was that it was thorough, maybe even overkill; the disadvantage was that there would be no way to know if the leak was fixed until we were under sail with a rail in the water.

Repairing the diesel was much easier. As the mechanic worked on the engine, I stood over his shoulder, watching his every move, and hoping to learn from his expertise. I felt negligent for not having learned how to fix the engine before there was a problem. It turned out that the trouble was caused by two clogged fuel filters. Once they were replaced, FUJIMO purred like a kitten.

CHAPTER 12

• • •

Can't Seem to Say Goodbye

An adventure is only an inconvenience rightly considered. An inconvenience is an
adventure wrongly considered.

—G.K. Chesterton

THREE DAYS LATER, WE HEADED back out to sea. I felt confident
that the seven tubes of caulking applied around *Sundance*'s entire circumference would put an end to the "wet-boat issue."

We left Honokohau, passing Kona on a southerly course,
once again headed toward Tahiti. "Take two." It was slow going
on the leeward side of the Big Island, where the massive volcano
serves to block out the strong trade winds, but once we were clear
of the island's southern tip, it was a completely different story.
Now, the unabated wind whipped up to a knock-your-socks-
off thirty to thirty-five knots. The transition from pleasant, light
breezes to gale-force winds was dramatic. We went from comfort one minute to rough, heavy weather sailing the next—wind
shrieking in the rigging, whitewater crashing over the bow. I put
one reef in the mainsail and shortened the headsails. We were on
a port tack, once again, with the starboard side of the boat plowing through huge twelve-foot waves. When you consider that a
basketball hoop is ten feet off the ground, you're able to gain a
better perspective on just how huge a twelve-foot wave looks like
when viewed from a trough beneath it.

Chas seemed energized by the conditions, but the Frenchman sat near me in the cockpit with his personal floatation device (PFD) strapped on tightly, hugging his guitar with white knuckles, his eyes like those of a deer caught in the headlights. It was now blatantly obvious to me that he had lied to come on board. He had never experienced heavy weather conditions before; he was useless . . . dead weight. And speaking of "dead," he had an awful smell to boot. Even in these high winds, I couldn't get his stink out of my nostrils. His pungent body order fouled up the entire cabin. Earlier, when I had questioned him about using deodorant, he'd said, "It is not Frenchman-like to use this thing." He was too scared to teach me French and smelled too bad for me to let him fix any of my meals. Since he was lacking even the slightest idea about how to sail a big boat in rough seas, he was an extreme liability.

I wanted him gone.

Chas went below to see how the caulking was holding up, and came back up through the companionway with a frown on his face. Crap, damn. Well, kiss my ass! We were taking on water again. "You'd best take a look yourself, Captain," Chas said.

I was startled by what I saw. We were leaking profusely. Water was filling the cabin at an alarming rate, much more rapidly than we had first experienced. *I think we are going to need some bigger buckets*, I thought. My caulking repair job was a miserable failure. If anything, it seemed to have made the leaking problem worse.

It was, of course, impossible to attempt to sail 2,000 miles while bailing water out of the boat.

I had a long moment with myself down in the cabin. I was feeling an onrush of emotions that hearkened back to my first passage with DH. I was discouraged, I was angry, and the feeling of bafflement at how the water was coming into my boat was making me feel impotent and frustrated.

All normal feelings, I reminded myself—but you can't afford the luxury of negative thoughts. Let's breathe for a minute and put all this into proper perspective. This is not cancer! This is nothing more than a temporary inconvenience. Deal with it! Don't let this temporary problem get the best of you. This, too, shall pass. You can certainly weather this storm. Do the best you can with what you have to work with. And here is a positive thought: it's much better to have a leaking boat close to land, rather than a thousand miles out to sea. This is no big deal. Get back to the marina and fix the damn leak!

After conferring with Chas, I made the decision to set a new course for the Hawaii Yacht Club in Honolulu. I wanted to find a professional to work on the leak, and I wanted to get the Frenchman off my boat.

The sail to Oahu was in a northwesterly direction, which put us on a starboard tack with a leak-free port rail in the water. It took us twelve hours to reach the yacht club without incident.

Back on the Aloha Dock, Chas headed for shore but I called to the Frenchman to wait behind with me. "We need to talk," I said.

"Yes?"

Once Chas was out of earshot, I said, "You haven't been in weather like that before, have you?"

He looked down at his feet, then back at my eyes. "No," he said.

"You've hardly sailed at all before this, have you?"

"Not much. Not really."

"How did you really get to Hawaii from Tahiti? Because I know you didn't sail."

"By airplane."

"That's what I figured. I don't want you on this passage. You don't have enough experience and you don't seem cut out for it."

"All right," he said.

He went below to gather his things, rather cheerfully it seemed. Which, I realized, shouldn't be too surprising; I would think that my boat was just about the last way he'd like to get back to Tahiti. He emerged with his bag and guitar a few minutes later, said, "See you," and stepped off the boat and out of my life.

I sat there for a moment in the wake of his stench, a little bit grateful for the leak after all. At least I had avoided another DH situation. *Au revoir, asshole.*

Even after such a short sail, *Sundance* needed tidying up— especially given the stench the Frenchman had left behind. I did my best to clean up his bunk and felt sorry for whoever would be sleeping in it next. And someone soon would: I still wanted a third crew member for this leg of the trip.

That afternoon, I went ashore to begin a new crew search. I wasn't messing around this time. Considering the contrast between Chas and the Frenchman, or Chas and DH, I could finally see what a difference it made to have an able-bodied person with relevant sailing skills on board. I knew about a person in Oahu whose status among sailors was legendary. His name was Buck McGee, and he was a delivery boat captain with over fifty-eight crossings under his belt. (In order to qualify as a "crossing," a passage must be over 2,000 miles.) Imagine having someone with *that* kind of experience on board . . . he could teach me a thing or two about bluewater sailing. There was just one problem, so the story went: Captain McGee was a pretty serious alcoholic. Still, he'd be worth talking to.

I wanted to meet Mr. McGee. As it turned out, it wasn't hard to find him. Just ask anyone in the marina, and they can steer you toward Buck. I found him sitting out on the jetty in a six-dollar folding lawn chair with a cigarette in one hand and a swollen, yellowed paperback novel in the other. There was a fishing pole at his feet, but it seemed he'd forgotten all about it hours ago. *Must be a damn good read,* I thought.

Meeting Captain McGee was a little bit like calling on Rooster Cogburn. He looked like he had staggered out here after sleeping in a cardboard box in the park. Long hair; full, unkempt beard; ruddy complexion; a black captain's hat perched on his head . . . too cool for school.

"Captain McGee?" I said.

"Yessir."

I introduced myself and told him I might be interested in

hiring him to crew for me to Tahiti. We talked for quite a while. It was hard not to like him instantly. He had an understated style, slow of speech with no sign of an ego. He downplayed his extensive experience at sea even though his life sounded like something out of a Joseph Conrad or Jack London novel. He told me he had made his first crossing after running away from an abusive home life, on a twenty-eight-foot sailboat from Long Beach to Hawaii, when he was sixteen years old. Now, he was fifty and he had never returned to Long Beach. Hawaii had been his home and base of operation for the past thirty-four years. He didn't advertise and he didn't hand out cards. All his business was by word of mouth and a handshake. No contracts, no lawyers. If he couldn't trust a man's word, he didn't want anything to do with him.

"I do enjoy having a beer from time to time," he said.

"I heard that about you," I said.

• • •

We met again later that evening on board *Sundance*. Buck said he liked the boat and was indeed interested in sailing with us to Tahiti. He wanted to see some friends there and he didn't have any deliveries scheduled in the immediate future; so far, so good. There was just one possible sticking point for me: the drinking. I had laughed it off earlier in the day, but now I knew it needed to be discussed.

"Listen," I said. "I'd be honored to have you on board. The only thing that concerns me a little bit is the drinking."

"Oh," he said. "That won't be a problem. I've got it worked out to where when I'm at sea, I only drink six beers a day."

I quickly did some calculating in my head. Six beers a day for a twenty-day passage; that amounted to 120 beers!

"Wow," I said a little sadly. "I just don't have room on the boat for 120 beers."

Captain McGee was noticeably disappointed and so was I.

We agreed to talk some more in a couple of days.

I had even less luck when it came to finding a professional boat repairman to tackle the leaking situation. I couldn't wait around forever, so I bought seven more tubes of caulking material. For the next four days, I did nothing except apply caulking to every conceivable source of the leak.

The day before we were planning to leave, Captain McGee suddenly appeared on the dock and asked permission to come aboard.

"Sure," I said. "What's on your mind, Captain?"

"Listen," he said. "I've been thinking. I'd really like to do this trip, and I understand your concern about the drinking and about carrying that much beer. What I'd like to do, if you haven't filled the crew position yet, is come with you with no beer at all."

"Is that, uh—could you do that?"

"Sure. I've been wanting to dry out anyway, so this will be the perfect way to do it."

He made it seem like no big deal at all. So I gave him the position, thrilled to have a sailor of such caliber join the crew of *Sundance*. I just hoped he wouldn't spend most of his time in his bunk in the throes of the *delirium tremens*.

• • •

Take three. We departed the Aloha Dock of the Hawaii Yacht Club without any fanfare. No horns blowing, no water balloons raining down, just another boat getting under way. I was confident this time we would be successful in making it to Tahiti. Third time's a charm, right?

We were barely out of sight of Oahu when to my astonishment Buck McGee strode into the cockpit, sat down across from me, and fired up a Maui Wowie joint the size of a Cuban cigar. I sat there staring at him for a minute, hardly believing my eyes. Make no mistake: I went to college in the sixties and have toked my share of the magic weed, but I could not imagine trying to sail my boat while I was stoned. My first impulse was to turn the boat around and deposit him back on the Aloha Dock. Yet he was a legendary sailor, and I was lucky to have him. This was a real dilemma.

"Buck," I said. "When you said you were drying out, this isn't exactly what I pictured."

"Oh," he said. "Don't let this worry you. Keeps me even-keeled and prevents seasickness to boot."

"Is it going to be a problem?"

"You watch me carefully, Skipper. If I ever seem like a man who's incapacitated, you can drop me at the nearest harbor. Or, hell, dump me overboard for that matter."

I decided to give him a chance. But he was right about one thing: I'd be watching him very, very carefully.

As the wind grew stronger, the starboard rail plunged into the water and I held my breath in anticipation. Chas and Buck were both below in the cabin, and I expected one of them to shout at any moment, "Abandon ship!" There wasn't a word from either of them, so perhaps my latest patch job had been effective. I engaged the autopilot and went below to see for myself. Where the water usually accumulated, it was damp, but not flooded as before. I was cautiously optimistic.

As we cleared the southern tip of the Big Island on this our third attempt at reaching Tahiti, the wind speed again increased dramatically to thirty-five knots off the port bow. We shortened sail and hung on for another wild ride.

We had little choice but to sail close to the wind, on a heading that made for a rough going. One of the challenges of sailing from Hawaii to Tahiti is that Tahiti lies southeast of Hawaii; going back eastward against the prevailing trade winds is quite tough. It's critical that you work your way well to the east before you cross the equator on your way south. This is called "getting your easting in." Experienced sailors know that if you haven't got your easting in before you reach the equator, you're in big trouble. At the equator, the prevailing trade winds switch from the northeast to the southeast. Those new trade winds will be directly on your nose as you attempt to steer a southerly course to French Polynesia. Remember, it's impossible to sail directly into the wind, so a sailor who hasn't got his easting in must tack, sailing a zigzag course that can double the miles and take twice as long to reach Tahiti.

In order to get our easting in, we were forced to sail hard on the wind, "close-hauled." This angle of sailing to the wind is not conducive to a comfortable ride. The boat heels way over and races along, smashing its way through the waves. Sailing from San Diego to Hawaii, the trade winds had been generally aft of the beam, a quartering wind, allowing us to sail on a comfortable "broad reach," riding with the waves instead of crashing through them. This was quite another cup of tea.

Wind direction, wind velocity, and the size of the seas all have a direct effect on the comfort level of those on board. And it is utter misery for everyone on the boat when the winds blow at gale force (over thirty-five knots), whitewater crashes over the bow and the boat fights its way through waves of fifteen feet or more. Here is what the sailing conditions were like: First, imagine that you are on a sightseeing tour with two of your friends over 2,000 miles of beautiful wilderness country. The vehicle for this tour is a large cement mixer truck that has a revolving tank where the cement is usually contained. Your tank is made out of clear Plexiglas for the purposes of this trip. The roads are four-wheel-drive trails, sometimes full of rocks, pitted with holes, logs strewn about, and parts of it completely under water. Your driver is a fucking maniac, and at irregular intervals your friendly tour guide shoots 100 gallons of ice-cold water into the mixer. The truck runs day and night at about five miles an hour. The mixer never stops turning. Welcome to *Sundance*, sailing to Tahiti. How are you enjoying the ride so far?

Having two excellent crew members certainly made the difficult circumstances much more tolerable. These guys were first-class sailing companions; no one complained about the conditions, they just went about their work. This gave me a great peace of mind to know I could have confidence in their ability to handle any situation when they were standing watch. For the first time on board of *Sundance*, I could go off watch and actually relax.

I was also pleased to have avoided serious seasickness on this passage. I felt a bit nauseous, but at least I was not hanging over the rail, tossing my cookies. Now, I don't know if it was one or some combination of the remedies I'd tried, or perhaps the result of inhaling the secondhand smoke from Buck's never-ending chain of joints. Frankly, I didn't care, as long as I wasn't puking my guts out.

I assigned Chas to be our navigator. Buck was our sail tactician, in charge of calling the sail trim and sail changes. I was the captain of the ship, although I felt a little silly in this position given that my crew had vastly more passage-making experience than I did. But I didn't take the attitude that I was in any way their superior. I had learned a valuable lesson from Captain Bligh. In the end, my role was simply to take responsibility for making the final decisions when it was appropriate. After all, it was my boat.

On the third day out at about 9:00 AM, we were laboring along through the same gale conditions (twelve-foot seas, one reef in the main, half of the headsail, and three-quarters of the staysail out), when we heard what sounded like a gunshot from up near the bow. Buck was at the helm, so Chas and I worked our way forward to investigate. With one look over the bowsprit, it became sadly obvious what had caused the sound. The bobstay had broken! The bobstay is a cable that attaches to the bow at one end and to the headstay at the other. Its purpose is to support the mast, the way a guy wire supports a radio tower. Without a secure bobstay, the mast will collapse from the strength of the wind's pressure. The fitting that secures the bobstay to the bow is close to the waterline; over the years corrosion had weakened the fitting, causing the cable to tear loose. *Houston, we have a problem.*

We immediately dropped the mainsail and furled in the

headsails. FUJIMO was mustered to action and we promptly changed to a downwind heading to take all the stress off of the mast. Once the boat was secured, we held a team meeting to discuss our options. Chas calculated our position to be 340 miles from the Big Island and over 800 miles from the small Line Islands to the west. *Sundance* was in bad shape; she needed to get to an intensive care unit immediately.

I carried a lot of spare parts, even backups for the backups. We did have some spare cable on board, but no way to attach it properly to withstand the enormous pressures when under sail. Sailing with no bobstay was never an option; we would surely lose the mast if we tried. The only feasible option was to motor 340 miles back . . . to Honokohau on the Big Island. Yes, reader, you're getting good at this. Honokohau was the place with the marlin blood, and this would be my third visit to that charming port of call.

Here I go again . . . I knew I had to get a grip and do my best to remain calm; for both my crew and for myself. As we changed course for Honokohau, I could feel my brain churning to keep this latest problem in its proper perspective. *Remember, you can't allow yourself to dwell on something that is out of your control. This is nothing more than another temporary inconvenience.* I directed myself to think about the alternative: imagine that you're halfway to Tahiti and *then* the bobstay breaks. There you are, a thousand miles from Hawaii and over a thousand miles from Tahiti. You can't sail on and risk losing the mast, and there is only enough fuel on board to motor 500 miles, at the most—too far out to sea to call for help—nobody coming to save you. Now there would be a *real* problem! In the end, I found myself feeling lucky that the bobstay had broken when it did. I was disappointed, but I didn't fall into a state of depression. As a matter of fact, I was quite proud of the way I dealt with the situation. Both Chas and Captain McGee were nonchalant about the whole thing, which certainly helped. "No big deal," Buck said, reaching for his lighter. "Let's go get it fixed."

I looked over at Chas. He was hunched over the GPS, smiling a little, immersed in the task of plotting out a new course for Honokohau.

· · ·

Eighty-four hours after the bobstay failed, *Sundance* was back at the big game fishing port of Hohokohau . . . for the third time.

I spent the first day ashore looking around for a craftsman with the skill to do the repair. This time I was lucky; I found a guy who said he'd come out and take a look at the boat that very evening. He quickly sized up the damage and told me it would take him four days at a minimum—three days for the necessary parts to arrive from Honolulu and, if we were lucky, another day for the new bobstay to be installed with a Stay-loc fitting. I took him at his word, and the three of us idled about on shore, waiting to see how things went.

I called Sally and told her about all our misfortune, taking care to omit the details about just how dangerous it would have been to spring a leak or break a bobstay in the middle of the Pacific. She took it all in with the bemused resignation that was becoming natural for her. She no longer asked me to come home and she no longer questioned what I was doing out here. I wasn't at all sure if that was a good thing or not. For my part, I didn't want to torture either one of us with effusive declarations of love or statements about how much I missed her and longed for home. When it was time to hang up, she simply said, "Michael? Take care of yourself out there, okay?"

And I said, "I will, baby. I love you and I miss you."

I hung up feeling conflicted. It was good that we were no longer heartbroken about not being together, but I didn't want either of us to get too comfortable with being apart.

The repair schedule worked out just as the craftsman had predicted. By the end of the fourth day, he had installed the new fitting, which would not be affected by the corrosion like the old swaged one. While he worked, we had replenished our provisions and topped up the diesel and water tanks. By the time he finished, we were ready to sail.

Take four. *Sundance* was ready to head off to Tahiti. *Fourth time's a charm.* Secretly, I couldn't help but wonder what the next catastrophe might be.

Nine days out of Hawaii, three days from the equator, I was on watch a little before midnight, hand-steering in moderate conditions. Normally when I'm at the helm, I automatically scan left to right, right to left, before me in a constant sweeping pattern. This time, I spotted the lights of a ship off our starboard bow quarter, surprising the hell out of me. After nine days, this was the first ship I had seen since leaving Hawaii. I watched the vessel's movement for a moment, and quickly determined that we were on a collision course. One of us would have to alter direction to avoid a disaster at sea. Using the handheld VHF radio, I hailed the oncoming boat. "Vessel located at 5 degrees south by 149 west. This is the sailing vessel *Sundance* off your bow. Do you have a copy? Over."

I waited a minute but got no response, so I made the call again. Soon, a distinctly Asian voice came on the radio, in heavily accented English. All the voice said was, "We see you."

Well, that was unsatisfactory. We needed to communicate if we were going to avoid a collision. With my dander up, I said, "Let me speak to your captain."

I was getting a little worried. Maybe this was not a friendly ship. Chas and Buck heard the limited conversation and joined me in the cockpit. Apparently they were having the same reservations I was, because Buck stepped past me mumbling something about manning the battle stations, and clutching our only means of defense, a baseball bat. Obviously, we could have changed our course, but we didn't want go to the trouble of adjusting the sails. It would have been much easier for the big engine-driven ship to just steer its way around us.

After ten or fifteen minutes, a booming voice came over the radio. "This is Captain Yang."

The long wait for the captain was unfortunate, because it had been enough time for me to really grow indignant and puffed up. Feeling like a big-time seafaring captain, I spoke into the microphone with all the authority afforded me by my nine whole days of water under the hull. "Captain," I said. "This is the sailing vessel *Sundance*, nine days out of Hawaii, with Tahiti as our destination. Give us the name of your vessel, how many days out, your home port, and where you are headed. Over."

This time I didn't have to wait for an answer. The captain came back immediately, in a much stronger voice (which I would not have thought possible). "We are the fishing vessel *Sun Hee*, 162 days out of Korea with thirty-six days to go, and a lot more fish to catch. Over and out!"

I felt like a little kid who'd just gotten his ass kicked on the playground. I was speechless. One hundred and sixty two days out, compared to our pathetic nine days! The fishing boat did change course, but I was the one who sailed off with my tail between my legs. I *hate* to lose a pissing match.

• • •

After ten wet, miserable days of riding in the cement mixer, beating to weather with a constant barrage of green water crashing over the bow, we reached the doldrums near the equator. Typically, there is little or no wind at all close to the equator, hence the term "doldrums." I was not about to complain. After a week and a half of pushing the envelope twenty-four hours a day, I was more than happy just to be dry and sitting on flat water for a change.

The water was so calm, in fact, that we could jump off the boat and swim, like we were noodling around on a lake. We always kept one person on deck, standing at shark watch. Jumping off of *Sundance* for the first time, I felt a thrill of uneasiness. It was a bit like doing a spacewalk, only without the tether; I was disconnecting from the vessel that had carried me through this foreign medium. As I paddled along-side the boat, it was hard not to think of the vastness of this ocean, both in terms of the depths beneath me with all their myriad mysteries, and with respect to the unimaginable distances out along its surface to the nearest land, to the nearest continent. It was the sphincter-tightening sensation of a man who finds himself in true wilderness.

With such a complete lack of wind, it was time to burn up some dinosaur juice. We started FUJIMO and motor-sailed for the next three days until we were edged up to the equator. I felt a childlike fascination staring at the GPS as I watched the degrees, and then minutes, of latitude descending to zero.

I had a great idea to pay homage to King Neptune; I would swim across the equator! As we approached, we lowered and furled all the sails and let the boat drift slowly with the current. Just before we hit 00 degrees and 0 minutes, I dove off the bow into eighty-degree water and enjoyed a leisurely swim across the imaginary line that circles our planet. It was one of those surreal moments of life, and I sent a spiritual postcard back in time to my eleven-year-old self: *Am now swimming across the equator! Lots to look forward to in life, kid. Love, an Older Version of You.*

When I came back aboard, Chas said that he had brought along a special treat to commemorate the crossing of the equator. He went below and came back up with three huge cigars and a bottle of rum. As we sat puffing our smokes, I said to the crew, "This sucks, doesn't it, boys?"

"What do you mean, Captain?" Chas said.

"Look around you. Not a single souvenir shop, as far as the eye can see. Where the hell am I going to get my T-shirt that says, 'I swam across the equator?'"

CHAPTER 13

• • •

White Squall and Landfall

*All men dream—but not equally. Those who dream by night in the dusty recesses of
their minds, wake in the day to find it was vanity—but the dreamers of the day are
dangerous men, for they act out their dreams with open eyes, to make it possible.*

—T.E. Lawrence

WE HAD CROSSED THE EQUATOR at 0'00S, 149'00W. We
hadn't quite made our "easting" goal of 145'00W, but we
were close; close enough that we could lay off the helm, move
off the wind, and settle the boat for a smoother ride. Eventually, we eased out of the doldrums with a fresh breeze filling in
from our new trade winds out of the southeast. At last, we had
successfully accomplished "getting our easting in." I would be
content never to hear the word, "easting" again in my life. The
average strength of the southeast trades is around fifteen knots,
although they will pipe up to twenty-five knots and more, depending on the location and intensity of the high pressure systems
to the south. Thirty knots is not uncommon. If you encounter
one of the localized squalls, you'd better be ready to handle forty
knots with vicious rain.

   Every day at exactly noon, Buck would sit in his favorite spot
in the cockpit, fire up one of his three handheld GPS units, and
ask Chas and me to guess how many miles we had covered in the
last twenty-four hours. This was a daily ritual that we all partic-

ipated in and looked forward to. Finding out the miles traveled in the past twenty-four hours was the equivalent to watching the lotto numbers revealed on TV. We would all take our best guesses and would either be excited or disappointed when Buck announced the figure. On a good day, the number would exceed 150 miles; on a bad day, the reading would be 100 miles or less.

We certainly did put in some 150-miles-plus days, which, of course, meant we were going very fast, at least seven knots. The drawback was, in order to go that fast, we had to have some ass-kicking wind blowing, which made for high seas and a rough, wet ride. I spent my days with the safety harness strapped tightly around my chest, holding on with both hands. It was nearly impossible to move about the boat without carefully balancing myself and proceeding in a hand-over-hand fashion. My nights were spent in my bunk, wedged between two large sail bags to lessen the effects of being slammed from one side of the bed to the other. I would lie on my back, jammed tightly between the sail bags, listening to the sound of the water rushing past the hull. It really was like sleeping in the tank of a cement mixer . . . or trying to. There was no such thing as REM sleep. The soft flannel sheets of home were a distant memory. A few times too often, I had come off watch, soaked from head to toe, too exhausted to extricate myself from all my cumbersome foul-weather gear, and had crashed into the bunk and promptly passed out. My sheets had thus gotten wet with saltwater numerous times. They always seemed damp and, even at their driest, felt prickly and itchy, like cozying up to sandpaper. Most of the time, though, after standing a four-hour watch in heavy weather, I didn't much care what the sheets felt like. I just wanted to get off of the helm, escape the nasty weather, go below, and crash. Often enough, I'd have just begun to doze when my treasonous bladder and prostate would start acting up, and it would be time for Mr. Happy to pay his respects to the green bottle . . .

But to my credit, I was showing signs of having learned from my experience. Back in Honolulu, shopping to re-provision for the passage, I had happened to see a garden sprayer in a hardware store. It held five gallons of water, and could be pressurized by using a handle to pump it up. I was struck by inspiration and purchased it on the spot. Now, when my face became too un-comfortable from getting soaked with seawater coming over the bow (stinging my eyes and filling my mouth with its awful taste), I pumped up my new sprayer and rinsed my face clean. Weather permitting; I could even take a complete shower with it.

We all had our little ways of enduring ocean sailing . . . and Buck's was to smoke more weed than Bob Marley. He burned off several joints daily. At first, I was concerned that he might not be able to function and would cause a horrific accident. So, as promised, I paid close attention to his every move for the first few days, and he seemed just fine—always happy, but never out of control. I didn't want him stinking up the cabin, though, so I asked him to perform his sacrament topsides, and he cheerfully agreed. He never missed a watch and never uttered a complaint about anything. In all ways except for the illicit drug use, he was the ideal crew member.

In some books I've read about sailing in the South Pacific, the crew cleats down the sails, turns on the autopilot, and lies in the sun drinking cool beverages as they leisurely float over gently rolling waves. Some even make the patently absurd claim that it is possible to read a good book. I think they must have been aboard the *Queen Mary*!

The only way I could lie down in the sun was if I was tightly strapped in with my harness. Otherwise, the "mechanical bull" would toss me onto the cockpit floor with the first decent-sized wave we smashed into. Or one of the rogue waves would decide to jump into the cockpit and drench me with a ton of water. This usually happened when I was trying to eat a sandwich. Take this hard-earned piece of seafaring advice: a sandwich is a magnet for rogue waves, so unless you want to get dowsed, don't ever get caught holding one in your hand.

Eating dry sandwiches? Reading more than a chapter of a

book without getting seasick? Are you kidding me? Don't believe any of the "cruising in paradise" articles you read in the sailing magazines; there's no such thing as *comfortable* bluewater passage—at least, not that I have experienced. The words *tired, cold,
wet*, and *hungry* describe the circumstances more accurately. I've
also read that it is "not the destination, but rather the journey!"
After a few days of heavy weather sailing, through one storm after
another, I'll say this: you show me a person who says he's enjoying
the journey and I'll show you a dangerous liar. Or, we might be
looking at a true masochist.

Want to make Neptune laugh? Tell him you are going to sail
across an ocean in a small boat. I consider any boat under one
hundred feet in length to be too small for me.

There were, if I must be honest, a few days after crossing
the equator that were marked by fluffy cumulus clouds drifting
over deep blue skies. Even so, the pleasant daytime weather was
made up for by what we experienced at night. During the day,
the sun heats up the surface of the ocean; at night, when the cool
air meets the warm water, Mother Nature puts on a show. If you
have the radar on, it is possible to see the previews of the coming
attractions waiting for you on the horizon. The radar screen will
show different-sized dark blobs during the day, and at night, they
appear on the screen as light shapes. Some look like snowballs,
others like crescent rolls back home in the local bakery . . . Mmm,
crescent rolls. It would be wonderful if bakeries had boats out on
the ocean. Every morning they could deliver fresh warm donuts.
Can't you just smell them? Can't you just taste the white frost-
ing on the roof of your mouth? Wouldn't you pay just about any
price for a fresh, warm jelly donut right about now? See, that's
how you feel when you're at sea. *Enjoying the journey*, my ass. But
I digress; let's get back to the lovely nighttime squall show.

The storm blobs that appear on the radar screen come in
two shapes. One will just wash the crusty accumulation of salt
off your boat; it carries very little wind and is quite friendly. The
other shape won't wash off your boat with as much fresh rainwater, but it very well might blow all the salty crud to kingdom

come, taking you and your can opener along with it. The trick is to remember which shape has the rain and which one has the wind. If you guess wrong, you could be in for a rude awakening.

• • •

At 2:00 AM, on the dog watch, I was hand-steering, enjoying a lovely blow of fifteen knots, sailing along at a decent six and a half knots. I had one reef in the main; we always sailed that way at night just to be safe. The headsail was three quarters of the way out, the staysail was all the way out, the helm was soft, and the boat was balanced nicely. It had been an uneventful watch . . . then I glanced at the radar screen. What I saw immediately sent an adrenaline rush throughout my entire body. On the edge of the screen, fifteen miles distant, loomed the mother of all blobs—the sinister kind. As it moved toward us, the storm filled out until it covered the entire screen. Looking for an escape route from such a large blow was fruitless. Anyway, *Sundance* is not fast enough to outrun storms, unless she has twenty-four hours' notice. Even then, it's questionable. And we had only minutes before this one would hit.

Chas and Buck were sound asleep in their bunks. I stuck my face in the companionway and screamed, "Get your lily-white asses up on deck as fast as possible! Time to man the battle stations! Get your foulies on; we are definitely about to experience some very bad weather!"

Anything that can fly across the cabin was lashed down, everything stowed, all the hatches closed and locked. I headed the boat into the wind to ease the pressure on the sails, and Chas and Buck put two additional reefs in the main. We furled the headsail and shortened the staysail until it looked like a diaper on the bow.

As we approached the edge of the storm, I remembered the movie *White Squall*, in which a wall of green water crashes over a 120-foot sailboat, the *Albatross*, sinking it and killing several of its crew. My adrenaline spiked up to "pedal to the metal" mode. *Nowhere to run, nowhere to hide! It's game time; let's get ready to rock and roll!* Just before a storm hits, you can feel a blast of cold air. If you don't have your foulies on by the time you feel the cold air, it's already too late; you'll never pull them on before the brunt of the storm slams you in the face.

Here it came.

The wind was fierce and wild, never driving from the same direction for any length of time—and yet, to avoid being hit with its full strength, I needed to steer about fifteen degrees off the wind. I stood at the helm, doing my best to maintain a steady course, despite the frequent changes in wind direction. Now the rain hit, blasting my face with such force that it felt like I was being shot point-blank with a dozen BB guns. I shielded my eyes to steal a look at the wind instrument on the bulkhead and saw a gust blow the needle past forty-eight knots. But at least the waves weren't too bad; the force of the rain hitting the water kept them to a minimum.

Either of my crew could probably have steered at least as well as I, but I stayed at the helm. If we were going to be dismasted, I wanted to be the one steering the boat. Was I scared? Oh, you bet your ass I was scared! Yet, I also found sailing through the teeth of a huge storm to be deliriously exhilarating. This, by far, was the most severe storm I had ever experienced at the helm of my own boat. We were faring well in it because we had followed the Boy Scout motto to always be prepared. There's no doubt that if we hadn't got the boat ready in time, we could easily have seen serious loss of property, maybe even loss of life.

The storm, which seemed to go on for days, lasted a total of two hours. Finally, I could see the monster moving off our stern port quarter. Once it started to pass, things went strangely quiet. Still shaking from the excitement, Chas, Buck, and I exchanged high-fives and congratulations. They had nice things to say about how I'd steered, which meant a lot to me. I walked the deck to assess the damage and was happy to see we had weathered this storm without breaking anything. I came away from that violent storm with a newfound sense of confidence in my ability to sail in any kind of weather. I didn't look forward to the next storm, but I did feel that I'd be up to the challenge when it came. And I would be able to comfort myself with the old adage, "This storm, too, shall pass."

• • •

Chas was the first to see land on the distant horizon. He let out a loud, "Land ho! Land ho!" I raced up on deck to see for myself. What he saw as land appeared to me as nothing more than a sliver of a storm cloud; it never moved nor grew larger as we got closer. "No, that's it," he insisted. "That's land."

When I realized he was right, I let out a whoop, and danced a jig only slightly less extravagant than the one on my passage to Hawaii with DH. When I turned around, Buck saluted me from his seat at the helm, and Chas just grinned.

"What's the matter with you guys? Aren't you thrilled to see land?"

"Sure," Chas said. "I just don't want to let my shore anxiety peak too soon. It'll be many hours yet before we're able to drop anchor."

True enough. Yet, it's impossible for me not to feel a rush of excitement when I first see land after being out at sea for any length of time. I guess that means that in my heart of hearts, I'm a true landlubber.

Before we reached shore, I knew that Mr. McGee and I needed to have a serious conversation regarding his Maui Wowies. French Polynesia has a zero-tolerance policy concerning any drugs entering its country. I knew that if they found so much as one seed of a marijuana plant, they would impound my boat and dump all three of us in jail. The justice system in some foreign countries is starkly different than that of the United States. You are considered guilty until proven innocent, not the other way around. It's not at all uncommon for a local customs officer to board incoming boats and search extensively for drugs—especially boats arriving from America. I, for one, never want to see the inside of a Polynesian prison.

I explained all this to Buck, and he listened respectfully.

"No problem, Skipper," he said when I had finished. "Fact is, I just smoked my very last joint. I was saving it for when we spotted land."

"I'm glad to hear you say that," I said. "Still, would you mind if I kind of did my own inspection, just to make sure you haven't inadvertently overlooked anything?"

"'Course not, Skipper. Knock yourself out."

So I did. I put myself in the shoes of a very pesky customs officer, and scoured the boat, peeking into every last recess I could think of. After two hours of searching, I was relieved to find no evidence of marijuana, not even a seed.

Now, after two 2,285 arduous nautical miles—approximately the distance from Los Angeles to Detroit—I could see Mount Orohena, the main peak on the island of Papeete, rising up 7,352 feet. I stood on the very end of the bow pulpit, reveling in an enormous sense of satisfaction. Tahiti has been the setting for innumerable novels and adventure stories that have come to be associated with the typical South Seas island paradise. I had dreamed of this very moment since 1967 while watching *Mutiny on the Bounty* in Ann Arbor, Michigan. Sailing into the azure blue waters, seeing the beautiful Tahitian girls dancing to the sound of the drums, watching as outrigger canoes full of natives paddled out to offer us heaps of fresh fruit. I was hoping to find the breadfruit plants still in existence. I could send some home to Sally so she might plant them in her garden. HMS *Bounty* had sailed into this very same bay on October 26, 1788. I entertained my long-lived speculation about whether Fletcher Christian might have secretly returned to the island, and, like a little boy, I stood in the bow pulpit imagining what it would be like to have a beer with him and swap sailing stories.

Sundance's anchor hit the water at eleven-thirty that night. We were safely in the harbor of Papeete, staring down a massive wooden sign that read:

POLYNÉSIE FRANÇAISE
PAPEETE
BIENVENUE, IORANA, WELCOME

With no further ado, we inflated the dinghy, dropped it over the side, and paddled ashore. (Sometime during the passage, I had thought up the name *Butch* for the dinghy; you know: *Butch* and *Sundance*.) Just getting some solid ground under my feet did wonders for washing away the sheer discomfort of nineteen grueling days at sea. Something to do with the restoration of one's natural rhythms, I'm sure.

The first thing I saw after coming ashore in this exotic country was a pair of familiar faces. It was two of our friends from Hawaii, walking toward us on the boardwalk—Captain Bert and his first mate, "Big Fred," off the sailing vessel *Arca*. They had departed Honolulu seven days after *Sundance* and, they told us, arrived three days earlier. I took that in stride. *Arca* happens to be a splendid, 100-foot Sparkman-and-Stevens-designed sailing yacht. Her glossy hull is dark blue, her varnished wood shines like an urn, and she is altogether an awesome sight to behold. Oh, and Captain Bert has a crew of seven—not including the cook. The owner enjoys wearing sweaters; therefore, Captain Bert sets the air conditioning—that is correct, reader: the *air conditioning*— inside the cabin at sixty-eight degrees. *Arca* slides through the ocean at over ten knots; we averaged 4.2 knots. They chowed down on filet mignon, while we feasted on MREs, instant soup, and saltwater sandwiches. The only time they got wet was when they took their daily hot showers; we had showers several times a day, compliments of Neptune himself sending waves over the rails. There is, all told, an enormous difference in making an ocean passage in a forty-foot sailboat, compared to a tranquil sail on a 100-foot yacht. They might have made considerably better time, but we had something they didn't: in the recesses of our minds, we could bask in the glory of knowing we had accomplished something *grand*.

I rushed to a pay phone. Sally picked up on the first ring.

"I did it, baby! I made it to Tahiti!"

"Oh, Michael, I'm so proud of you. I'm so happy for you."

And she was. I could hear it in her voice. Of course, she couldn't fully appreciate what an accomplishment it was, but I had been keeping her informed of our progress by e-mail. Typing in the cement mixer had been a challenge, though, so most of my e-mails were truncated missives that read more like text messages, just giving our position and an "all okay."

Everything was fine at home. But now I suddenly found myself missing Sally rather painfully. Before she hung up, I said, "Why don't you come down here to Tahiti? It's beautiful here."

"Yeah? When should I come?"

"Early June."

"All right, Michael, I will."

I skipped away from the pay phone like a schoolboy with a new crush. My woman loved me, she supported what I was doing, she was happy for my successes, and she was coming to see me in this island paradise! There is simply nothing more than a guy could have asked for. We were coming to grips with my journeying rather well, I thought. It wasn't a panacea for our struggles, nor was it going to rupture our relationship. It just was what it was. And it felt really good to know that.

Captain Bert and Big Fred joined us for a late-night coming-ashore pig-out session. I stuffed my face with a large steak with chips (French fries), and we stayed up late drinking way too much rum and, as the Hawaiians say, "talking story."

In the morning, we awoke to a steady rainfall on *Sundance*'s decks. I radioed the customs officials to request a formal entry into Tahiti. We had broken all the rules by going ashore the night before without first clearing in with officials, and we would have been in big trouble if we had been caught. Now they told us they didn't want to venture out to inspect our boat, due to the inclement weather. Instead, would we mind making our way to their office with all of the necessary documentation papers?

Would we *mind*? Hell, no, we wouldn't mind. I was thrilled not to have *Sundance* subjected to a strip search. The process of clearing in is tedious as hell, requiring the exact same paperwork to be completed in three different offices: Customs, Immigration, and the Office of the Port Director. If we could skip even one step in the process (the laborious vessel inspection), I was all for it. Even as it was, it took us all day to clear in. Efficiency is a concept that has not yet reached the French officials in Tahiti. It kind of took some of the romance out of our landing, I'll tell you that. I doubt Captain Bligh was subjected to any of this.

Now that we had officially gained entrance to French Polynesia, I requested permission to relocate *Sundance* from the main harbor to the Marina Taina, some twelve miles around the island. There we would be able to tie up in a slip and start repairing all the things that had been damaged during the passage.

As I walked out of the customs office with my "permission slip" in hand, I saw Buck and Chas talking to two young ladies on holiday from Paris. They were pretty attractive—medium height, short brown hair, nice tans. Not quite Catherine Deneuve, either of them, but far from ugly.

"Skipper," Buck said. "All right if these ladies ride over to the marina with us?"

"Sure."

The five of us climbed aboard *Butch* and labored over to *Sundance*. Chas was in charge of pulling up the anchor. It was always cool to hear this ex-Navy man call out, "Anchors aweigh," but I think he did it with a little more gusto than usual for our new friends.

As we motored out of the harbor, Buck stood beside me as I steered, providing an extra set of eyes. Exiting a harbor can be demanding; you have to be on the lookout for other vessels, you have to find the navigational markers that show the way out, and you have to watch the water for any obstructions. Chas and our two passengers were standing up on the bow pulpit enjoying the ride. Suddenly, like something out of an adolescent fantasy, each of the girls casually removed their tops, exposing two pairs of small, peach-like breasts. Chas swiveled his head around to look back at us with a huge grin on his face, proudly, as if he were somehow responsible for the spectacularness of the breasts in question. Buck looked over at me and said simply, "What*ever*, dude!"

I knew that Captain Bert on *Arca* was moored at Marina Taina, so as we got closer, I used the VHF to let them know we would be arriving shortly. "Come up on your stern," I said. "I've got something I'd like you to see."

As we first entered the small bay, Bert and Fred had a difficult time making out what was on our bow. I saw them leave the stern and reappear shortly with two sets of binoculars. Once they could make out our proudly bare-breasted guests, they started clapping and Bert gave three loud blasts on the ship's horn. *Sundance* had made a grand entrance to her new home, Marina Taina.

As soon as we were tied up to the dock, Buck jumped off the boat and charged toward the marina office at a dead run. "What the hell is he up to?" I said.

Chas shrugged, and we set about cleaning up the boat.

Half an hour later, Buck came walking back toward the boat, pushing an enormous wheel barrel overflowing with heaps of Hinano beer and ice ... looked like his dry spell was officially over.

We enjoyed the afternoon drinking cold beer and watching the now-totally-naked girls lounge about on the boat. When it started to get dark, Chas took me aside and said, "Captain, I think it's only chivalrous for Buck and me to escort the girls back to their hotel. Would that be all right?"

Of course I told him that would be fine, and I didn't see hide nor hair of them until they returned about noon the next day, each with a big smile on their face.

Buck McGee had a flight back to Hawaii the next day. He was an exceptional sailor and good company; it pained me to see him go. I had been unbelievably fortunate to have him with me. Exchanging the Frenchman for Buck had been the best thing to happen to me so far. Thank God for *Sundance's* leaks!

Chas, too, was a gem—a wonderful companion and an incredible sailor. Plus, he did not whistle! I was pleased and relieved when he told me he'd like to stay on board and continue sailing on *Sundance*.

· · ·

I have already mentioned that, as a young man of twenty-one, I had the extreme pleasure of being a professional water-skier with the Tommy Bartlett International Water Ski show in Wisconsin Dells, Wisconsin. I was a student attending Trinidad State College in Colorado on a football scholarship, and this was my summer job—a dream job. I was getting paid $100 a week to do what I loved. I would ski barefoot, skiing off jumps flying over one hundred feet through the air, ski with beautiful girls climbing up on my shoulders, drive small boats off ramps. I worked four shows a day, six days a week. Man, I was right up there bumpin' heaven. The show also included three other acts: the Dancing Waters, a comedian and a Tahitian Drum Dancing group of three girls and five men. Until then, my only exposure to Tahitian dancing had been in the *Bounty* movie, never in person. I was thoroughly captivated by the beauty of these young women and the way their hips moved to the beat of the drums. I never missed their act.

Eventually, I became friends with one of the girls, Claudine Dupree. Her father was French and her mother was Tahitian. She was stunningly beautiful—long, straight black hair down to her hips, sea-green eyes, soft skin the color of coffee with just a touch of cream. She walked with the grace of a panther softly slipping through the jungle. But when she danced to the rhythm of the drums, she was no longer a panther; she was a cyclone of perpetual motion, and I couldn't take my eyes off her. Our casual friendship deepened over the coming weeks, until we were sharing the same bed. The fling was brief, but I had never forgotten Claudine, who had held a special place in my heart since those warm summer nights in 1961.

On a lark, I asked the marina manager if he had ever heard of a lady named Claudine Dupree. I almost fell off the boat when he said, "Yes, I know her daughter. She lives in Papeete."

A few days later, he showed up with a phone number for Claudine. I called, and was thrilled when she said she remembered me from Wisconsin. We planned to meet for lunch the next day at a lovely hotel with a restaurant overlooking the deep blue waters of the bay. The anticipation of seeing my former summer lover caused my hands to sweat and my mouth to go as dry as a sandbox. Too nervous to sit, I paced around in the jungle-like lobby of the hotel. Then she walked in, and I felt my heart sink right to the bottom of my ass.

Could this possibly be the gorgeous Tahitian poster girl I was sleeping with, just forty years ago? No. There must be some mistake. Maybe this lady was her grandmother. Oh, the years had not been kind to Claudine Dupree; she looked a hundred years old! She was roughly the size of a defensive tackle for the Green Bay Packers. Her hair was thinning and mostly gray, and her once-smooth skin had wrinkled like last week's newspaper. The poor thing was also missing two front teeth. She held a cigarette in one hand and a bottle of beer in the other. I felt like I was going to have a massive coronary right there in the jungle lobby. Instead, I squared my shoulders, walked over to her, and gave her a hug. When she was looking at my face, I couldn't help noticing a flicker of disappointment there. We had a pleasant lunch, talking about old times and about our families. When I got back to the boat, I looked at myself in the mirror and laughed for about ten minutes straight. For someone who had last seen me as a twenty-one-year-old waterskiing hero, I supposed I probably looked like the Grim Reaper.

• • •

Papeete, population 4,000, is a modern city, or at least, modern for a South Pacific island. It is built around a coastal lagoon in the northwest corner of the island. My best description of run-down Papeete is, "Tijuana with a French accent, only much more expensive." It's a good jumping-off point for those visiting French Polynesia, but not a city one would want to spend much time in. The currency is the French Pacific Franc, and everything is extremely expensive. One bottle of Budweiser beer will set you back twelve dollars; a bottle of the local beer, Hinano, only costs five dollars and sixty cents, and, when cold, it tastes pretty good. If you don't have a car in Papeete, you ride Le Truck, an old, oversized pickup truck with benches over the bed for passengers to sit on. Not particularly comfortable, but it beats hitchhiking.

Our marina was about ten miles from town, so one evening, Chas and I rode Le Truck into town to get a bite to eat. After dinner, we were sitting on the Quay, sipping Hinano and studying the variety of hailing ports of the boats tied up to the wall. There were lots of boats that had sailed from Europe: England, Germany, France, Spain, and Sweden. We had met a man named Joe Katsafarers, who enjoyed talking to the visiting "yachties." Joe was a member in good standing of the Dock Committee. He had sailed into Tahiti in a small boat from his native Greece, planning to spend a month or so. That was thirty-two years ago. He was short and overweight, with a full, snow-white mustache, weathered olive skin, and one gold earring in his right ear. A black captain's cap covered his bald head; he was the quintessential old sailor with a million miles under his hull and a million stories to tell. Every island seemed to have at least one interesting expat hanging around the docks, anxious to talk story with the incoming boats. Joe was a wellspring of local knowledge.

During the conversation, I noticed two gorgeous Tahitian girls walking toward us, and of course, Chas's eye wandered toward the two stunning beauties. I didn't blame him; they looked like they belonged on the cover of a Tahiti travel brochure. Once they got closer, Chas excused himself from our conversation, stepped over to them and, in his best attempt at French, said, "Good evening, ladies. Do you speak English?"

When one of them opened her mouth to speak, out came a deep, raspy voice that sounded more like Willie Nelson's than that of any Tahitian beauty. I damn near fell off the quay. The other one said something in a near-baritone, and Chas's jaw swung wide in total shock. These were not girls; they were boys that looked like girls! Chas stammered an apology, but they were already walking away, apparently accustomed to such encounters with foreigners.

Poor Chas was deathly embarrassed. "I—I want to go home now," he said.

Joe clasped his hands together and doubled over with laughter. When he could speak again, he said, "You've just had your first run-in with Tahiti's third sex. They're called the *mahu vahine*." He went on to explain that Polynesians typically have large families with seven, eight, sometimes nine children. A longstanding tradition dictates that the firstborn child in the family be raised as a female—even if it happens to have been born a male. That firstborn will grow up to assume the role of surrogate mother, with the responsibility of caring for all the additional babies. The mother's job is to continue to have children. These boys/girls have a special status within the community and are looked upon with a great deal of respect. "So," Joe said, "Remember: what you see in Papeete is not necessarily what you get! You might be in for an unpleasant surprise."

May I just state for the record that I was the firstborn in my family, and that I am endlessly pleased that I was born anywhere but Tahiti.

• • •

It has often been said that sailboat cruising is the art of doing boat maintenance in exotic ports. Working on the boat in a foreign country is challenging—can't speak nor understand the language, don't have a car, and can't find the necessary parts to do the repairs. Plus, there's no one to call for help. During my years of owning sailboats in Newport Beach and San Diego, I had grown accustomed to picking up the phone and calling someone to fix the problem, any damn problem, just call somebody. Out here, far from home, there was simply no one to call. I was forced to become a diesel mechanic, a plumber, a painter, an electrician, a single-side-band radio operator, a sail repairman, a cook, a dishwasher, a housekeeper, and the fixer of the head. In case I have not yet made this clear, I will readily admit that I am not mechanically inclined, nor did I (or do I) have any desire to become proficient in the art of boat repair. I just wanted to go sailing, not become a jack-of-all-trades. But the work was never-ending; something always needed tending to. I drew up a work list and posted it on the navigation table. A sample excerpt: Replace flapper valve in the head; repair solar panel junction box that started to smoke and then flamed out while at sea; top off eight batteries with distilled water.

Let me tell you about watering the batteries. They are located (*hidden*, one might better say) under the cockpit floor. To reach the batteries, you must remove a section of wood paneling in the starboard bunk. In order to get at the paneling, you first have to take out the mattresses and stow them in the cabin. Now the batteries are visible, but not reachable. This is where I needed a midget from Cirque du Soleil to squeeze into this small space with a flashlight in one hand and a large water bottle in the other. It was always hot, nearly ninety degrees, with ninety percent humidity, so every time I performed this hateful task, sweat streamed into my eyes, making it even harder to see. And it wasn't just a matter of reaching in there with a water bottle and filling a single hole, the eight batteries held a total of 128 receptacles that needed to be topped off. I would have loved to hire a little person to work full time on *Sundance*. I wondered if I could convince one to come on board in exchange for MREs and passage to exotic ports.

I was delighted to see a McDonald's within walking distance of the marina. I'm not normally a fast-food guy, but I was jonesing for my own cheeseburger in paradise—or, more accurately, my own Big Mac with fries and an ice-cold Coke in paradise. The restaurant stood adjacent to a public beach that was popular with the locals. As I stood in line thinking about the Big Mac that would soon be mine, I saw out of the corner of my eye that three young, attractive girls were walking up from the beach toward the restaurant. No *mahu vahine* were these. I could tell, because they were topless. They strode into Mickey D's (No shirt, no shoes, no problem!) and took their places in line directly behind me. Never having spent time in a country where the sight of a topless woman is anything less than scandalous, I stood there laboring under a foreigner's taboos. What was the proper etiquette in this situation? Would it have been permissible, for example, to turn around, take a long look, and say, "My word, ladies. I must tell you, your breasts are simply splendid?"

It was my turn to pay. I was so conflicted, but so happy. A Big Mac with fries was $13.75. Magnificent scenery while you wait. Tahiti! In just my first couple of days, I'd had naked girls sunbathing on my deck, I'd seen beautiful hermaphrodites, and now, three topless lovelies were placing their orders a few feet away from me under the beneficent gaze of Ronald McDonald. *Toto, I've a feeling we're not in Kansas anymore.* My buddies back home were never going to believe this.

Grandson Alexander and Sedona in the cockpit of *Sundance*.

At the navigation station—on the computer.

On *Sundance* shortly after making landfall; Hilo, Hawaii.

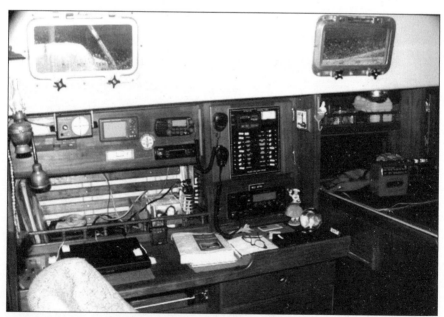

My naval station: My laptop, and from the upper left: emergency radar detection, which alerts me if any ships are in the area; primary GPS; VHF radio and mic; CD player; main electrical panel; single side band radio; various good-luck items.

Sundance; Cook's Bay, Island of Moorea.

At anchor; Bora Bora.

On the helm, dressed in heavy-duty foul weather gear during a
lull in a storm.

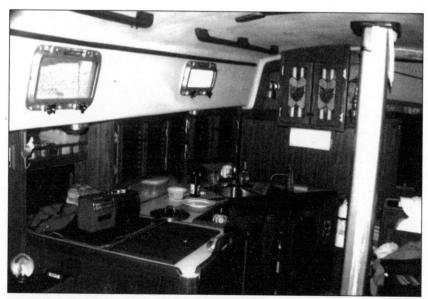

The galley.

Sundance under full sail; Bora Bora.

Bora Bora.

Lady delivering flowers to the church on her scooter; Aitutaki, Cook Islands.

Birthday party for a young girl and her friends; Aitutaki, Cook Islands.

Looking aft from the bow pulpit of *Sundance*.

The view from the cockpit looking off the port side—checking out the large waves.

Sundance getting a lift out of the water; Vunda Pt. Marina, Lautoka, Fiji.

Sundance sitting in her cyclone hole; Vunda Pt. Marina, Lautoka, Fiji.

Native woman; Tonga.

Daughters: Kasey on left and Kelly on right. Safety harness on, ready to take to the high seas.

At anchor; Port Resolution, Vanuatu.

Taking a break with the natives; village of Ireupuow, island of Tanna, Vanuatu.

Being surrounded by the natives of Erromango; Vanuatu.

Mother and daughter; Erromango, Vanuatu.

Daughters Kasey and Kelly with the natives; island of Erromango, Vanuatu.

Yasur volcano; Tanna, Vanuatu.

Yasur volcano; Tanna, Vanuatu.

Sally and me; Great Barrier Reef, Australia.

Sally and me with my new best friend—a koala bear; Australia.

Jungle and me day sailing; Bora Bora.

Standing at anchor; Bay of Islands, New Zealand.

Bay of Islands, New Zealand.

Bay of Islands, New Zealand.

At anchor in the Bay of Islands, New Zealand.

CHAPTER 14

• • •

Changes in Latitude

In the soul of man there lies one insular Tahiti, full of peace and joy, but encompassed by all the horrors of the half-known life.

—Herman Melville

WE PLANNED SALLY'S TRIP TO Tahiti to coincide with Father's Day, and I was honored that her son, Jeff, would be joining us. I had felt completely content in Tahiti until the day of their arrival drew closer, and then I realized I was becoming increasingly overwhelmed with anticipation. This suggested that I was maybe just getting better at fooling myself about being a solitary man and an adventurer—perhaps, after all this time, what I wanted deep down inside, was still to be with family.

I was getting my wish. I stood in the airport with my face against the glass and watched them walk off the plane together. My heart skipped a beat. It would be another forty-five minutes before they worked their way through customs, and I paced eagerly around, certain it was taking hours instead of minutes. When they finally walked out of the customs office, I charged at them like I was trying to sack a quarterback. Sally and I hugged, kissed, and hugged some more. I had a desert thirst for Sally's hugs. It gave me such a warm, secure feeling that I never wanted to let her go. Jeff was standing there with a good-natured smile on his face, and I turned and gave him a solid hug too. He was a tall, good-looking young man, thirty years old, with an air of confidence and an easy smile. Look what a lucky guy I was. I grabbed their bags and hustled them out of the airport, lest the customs people change their minds and take my loved ones away from me again.

I wasted no time getting Sally and Jeff aboard *Sundance*. "Here's the plan," I said. "We'll set sail in the morning. Papeete is nothing. I want to explore some of the good stuff with you guys."

I'm sure my eagerness amused them both. To them, having just flown in from Los Angeles, Papeete must have seemed plenty exotic and picturesque, yet, I was chomping at the bit to put it astern, as if it were Newark. "Michael," Sally said, "I don't want to be a wet blanket, but remember what happened last time? Can we keep the sailing to a minimum?"

"Of course, baby. I won't put you through anything like that again. We're just going to do an easy twelve-mile jaunt to the most beautiful place in the world. It'll be worth it, I promise."

The next morning, I distributed seasickness patches and hoisted the sails, and we escaped the vortex of the big city. Destination: Moorea. And for once, the gods smiled on me and did not make me eat my words. We had a nice, easy, twelve-mile sail to the northwest, with a slight breeze and very little wave action. Sally would not be forced to relive her Hawaii nightmare in front of her son and Chas—just a comfortable, smooth sail in paradise. All on board were happy.

Moorea was everything I had promised, and more. Without question, sailing into Opunohu Bay, I was treated to one of the most beautiful sights I have ever seen. When the author James Michener first came to Moorea as a seaman in the U.S. Navy during World War II, he was so impressed with the natural beauty of the place that he declared it to be the most beautiful island in the world. It is said that his first sight of Cook's Bay inspired Bali Hai in *South Pacific*. Every view of Moorea shows evidence of its volcanic past. Blankets of lush green foliage cover the sheer peaks that climb to a sapphire blue sky. When you picture the perfect island paradise, you're picturing Moorea.

We spent the first blissful night anchored in Robinson's Cove at the head of spectacular Opunohu Bay. Mel Gibson filmed much of his film *The Bounty* in this very bay, and my old friend Captain Cook also dropped anchor here. I've awakened to some lovely circumstances in my day, but I can't imagine anything better than waking up in Sally's arms, climbing through the companionway together, and stepping up on deck to the sight of such breath-taking beauty and wonder. After a breakfast of fresh fruit, coffee, and a French baguette, we took *Butch* to a sandy spot on shore and enjoyed a walk up the hill to Belvedere Overlook, where we had a great view of both bays, Opunohu and Cook's, glimmering beneath us like jewels.

"Let's go over there," Sally said, pointing at Cook's Bay.

"You got it."

We hiked back down to *Sundance*, started FUJIMO, and mo-tored for two hours to Cook's Bay, all four of us staring slack-jawed at the scenery and exhausting our supply of superlatives to remark upon its beauty. We dropped the hook in twenty-five feet of crystal clear water off the historic Club Bali Hai. As soon as we stepped ashore, Sally made a beeline toward a row of thatched-roof bungalows, and within minutes, had reserved one for the two of us. It was built on stilts that sat directly over the water, with an incredible view of the mountains and the bay.

That afternoon, we all walked together into the small village of Paopao, as impressed by its provincial charms as we'd been by its spectacular setting. Life on this island was easygoing, a throwback to earlier days. We felt like we had stepped back a hundred years in time. Dogs roamed free, grinning cautiously like amiable small-time crooks, looking as if they all came from the same mother but with fathers of different colors. Roosters ran freely and crowed day and night, an old familiar sound that startled me into confronting just how much the world had changed since I was a child. And the children—they tore around barefoot, wearing nothing more than shorts, freer than the dogs, and not a store-bought toy in sight. Which, of course, made for some very, very happy kids (but try explaining that to an American child). They made up their own games out of whatever they could find; they knew their neigh-bors; they knew their first cousins, their second cousins, and their third. We saw not a single stoplight, which would have been over-kill anyway, given how few cars were on the road. Most people, if they weren't walking, puttered about their errands on little motor scooters. There was only one gas station.

While walking around, we spotted something that absolutely baffled us. In many of the front yards of the small cottages, stood what looked to us like gravestones. Could they be, right in the front yard? That evening, we met one of the natives in the hotel bar. After a couple glasses of wine, Sally asked him to tell us about the gravestones in the yards. He was happy to explain their age-old custom: upon the death of a loved one, the remaining family members gather to discuss where the deceased should be buried. The tradition dictates the following: if the person was held in high esteem by the family, they were honored by being buried in the front yard. If the deceased was not held in high esteem, but was decently well liked, they could be buried in the side yard. However, if the deceased was overtly disliked, there was only one place left for them: in the backyard, next to the chicken coop. This may explain why all the natives are so friendly; no one wants to be disliked and end up buried next to the henhouse.

That night, Sally and I returned to our bungalow, and Chas and Jeff, who had hit it off nicely, camped out on *Sundance*. We were pretty exhilarated by our day of shared discoveries. This was exactly the kind of thing I had had in mind when I first conceived of my adventure, and to have Sally along for it was just ideal. We spent a magical night in our hut, where there was yet another surprise waiting for us. Beneath the hut was a huge deck with a glass floor above the water, and to our delight, the scene was illuminated by underwater lights. We sat in each other's arms, thrilled to be together, thrilled by our wonderful day, watching as thousands of multicolored fish darted about beneath our feet.

The week sped by, each day as exciting as the one that had gone before. I was euphoric, holding hands with Sally as we walked through the village, laying in the sun, on the beach, and sitting on the deck of the bungalow looking at such a breathtaking view of the mountains coming down to the blue water of the bay, snuggled on our glass deck and watched the fish play. And then, suddenly, it was time for Sally and Jeff to leave Moorea. I was thoroughly crushed by this development. Some part of me had actually grown convinced that this interlude was never going to end.

I found myself repeating the Kris Kristofferson lyrics, "Was the going up worth the coming down?" I had really set myself up for heartbreak this time. I drove them silently to the airport, dreading another gut-wrenching goodbye. I had to force back the tears, be strong, and show Jeff how a real man says goodbye: with a smile on his face, even though he is crying inside.

To take my mind off things, I walked to the dock where *Butch* was tied up, climbed in, gave a yank on the little outboard motor, and went for a ride in the bay. I was in one of the most beautiful places in the world, but it was impossible for me to appreciate it without my Sally. I was buggered up bad. I felt lower than whale shit. That night, my bunk felt vast and empty.

The next morning when I came up on deck, the first thing I saw was the bungalow over the water where Sally and I had spent the last four nights. I literally began to shake, remembering how fine it had felt to sit on the porch holding hands, drinking in the view. It was more than I could take; it hurt too much to spend another hour in Moorea.

I heard Chas moving around below, so I went to the companionway. "Chas? All right with you if we move on this morning?"

"Whatever you say, Captain."

Before he was finished dressing, I pulled up the anchor, and *Sundance* put gorgeous Moorea on her stern.

• • •

We sailed ninety miles to Huahine, an undeveloped island of 6,000 residents. It's considered the least spoiled of the major Society Islands, which suited my mood just fine. No tourons, no crowds, nobody getting under my skin. Chas promptly met a young lady from another boat, and I didn't see him for almost a full day. When he returned, I could tell something was up. "Captain," he said, "will you be staying around here for long?"

"I don't know, Chas. I haven't got much of a plan. Why? What's on your mind?"

"Well, I've met this girl. She's sailing on to Bora Bora. Would it be all right with you if I joined her, and then we could meet up when you get there?"

I smiled. "Of course," I said. "I'm happy for you, you devil."

He packed his things and was gone that very evening. Once again, I was alone on my boat. My big, beautiful, expensive, empty boat. What was I doing here? I wanted to be with Sally, that much was painfully obvious. Going home seemed to make a lot of sense. And yet I had already tried quitting once, and clearly I wasn't cut out for that.

I then realized that, no, quitting was not an option, especially since I'd made it through the really difficult part of my trip. I was not blind to the irony of my situation: this was supposed to be the fun part, the reward for the long, difficult open-ocean passages. All around me was a world of paradise islands, with easy sailing between them. I needed to stop moping and embrace this opportunity to sink my teeth into the world's finest pleasure cruising.

In that mood of forced merrymaking, I set out on a two-month interlude of island-hopping, exploring the South Pacific Islands of Huahine, Raiatea, and Tahaa. Each was unique; each had its own particular charm. Huahine shows a more natural, unspoiled Polynesian lifestyle. No rat race, not even a McDonald's; the biggest commercial venture is a black pearl farm. I bought some of the striking pearls with the idea of giving them to Sally and my daughters as unique Christmas presents.

Every island had a dancing group that practiced most evenings. Attending those practices was what first coaxed me back out of my shell, and they soon became the highlight of my days. *Sundance* was usually anchored off the village in sixty feet or so of deep blue water so clear that I could see the anchor sitting on the bottom. I would wait to hear the sound of the drums over the crowing of the roosters. This was the signal, the call to tell everyone that the session was about to begin. I would jump in *Butch* and motor to shore for an entertaining evening watching and listening to the natives practicing their routines. The entire village took part in the dancing: little girls all the way up to great-grandmothers performed the dance, and little boys all the way up to great-grandfathers either danced or played instruments. The groups were practicing for an all-island dance competition to take place on Bora Bora in late August. There was a great deal of pride involved in the competition; it was an enormous honor to be the very best dance group in all the islands.

And so I began to fall into the rhythm of this quiet place. There was no television to watch, and no shopping malls to see. It wasn't possible to cruise Main Street, because no one owned a car and, besides, there was no Main Street, only a dirt road. Dancing was the primary source of entertainment here before Captain Cook arrived in 1777, and it remained so today. I tried to make myself as inconspicuous as possible, sitting off to the side, making sure I was not going to be in the way. I always carried a pocketful of hard candy for the kids. Once they realized I was the white man with the candy, they always came over to say hello and get their treat. Kids have a way of making you feel like you belong in the world, and these kids were great, friendly, and so curious. On the first night, a giggling little girl said, "What is your name?"

I raised my eyebrows and said, "Fletcher Christian. I've come to your island in search of the beautiful breadfruit plant. Have you seen any?"

The girl shrieked with delight and ran to her parents. She whispered something in her father's ear, and the father threw back his head and laughed. A moment later, the whole family came over to introduce themselves, and I fell into a wonderful conversation with them. It worked so well that it became my standard routine, to be repeated at many dance practices on many islands.

The Polynesian people I met were universally warm, friendly, and genuinely interested in my boat and me. They live a stress–free lifestyle, refreshingly uncluttered by man-made distractions. They are not assaulted by a barrage of marketing everywhere they look or listen, and thus, are not enslaved by the massive importance Americans place on the material aspects of daily life. The kids have never seen an iPod, and they don't spend day after day inside the house, in their rooms, playing video games. They have never been to a mall and don't own a pair of shoes, but they are happy for all the right reasons. I wanted to bring all eight of my grandchildren to the island to have them experience this lifestyle. I have no doubt that if I did, they would grow up with a much more meaningful set of values. Call me naive if you wish— *oh, look at the rich American telling the have-nots how much better off they are without all the shiny things he gets to enjoy*—but I've seen enough of both sides of the divide to know that money and material objects can destroy the soul. Opulence can wrench families apart, and even our middle-class values no longer sufficiently emphasize togetherness, family, neighbors, human relationships. By our standards, the Polynesians are poor, very poor. But, if you asked them if they feel poor, they would laugh and tell you they are not poor but happy, very happy, with the only way of life they have ever known. I have no statistics to support this supposition, but I am sure that, given the lower rate of stress, the Polynesian people live happier and longer lives than the folks back home in the Mecca of materialism, Orange County, California.

Most of the islands in the South Pacific are surrounded by coral reef barriers that run roughly parallel to the shore. The reef will be pierced by a channel, which is usually referred to as "the pass." To make landfall, you must complete a passage through the pass in order to reach the body of water inside the lagoon. Getting through a pass was a new and frightful experience for me. It can be extremely dangerous, as coral is unforgiving. There are a lot of factors one must take into consideration before attempting to clear any pass. First, it's important to know the state of the tide. Fortunately, the tidal range in these islands is less than one foot, but even that much depth can make a difference in some passes.

You also need to know what currents you're dealing with; currents can sometimes be strong and particularly close to the pass and can suck you off course and into the coral. It's important, too, to pay attention to the position of the sun; it's critical that the sun is high overhead when you make your attempt. Otherwise, shadows or simply the angle of light will make it impossible to see all of the ever-present coral formations that rise up from the ocean floor like small mountains, called "bombies." If you fail to account for one of these factors and collide with a bomby, you can pretty much figure on your boat ripping apart. The majority of the boating accidents that occur in the South Pacific happen as a result of hitting reefs.

As you might imagine, the best idea is to have a crew stationed on the bow serving as a reef watch. But now that Chas was off with his new girlfriend, I was alone. Taking *Sundance* through a reef pass was a consistently anxiety-provoking experience, one that scared the hell out of me every time I had to go through one. I would rehearse in my mind all the potential catastrophes, trying to fit them to my general escape plan. It was FUJIMO's job to power us through, at just fewer than five knots, but the mainsail was up just in case. If FUJIMO stopped running in the middle of a narrow pass with huge reef formations on either side, what would I do? Step one would have been to crap my pants, most likely. Next, I would drop the anchor to secure the boat, and then scream for help like a kid who'd just dropped his candy bar in the sand. Once I had regained control (of boat and bowels), I would use the VHF radio to call for help.

That is correct: it wasn't much of a plan.

Sailing in San Diego, if you needed to call for help, someone would be at the scene within minutes. In Bora Bora, you would be more apt to get help if you issued the distress call in French, and still, you might be sitting there for hours waiting for someone to come. The next alternative, if the wind was aft, and the tide was moving inland, would be to sail on through with a gash in your hull. For some reason, I couldn't picture this scenario without imagining the cartoon character Pink Panther at the helm, sailing resolutely forward as the water swallows up his boat, then rises up his chest, his chin, his forehead . . .

Fortunately, neither of these scenarios ever took place. I was somehow able to clear every pass, but it never became any less stressful. Every time I entered a lagoon, I could feel the adrenaline dissolving away in a sudden rush of exhilaration and gratitude.

By the time I reached Bora Bora, I had shaken my funk and was truly having a good time. Except for the stress of navigating the passes, I was in hog heaven, lazing around, making casual friends among the natives and among my fellow boaters—taking it easy. Especially at first, this easy routine did not make me feel sluggish; I had, after all, paid my dues, in a hard way, by sailing here. The sea had now begun to fulfill its promise, to answer my need to break away, to escape the ordinary, to have an adventure.

Like Moorea, Bora Bora enjoys a reputation as the most beautiful island in the Pacific. Its sculptured, twin-peaked central mountain is surrounded by a deep lagoon inside a magnificent barrier reef with ocean swells breaking into plumes of white spray. With the roar of the barrier behind me, I could breathe my customary sigh of relief and relish the moment. I had successfully slid my way through the Te Ava Nui pass, and was now nosing along inside the lagoon where Captain Cook stopped on December 8, 1777. It felt surreal, seeing the mountains reaching high into the clouds, crystal clear water, water in dozens of shades of blue and turquoise, and above me lush green forest with the Hibiscus blaring along the hills. This was truly a Polynesian jewel to behold.

The Bora Bora Yacht Club was a short distance off the bow. I eased *Sundance* close to a vacant mooring ball until I heard the sound of them kissing hello. Rushing forward with the boat hook, I snatched the mooring line, secured it to a cleat on the bow, stood up, and took another long look around. "You are in paradise," I told myself. "Bora Bora. Bora Bora, mister! A long, long way from 34 Water Street, Ypsilanti, Michigan." And, for that matter, a long, long way from Bluebird Canyon, falling asleep in front of the TV in my leather recliner.

• • •

The Bora Bora Yacht Club looks like any other yacht club in the South Pacific—unpretentious, one small building, a bar, a food service, and usually an outside shower, sometimes with hot water, sometimes not. South Pacific yacht clubs are refreshingly modest compared to the edifice yacht clubs in the States. Not one member owns a blue blazer; these little clubs exist for the sole purpose of accommodating visiting yachts from all over the world. The scenery is breathtaking, but it's the people you meet who make the experience unforgettable. There's an instant camaraderie with other cruisers. Time is spent comparing the rough passages, the storms we had to fight through, the equipment that was damaged, and where you will be headed next. I missed talking to my friends back home, so it was particularly satisfying for me to bond with new people. Every morning at eight, there was a VHF radio conversation, called the "cruiser net" (short for network), between all the boats that cared to participate. It was like an old party-line phone; everyone could listen in to all the conversations. This radio net replaced the newspaper in my morning routine. I listened—and sometimes chimed in—as people shared all kinds of information: a good restaurant to try, the best shop for finding a particular part for the boat, and most significantly, the weather. Yachties' lives revolve around the weather.

Speaking of "yachties," I was shocked the first time someone called my boat a *yacht*. In this part of the world, any sailboat is referred to as a yacht, unlike in the States, where a boat has to be huge before anyone would use that term. Most mornings during the cruiser net, one of the *yachts* would announce they were hoisting the daily cocktail hour on their boat. Five o'clock would see a convoy of dinghies headed toward the host boat, all the yachties making their way to the cocktail hour.

One evening while enjoying a "sundowner" on a friend's boat, I noticed a guy talking on an unusual-looking phone. It was much larger than a common cell phone, with a fat antenna. His name was Chris Kingsley off s/v *Amanda Star* from England. He was talking to his wife in London on an Iridium satellite phone! Instantly, I knew I had to have one. As soon as he hung up, I button-holed him.

"Where do I get one?" I said.

"Actually, I've got another one that I'll sell you if you like."

"How much?"

"Sixty thousand CFP." (Which came out to $600.)

"Sold," I said.

I would have paid twice as much for the freedom to talk to Sally from anywhere in the world anytime I wanted. We arranged to meet the next morning to complete all the paperwork. Chris gave me a PIN and a strange new seven-digit phone number. My credit card would be charged $1.30 per minute, but it would be worth every penny. By noon, I was delighted to be talking to Sally on my new satellite phone. E-mails had been nice, but there was just no substitute for hearing Sally's sweet voice.

• • •

August tenth would be my birthday. Hard to believe that a year had flown by since that fateful sixtieth birthday party that had launched me on this adventure. Here I was, turning sixty-one, another year older, and yet I was mostly untroubled by this development. Time well spent is not to be regretted, and I had, to use Thoreau's phrase, lived more deliberately during this year than ever before. At every step of the way, I had made careful decisions designed to create a life packed with meaning and in-tensity, to do what was best for me and my family. I may not have always chosen correctly, but at least I had not drifted passively along. That was all that anyone could hope for, and, I had learned that process of self-questioning and careful decision-making must never end. There was no finish line. In order to keep my life meaningful, I must not stop asking myself, "Is this the right place for me now? Am I headed in the right direction? Am I making the wisest use of my time?"

I wasn't even, in fact at all, sure that drifting around alone in the South Pacific was the best thing for me, or at least that it could continue for very much longer; but I resolved to set aside my soul-searching and enjoy the fact that my best friend, Marine fighter pilot Jeff "Jungle" Devlin, was coming to Bora Bora to help me celebrate.

I met Jungle when Sally and I were living in Newport Beach. He walked his female Golden Retriever, Pearl, the same time and place each morning that I walked Sedona. It was Pearl and Sedona who hit it off first (we liked to think they were boyfriend and girl-friend), and soon Sally and I became good friends with Jungle and his wife, Leslie. On Fridays, Sally and Leslie would enjoy shopping at the malls in Newport Beach while Jungle and I played golf at the Marine base's private golf course. After a round, we would go the FA-18 simulator; Jungle was teaching me to fly the Hornet. It was, of course, only a simulator, but the experience felt like we were actually flying. It was one of the greatest thrills of my entire life.

I quickly developed a deep respect for Jungle. The FA-18 guys are considered rock stars, among the best fighter pilots in the world, and I was humbled when Jungle let me into his circle of friends. It was even more thrilling that they gave me my own call sign, "Cos." Although I'll never forget the embarrassment I felt soon afterward when, over a round of golf, I said, "Hey, guys. I've been thinking about it, and I think I'd rather have the call sign Razor. What do you say?"

They looked at me like I had just made nasty comments about their mothers. "No," Jungle said quietly, shaking his head. "Nobody gets to choose their own call sign."

That was Jungle—confident, soft-spoken, firm. Not only was he one of the best fighter pilots in the world, he was the personification of an officer and a gentleman. If I ever had a son, I would want him to be just like my friend Captain Jeff Devlin. Our friendship continues to this day.

Jungle arrived in Bora Bora, grinning and ready for some serious fun. Unfortunately, he was on a tight schedule, with only three days to spend on *Sundance*, so we packed our days as tightly as possible. We swam with manta rays, snorkeled on the edge of the reef, downed Bloody Marys at the famous Bloody Mary's bar. Just as my interlude with Sally had come to a too-quick ending, the fun time with Jungle ended far too soon. Once again, the adventure was much more meaningful when I could share it with someone of significance in my life, and once again, the departure of that person of significance left me wondering just what I was doing all by myself on the far side of the planet.

Just a few days after Jungle headed home, I was sitting on the boat in a bit of a funk when Chas showed up after a long absence. I was happy to see him; he was like an old friend now.

"Captain," Chas said after accepting a beer and settling with it in the cockpit. "I've got to tell you something that you might not be too happy about."

"Oh," I said. "Here we go, huh?"

"Yeah. I believe I'm in love, Captain."

"Well, why wouldn't I be happy about that?"

"I'm asking if I can jump ship to sail with her."

"Well, that's the part I'm not happy about. But I'm thrilled as hell that you're in love. You're a good man, and she's a lucky young lady."

"Thank you, Captain."

"I mean it. Of course I'll miss having you on board. You're a treasure of a crew, and I'll always be grateful for your company."

I could see I was making him squirm a little, so I wrapped up my little speech. "I hate to see you go, but that's just me being selfish. You've got to go, follow your heart, and enjoy this wonderful moment of your life."

We shook hands, and Chas stepped off the boat and walked out of my adventure. I really was happy for him, but now I was truly alone.

• • •

On the sixteenth of August, 2001, at ten in the morning, I hoisted the anchor, motored away from the Bora Bora Yacht

Club, and raised *Sundance's* sails. It was time to put French Polynesia astern. I was sad to be leaving, but I felt the need to be under sail. I'd spent ninety-one days and called on six different islands. I could understand why the crew of the *Bounty* had been so reluctant to leave these beautiful islands with their pristine lagoons and friendly people. (Yes, even the French were friendly.) But now, it was time to continue on toward New Zealand.

"We need the tonic of the wilderness," Henry David Thoreau wrote, and it was certainly true now for me. It was impossible to clear my head and figure out my next steps when I had fallen into what amounted to a routine as static and lazy as any: landlubber's radio net in the morning, cocktail hour at five, dance practice in the evening, shooting the shit with other cruisers at night, dozing off in my bunk. If anything, it was more sedentary than my lifestyle back home—at least there I had walked the dog and gone to the gym.

The sea—anchorages on isolated islands—that was the kind of wilderness Thoreau had in mind, and I was finding it much more than a luxury. It had become a necessity, something I needed the way we need vitamins. Maybe I was becoming a real sailor after all. Wilderness provides an antidote to our daily lives. Restores our balance. Revitalizes our senses.

<u>Captain's Log</u>

17 August 2001. Course 249' true, speed 4.2 kts. Seas lumpy, confused, swell west two to three feet. Wave pattern, E-SE, sky 75 percent clear with fluffy clouds. Air temp. eighty-one degrees; sea temp eighty degrees.

Miles covered past twenty-four hours: 110. Miles to landfall: 315.

Destination: Aitutaki, northernmost of the Cook Islands.

Sundance was once again dancing on the open, cobalt ocean. At the moment I made the above log entry, she was enjoying a slow waltz with light trade winds, a full main, full headsail, and staysail on a broad comfortable reach. I could feel my "shore funk" beginning to dissipate. This might have been the finest day of sailing I'd experienced since leaving San Diego. *It can't get any better than this.* I spent my time daydreaming of all the ships that had sailed this same route, from Flinders aboard the *Investigator* to Darwin aboard the *Beagle. How many have gone before me? When did the first ship sail through these waters?* It was a question that may be impossible to answer, but was fun to ponder.

The previous night, with no moon, the sky had flamed with a gazillion stars, seemingly close enough that I could reach out and scoop up a handful. The Milky Way sprawled across the heavens like one colossal star. A constant barrage of shooting stars took away my breath, better than any fireworks show at Disneyland. Alone on the ocean, with the autopilot steering and the radar alarm activated, I stretched out on the leeward seat, watching the light show in the sky like the luckiest guy in the world. I slept the sweet sleep of the innocent.

The next morning, I woke up and typed the following e-mail:

August 18, 2001 Notes from the Captain's Log

Dear family,

Happy to report that I was able to grab four hours of uninter-rupted sleep in the cockpit last night under the stars. The air is warm, not hot; the seas are lumpy, yet not offensive. The boat is free from any leaks. All gear is working well (knock on wood). Have cold water and pop to drink and thanks to Sally, I have homemade chocolate chip cookies she sent as a birthday present. My only wish is that each of you could be here to share this fan-tastic day of gentle sailing on the ocean. Today, I am the furthest away from any major land mass that one can be on this planet, and I am content. It's 3,000 miles to the U.S.A., 2,500 miles to Aus-tralia. South America lies 3,600 miles to my So' east. I am plunk in the middle of the largest body of water in the world—sixty-five million square miles of Pacific Ocean. There is no traffic, no advertising, no 7-11 stores, no TV, just my boat and I . . . makes one feel pretty insignificant, and yet, somehow strong.

Love & Hugs. All of the Best,

Michael, on board s/v *Sundance*.

The weather gods smiled upon me for five splendid days of carefree sailing and drifting along with soft trade winds over a turquoise sea. Now Aitutaki was in sight. I was excited for two reasons. First, Gordon Wiles, a dear friend of mine in Newport Beach, had told me about his experience of flying into this island on a Pan American Clipper. This was a scheduled refueling stop for the massive planes servicing the famous coral route between North America and the South Pacific. Gordon had shared his fond memories of his time in Aitutaki and encouraged me to be sure to call on this island.

Second, some friends I'd met in Bora Bora—Ariel and her husband Terry, from s/v *Stella* out of Toronto, Canada—were planning to stop here and had asked if I would join them. The challenge of stopping at Aitutaki was the difficult pass you had to clear to reach the lagoon. The cruising guide to the Pacific Islands states, "Does not have a harbor for ships or boats. The pass through the reef is too shallow for most boats." This discourages the majority of yachties from bothering to try, which means that fewer than a dozen boats each year attempt to make their way through the shallow pass. My new friend, Terry, had come up with a great idea; he would use his dinghy and a handheld depth sounder to chart a course through the pass.

I found the pass and lay off it at a safe distance. I was able to quickly raise Terry on the VHF, and he promptly appeared in his dinghy, waving broadly like I was his long-lost brother. We exchanged quick hellos, and Terry motored forward, successfully guiding me through the treacherous pass and into the lagoon.

The people of the Cook Islands are Polynesian Maoris, a blending of the people of Tahiti and the Maoris of New Zealand.

They are self-governed, with free association with New Zealand. Their basic language is Maori, but everyone speaks the Queen's English. After going ashore in *Butch*, the first person I met was the customs officer, Bob. Most customs officers show zero personality. They only want the facts, with no exchange of pleasantries. Bob, to the contrary, stepped aboard *Sundance* and said cheerfully, "Hello, sir. Thank you for visiting our island!"

I was instantly charmed. Customs Officer Bob and I kept up a convivial chitchat all through the clearing-in process, which wasn't long: the paperwork that normally takes all day took just thirty minutes. The next day as I was sitting in his office, I noticed a very old set of golf clubs in the corner of the room.

"Do you play?" I said.

Customs Officer Bob smiled widely. "Yes, I do," he said.

"Where?"

"We have a golf course here on the island," he said proudly. "Would you care to join me for a round tomorrow morning?"

"Oh, I would absolutely love to. But I can't. I didn't bring my clubs."

"No worries, mate. You can use my clubs. And I have a ball that you can borrow."

I left the clearing-in session feeling truly welcomed. I had been in-country for thirty minutes, and already I had a golf appointment, and with the customs officer, no less. On the way back to the boat, though, it occurred to me: *Did Customs Officer Bob really just offer to loan me* a ball, *as in,* one? *I can lose a dozen balls in a single round. What if I lose his one ball?*

The population of the island was about 2,000 people. Customs Officer Bob had told me that there were very few cars; most everyone rode small motorbikes, and renting one would be the best way to see the island. I rented one right away and tooled around for a spell before I spotted an ice cream shop on the outskirts of the village. I love ice cream and regularly sought it out soon after reaching land, so the discovery of this little shop was great. I ordered my normal two scoops of chocolate with peanut butter and looked around. Across the road from the shop stood a lone picnic table where four older men sat eating ice cream cones. I walked over to them.

"Hello, gentlemen," I said. "Mind if I join you?"

They all smiled rather winningly at me, and one of them said. "Of course you may join us. But you must understand that this is a table of great intelligence."

Another of them winked at me and said, "We have been meeting at this table for thirty years now, waiting for a man of great intelligence to join us. It has been thirty years of great disappointment. And now, finally, you are here. Come and join us."

I almost dropped my ice cream cone, I was laughing so hard. Thus, for a brief time, I became a regular at the Table of Great Intelligence; during my time on Aitutaki I met with my new friends every morning for a cup of coffee and wonderful conversation.

In the middle of the village a signpost pointed the direction to various cities, showing the mileage to each. Los Angeles: 3,957 miles. Honolulu: 2,414. Sydney: 2,760. Auckland: 1,725. The sign was there to provide a navigator with instructions for the next leg of his voyage through the Pacific. The short version: *It's a long haul to anywhere, baby.*

The next morning, after having coffee with the boys at the Table of Great Intelligence, I steered my motorbike over to the golf course to meet up with Customs Officer Bob. There was no valet parking in front of the thatched-roof clubhouse, no one to carry the clubs to the driving range—there was no driving range, for that matter. It was unlike any golf course I had ever seen. The fairways were hacked pathways through the jungle, boasting a little grass underfoot. The greens were not putting surfaces but the same fairway grass cut a little shorter. Bob greeted me cheerfully. "Welcome to golf on Aitutaki," he said. "You'll probably find it different from what you're used to back home."

Now there was an understatement. Before us stood a throng of people waiting to tee off, and I had never seen a group of golfers like this. Far from your typical duffers, these were villagers of all ages: grandmothers, grandfathers, mothers, fathers, and kids from teenagers on down to toddlers. And not a pair of golf spikes in sight; pretty much everyone except me was barefoot.

"It's always like this on Thursdays," Bob said as he saw me eyeing the crowd. "That's the day anyone and everyone on the island who plays golf shows up for their weekly game."

When it came our turn to tee off, Bob said, "Here, you go first." He handed me a ball. It had the word "BOB" written on it in permanent marker. So this was my loaner. I was beginning to get the sense that Bob was a little anal-retentive when it came to his golf balls. I set it on the tee, selected one of Bob's clubs, and peered down the fairway.

"Bob," I said. "I can't see the first green."

"Can't you?"

"No. I do see a number of people walking about on what looks to be the fairway."

"Perfect," Bob said. "Aim at them."

"Aim at the people?"

"Yes—that's where the green is."

"Ah, what if I hit somebody?"

Bob laughed. "Just go ahead," he said. "Don't worry about them. They're used to getting hit once in a while."

Feeling slightly criminal, I went ahead and drove the ball down toward the crowd, and they rather miraculously looked up in time to step out of the way of my BOB ball.

I had never seen so many golfers having such a good time. They were serious about their game, but would laugh at bad shots and applaud loudly for good ones. Their equipment looked like it belonged in a golf museum. No one—no one at all—had new clubs. These folks had managed to strip away all the cultural nonsense surrounding golf—the vying for status, the expensive clothes, the trappings of the clubhouse, the big shot execs talking shop—and boil it down to its essence: a really fun and challenging game. I was enchanted.

At the conclusion of the round, everybody gathered at the little shack of a clubhouse, and cold drinks and snacks were served. The conversations that ensued sounded very much like any you'd overhear at a fancy country club: people ribbing each other over bad shots, teasing each other for losing balls, vowing that they'd play oh-so-much better next time out. This was neither Augusta nor Pebble Beach, but I daresay the people who play the course in Aitutaki have at least as much fun.

During the post-round merrymaking, two teenage boys showed up with a woven grass basket filled with golf balls. "What's this?" I said to Bob.

"Just watch."

Everyone suddenly stopped talking. One of the boys pulled a ball out of the basket, turned it until he could read the writing on it, and said, "Mary."

Mary stepped forward, and the kid handed her the ball she'd lost the week before.

The kid pulled another ball. "John," and John came forward.

I watched, delighted, as the boys returned about two dozen balls to their rightful owners. Once a week, Bob explained, kids walk through the surrounding jungle looking for errant golf balls; if they didn't, the sport would pretty quickly die off in Aitutaki.

Without question, this was the most enjoyable day I had ever spent on a golf course, or ever expected to. In December, once I was back in the States, I sent 100 new golf balls, two balls per person, to Customs Officer Bob as a gesture of my appreciation for the islanders' hospitality. I have continued this tradition of sending the balls every year at Christmas time. Aitutaki is an island of unsurpassed natural beauty and tranquility, but the true beauty of this island in paradise is the openness and generosity of its people.

• • •

After a brief stop at the small island of Niue, known as the "Rock of Polynesia," I made an uneventful 365-mile push toward the Kingdom of Tonga. Tonga consists of 176 islands; my destination was Neiafu Harbor in the "Neiafu fjord" region within the island group of Vava'u. Pulling into the harbor was like old home week; there were seven boats anchored here whose owners I had become friends with in Bora Bora. After some much-needed time alone, I was once again looking forward to the sundowner cocktail hour and the sharing of sea stories. Tonga had a much different feel than the islands I had called on previously. It is ruled by a king and has never been colonized by a European power. The dark-skinned Tongans are relaxed, easygoing, never in a hurry to get anywhere or do anything. The buildings all look run-down, as if someone has been meaning to repaint for a decade or so but just hasn't quite got around to it. Tourism is relatively new to Tonga. Luckily, there are no luxury resorts and no fancy restaurants, and the Kingdom of Tonga largely remains an unspoiled tropical paradise, with stunning coral reefs and quiet, white sandy beaches.

Tonga and Niue are two of only three locations in the world where one is allowed to snorkel with humpback whales, and I planned on taking advantage of the opportunity. The Southern Humpback Whales migrate to Tonga from Antarctica, a distance of over 6,000 miles. Tonga's warm waters make ideal mating and calving grounds for these splendid creatures. Terry and Ariel, off s/v *Stella,* joined me on a twenty-six-foot tour boat that motored out to one of the whales' favorite hangouts. The skipper of the tour boat respectfully cut the engine back to an idle as he eased the vessel into position. I could see the animals lolling about in the clear water beneath us. God, they were gigantic—the size of my boat! We donned snorkels and fins, and then sat anxiously on the side of the boat listening to the skipper's instructions, which were minimal: get in the water, swim with the whales, and don't do anything stupid.

What would qualify as stupid? Suddenly, the very idea of getting into the water among these beasts seemed quite stupid, indeed. I couldn't get over their size. I raised my hand. "Uh, just how big are those whales, Skipper?" I said.

"Some are more than forty feet in length," he said, "and they can weigh twenty tons."

Great. *Bigger* than my boat. I went from being nervous to being outright scared; but it was too late to back out. The skipper was motioning for us to get in the water. Even as I deliberated, Ariel and Terry were throwing themselves over the rail, as eager as if they were going to pet some puppies. Aw, hell with it.

I backed into the water, overcome with the distinct impression that I was doing something woefully inadvisable. *Maybe there's a good reason why you can't do this in most countries,* I thought. I cleared my snorkel and peered out through my goggles. Ahead of me, the great charcoal flank of a big female hung suspended in the wavering water like a stage curtain, and with considerable trepidation I eased toward her. One thing I would not do was make any sudden movements and spook her.

A few flicks of the fins and I was almost on top of her, close enough to reach out and touch her. I heard my blood in my ears. *What if she's not in the mood? What if she's the horse and I'm the horsefly? One flick of the tail and she can send me to outer space.* Slowly, shyly, I reached out a hand and placed it softly on her back. She moved slightly, aware that she'd been touched, almost reciprocating the way a dog or cat acknowledges petting. I kept my hand on her, and slid it up as I nudged my way toward her head. There. Now I was looking into her eye.

Holy Christ Almighty.

It was like time itself had frozen. I had my palm against a living, breathing dinosaur, an old, wise life form that had been here before humans and that knew the secrets of the deepest, most mysterious parts of the planet, the places our species has yet to understand. I kept my hand on her for what was probably three minutes, which felt like it was there all afternoon. Suddenly, I wanted to do more than touch this whale; I wanted to embrace her, to thank her, to somehow convey my awe. Instead, I let my hand slip off her and I kicked my way gently over to another member of her family.

For the next thirty minutes, I forgot who I was and where I was. I know what it is to be absorbed in an activity, but this was different, something more like nirvana. It was almost an out-of-body experience, floating around and paying my respects to one whale after another.

On the boat ride back, I was speechless with astonishment and humility. One of the largest mammals in the ocean turns out to be gentle, trusting of the human, sharing its home of crystal clear water. Something about such a massive animal making itself vulnerable to one of my kind, given everything that we have done to wreck the planet—words will never describe being with these majestic creatures. I don't think my life will ever be the same.

• • •

Tonga has a number of spectacular anchorages, but it didn't take long before I was feeling the effect of being "islanded out." Boat friends are great, but such friendships lack a key ingredient: longevity. For someone as sociable as I, it became more and more painful to watch my new friends pulling up the anchor and heading off to their next destination. Often enough, I'd enjoy an evening on a friend's boat only to awake the next morning and see that they had gone. Maybe I'd meet them again in the next bay, or maybe I'd never see them again. I never got accustomed to the transitory nature of these temporary friendships.

. . .

CHAPTER 15

Almost Paradise

To a father growing old nothing is dearer than a daughter.

—Euripides

MY NEXT PASSAGE WOULD TAKE me to the island of Vanua
Levu in Fiji, about 535 miles to the west. Sailing from
Tonga to Fiji on the lay line (also known as a *straight* line) is seldom attempted, since it requires negotiating one's way through
a minefield of uncharted reefs. It is extremely dangerous; many
boats and lives have been lost in these treacherous waters.

One evening in Tonga, I was listening to the nightly Pacific Seafarer's net on the single-side-band radio, when I heard a
hysterical Mayday call. My heart skipped. *Mayday* is a word no
yachtie ever wants to hear. A forty-foot sailboat had run into a
partially submerged reef 200 miles from Tonga on their way to
Fiji. I listened in horror as water began filling the vessel. The life
raft was inflated and the crew abandoned ship. It took less than
thirty minutes for the boat to sink.

This was one of my never-ending concerns. Stories similar
to this are way too common. We think of the ocean as empty
and deep, but there are all kinds of hazards floating around out
there. Metal containers fall off ships, logs bob hidden in the
waves, even whales sometimes float invisibly just beneath the
surface and have been known to cause accidents. I had already
come to grips with the possibility of meeting with a submerged

or floating object; I had accepted it as a danger beyond my control. But listening to that radio call had been enough to extinguish any inkling I may have had to try the direct route to Fiji. I wanted no part of it, even after I learned the next day that the boat's two survivors had been rescued by another yacht in their vicinity. My plan was to sail an extra 150 miles to avoid the perilous reef system.

The six-day passage was uneventful, with only a few squalls to fight through. With each successful passage, I was gaining more confidence in my ability to sail and navigate. *Sundance* and I were getting along better and better. At last, I had begun to feel competent as a single-hander, not desperate for a crew to save me from my own inexperience. Each crossing got a little bit easier. I've always been a firm believer that you can't do well what you don't do often. It makes no difference what the activity—sailing across oceans, solving complicated math problems, or making love. If you don't do it often, chances are you won't do it very well. And these days, I was sailing very, very often.

• • •

Fifty percent of the population of Fiji is made up of East Indians, the descendants of laborers brought to the country by the English to work in the sugar cane plantations; they now run the country's commercial businesses. Forty-five percent of the population is Fijian, with the balance made up of other Pacific Islanders and Europeans. Fijian chiefs still rule, and the old ways remain in effect, with the notable exception of cannibalism, which the missionaries had pretty much managed to squelch by the time Fiji became a British colony in 1874. The Fijians do not like the Indians and have prohibited them from owning property. Unsurprisingly, the Indians do not like the Fijians, either. The political conflict is never-ending, with an ugly coup occurring every few years. If you ask an Indian what he thinks of a Fijian, he will tell you, "They are lazy." Ask a Fijian what he thinks of an Indian, and he'll tell you, "They can't be trusted."

It's a shame that these two groups of dear people are living with such dislike for each other, without a constructive resolution in their future.

Vinaka means "Thank you" in Fiji. *Bula Bula* means "hello." I found it disproportionately fun to say *Bula Bula* when greeting someone, although it made Sam The Sham's song *Wooly Bully* get stuck in my head for the first few days.

There are over 300 islands in Fiji, making it a popular sailing ground, with secluded bays, sweeping remote beaches, and traditional villages. *Sundance* and I had lots of options. I was on the hook listening to the morning VHF radio sked when I learned of a popular marina called Vunda Point, located between the cities of Lautoka and Nadi. Its location and services sounded perfect for *Sundance* and me, so we made our way there.

I tried to settle back into my island routine, but this time, I struggled to shake the restlessness and homesickness that had taken over. I couldn't shrug off the thought of how stupid it was for me to be sitting on a white sandy beach all by myself, while all the significant people in my life, who I loved so very much, were going about their business half a planet away. The satellite phone had indeed been money well spent—it was a blessing to hear Sally's voice every day—and yet, predictably, we were running out of things to say to each other under the circumstances. Our conversations had taken on a formulaic structure, and they often left me feeling like I'd just missed talking with her—like I'd spoken to someone very similar to my Sally, but not quite to the woman I loved, if that makes any sense. Sometimes I actually dreaded speaking with her because of the empty feeling that came when I hung up the phone. Plus, she had recently begun making strong suggestions that my foolishness had gone on long enough and that it was now time for me to come home and give up the sailing life.

On the morning of September 12 in Tonga—September 11 back in the States—the VHF radio came alive with nonstop chatter about airplanes having flown into the Twin Towers of the World Trade Center. I sat stricken, listening to the reports, the voices reaching hysterics, and feeling the overwhelming need to go home—now. I called Sally. She was terribly upset. No one knew if the terrorists would strike again, and if so, where. I tried to reassure her, but I felt helpless. When I tried to book a flight home, I found that it was impossible. There was nothing to do but sit alone on the other side of the planet while my country was under attack and in mourning.

• • •

In the following days, I felt like part of me had died. I abandoned my routine and just sat listening, following the news, numbed by the world events unfolding so far away. My original plan had been to sail on to New Zealand after spending a few weeks in the islands of Fiji, but I had no heart for it. Not that it mattered anyway; somehow I had overlooked the approach of cyclone season. It had snuck up on me this time, and would be here in just a few weeks, about the time I'd planned on making the push to New Zealand.

Although I had grown as a sailor, I wasn't looking forward to the 1,259 miles of infamously dangerous ocean to reach New Zealand—even in normal conditions. But now it was October, and the cyclone season runs from November to March. (A hurricane in the Southern Hemisphere is called a Cyclone; in the Orient, it's called a Typhoon.) No matter what you call it, no sailor with any intellect would ever be caught on the ocean during cyclone season. I hadn't realized it when I'd chosen Vunda Point, but that marina is a favorite place for cruisers to wait out the season. One morning, while taking a walk around the place, I saw a number of sailboats sitting in deep holes in the ground. It didn't take long to figure out they had been placed there to survive the coming cyclones. I had an epiphany followed immediately by a sudden burst of pure joy. Air travel to the U.S. had opened back up. I could safely park *Sundance* in one of these holes and could go home . . . and soon, very soon. As soon as the prospect of going home began to seem like a possibility, I felt suddenly racked by a full-on case of homesickness.

I ran back to the marina office to see if they had a spot available for my boat. When the manager said, "By all means," I was so excited that I instantly found a pay phone, called a travel agency, and booked a flight to LAX. I was going home!

Three weeks later, after intense work preparing *Sundance* for her hiatus, I watched as a backhoe dug a fissure the same size as the hull and deep enough so the boat sat in the opening with just two or three feet of hull exposed above ground. Using a travel lift (a piece of equipment that looks more like a prehistoric monster than a machine, designed to move boats around the shipyard), workers hefted my baby up and gently lowered her into the hole, the keel coming to rest atop a bed of large timbers. There they cushioned her with lots of old rubber tires along the hull, to keep *Sundance* stable in her nest and protect her sides from the dirt . . . and there she sat, hunkered down for the season, as secure in her new temporary "grave" as any boat can be. I took one last look, beelined it to the airport, and caught a ride to LAX on a gigantic silver bird named Qantas.

Back home in California, the land of fruits and nuts, the pace of life was almost too alien for me to comprehend. It was wonderful, of course, to be with Sally: to see her beautiful face, to feel her touch, to hold her in my arms and feel safe once again. It was pure bliss to hug Sedona: to smell his fur, to see his big brown eyes looking directly into mine, to make him smile by scratching behind his ears. I was thrilled to spend time with my four daughters and eight grandkids. Once again, I had a chance to savor the luxury of what I used to take for granted: sleeping in my own bed, enjoying a home-cooked meal, and soaking in all the comforts of home.

And yet, because I had seen this movie before, I knew that such spells were short-lived. It didn't take long before the comforts of home gave way to a kind of culture shock. I had been kicking back in a very, very slow and quiet place. Now, within the L.A. basin, which includes a circle of fifty miles around L.A., I was part of a swarm of some twenty-six million people! Life in the fast lane includes holding one's own in six lanes of traffic, hurtling along at somewhere between zero and ten miles per hour much of the time. How is it that painfully slow traffic can make life seem too fast-paced? I'm not sure how, but for some reason, it can. Slow traffic is the result of what I call TMP: Too Many People. And TMP affected more than traffic. I'd been longing for a cup of my favorite coffee at Starbucks, but was irritated when I counted the number of people standing in line ahead of me. I was number fifteen. I had a rather foolish thought that could only belong to someone who had just arrived from the remote South Pacific: *How can it be that all these people want coffee at the same time I do?* Later that same day, I had the urge for a sub sandwich and was number fourteen in line. *Gah*, I thought. P*eople in Southern California must stand in line to die.*

I was not adjusting well to shore life; contending with all the landlubbers was driving me slightly crazy. People talked too fast, walked too fast, and drove too fast every chance they could, speeding from one stoplight to the next, only to have to sit there like everyone else when it turned red. No one seemed to smile; friendships appeared superficial. What I saw around me seemed more like acquaintances than true friendships. *Maybe,* I thought like a total naïf, *if these people could experience the lifestyle in Aitutaki, they might be able to develop a better feeling for a more meaningful, more rewarding life than their obsession with life in the fast lane.*

I had come to a tough place in my thinking. The truth was, I was content neither here at home nor back in the South Pacific. In its way, life on the boat in paradise was wonderful, but sitting on a white sandy beach all by myself left me sorely homesick for my loved ones. Yet, now that I was home, the complexities of a comfortable shore life left me discontented, and even my home life was quickly losing its magical sheen, just as I had known it would. I was perplexed; the answer to this paradox was not within my limited powers of discovery.

After I had been home for about ten days, Sally caught me moping. This time she didn't wait to confront me. "Wishing you were back in the Pacific?" she said.

"Part of me," I confessed. "I tell you, baby: when I'm there, there's nothing I want more than to come home. But then I start to miss it."

"That's obvious."

I knew it wasn't what she wanted to hear, but I said it anyway: "What I really wish is that you were there with me. Then it would be perfect."

Her reaction surprised me a little in its harshness. "Well, it's not what I want. Okay? You want to do it; I don't. I'm happy here trying to live the life that we planned on. If you need to keep going back to sea, that's your issue."

Of course she was completely right, but it didn't change the fact that it was already time for me to start making plans for my return to Fiji. It wasn't just that I had come to enjoy sailing; there was still a big part of me that had an issue with the F-word (failure). It seemed like I wouldn't be fully satisfied with myself until I had either completed my circumnavigation or reached a point of personal growth where I could honestly say that I had finished my adventuring, had developed the freedom and ability to be out in the world alone, happy with my own company.

I could not leave *Sundance* sitting in her grave forever. I must return to Fiji. I had the feeling of a kid that had ridden his bike too far from home and didn't know how he was going to get back. *Just sail on, old boy. Sail on.*

Before leaving San Diego, I had dinner with all four of my daughters. They raised their glasses to toast my safe voyaging, and I took the opportunity to invite them all to come visit me aboard *Sundance*. "Really," I said. "I want you all to join me anywhere, anytime, on this adventure. I will gladly pay for all your expenses. There's nothing that I'd love more than to show you girls around paradise aboard *Sundance*."

It was a beautiful dream, but I was talking to four married women with children. The chance that any one of them could escape their responsibilities for a trip like that was far-fetched enough, never mind all four of them at once. Still, being a fond old fool, I was hopeful.

· · ·

Once back at the Vunda Point marina, I was relieved to see that *Sundance* had survived the cyclone season without the slightest bit of damage, but she looked pathetic sitting in a hole in the ground; it was like seeing a prizefighter in a hospital gown. She belonged in the water, not in the dirt.

Despite the lack of damage, the list of work that needed to be completed was extensive. It included the following: checking out a strange noise emanating from the helm; relocating the Trace regulator that controls the juice from the eight solar panels (it had gotten wet and experienced a small fire); replacing the broken timber that supports the bow pulpit (a major job); applying more caulking to the rub rails; varnishing all the bright work; and applying three coats of anti-fouling paint to her hull. I was unprepared for the amount of endless work it required just to keep the boat afloat. I was more accustomed to hiring someone else to do my dirty work . . . but that wasn't an option out here in paradise. Yes, I had help with some of the work, but most of it was mine alone to do. And yes, I gained a certain sense of accomplishment when a project was completed, but the work was never-ending, and any trifling of accomplishment was not enough reward to excite me. I spent more time working on the damn boat than actually sailing. This wasn't part of the dream, but there was no alternative.

It amazes me that sailors have not yet figured out that boats and saltwater are highly incompatible. I will say, though, that Fiji is an excellent place to do boat repairs; the wages are low and one can find skilled workers for the technical stuff. But the weather makes the smallest job difficult because it is so very hot and humid. Daily temperatures are close to one hundred degrees and the humidity is always in the nineties. If you so much as blink, you will start sweating. On most afternoons, a rain storm will blow through; but these rains provide no cooling relief, they just turn the place into a sauna bath. During those days of hard work, I would stand under a cool outdoor shower at least three times a day.

The marina did have two coin-operated washing machines. This was a luxury; I was accustomed to washing my dirty clothes in buckets, whenever and wherever I could find fresh water— usually on the dock of a yacht club. One bucket was filled with soapy water, the other was used to rinse. For the wash cycle, I would jam my foot in the soapy water, applying pressure to the clothes, doing my best impersonation of a plunger. The part I loathed was the wringing-out cycle, twisting each article by hand, using every ounce of strength in my fingers and forearms, to ensure that they would dry properly when I hung them on the lifelines of the boat. Sheets and towels were the most challenging, because of their size. They always left my fingers sore and tired. Simply dropping a quarter into a washing machine was a true luxury.

Sleeping was another challenge. The excessive heat made it impossible to sleep without two turbo fans blowing directly into my bunk. I waged constant battle with the mosquitoes (called *mawzies* by the locals) and the ever-present no-see-ums (similar to a sand flea). The mawzies, of course, made me worry about malaria. Even though I slept under mosquito netting, the little buggers found their way into my bunk, buzzing in my ears, waking me from a sound sleep in the middle of the night. Coming within earshot of *Sundance* during the wee morning hours would have been an education in cussing even for the saltiest of sailors.

• • •

The Vunda Point Yacht Club was a small, open-air building with a grass-thatched roof that sat next to the water. There was a small bar with eight plastic chairs and five plastic tables, each with seating for four. The etiquette was this: you say to the lady bartender, "Please pass the bug spray." She hands you the repellent and you excuse yourself and step off to the side so the spray doesn't light on anyone's face at the bar.

Every evening, I would join other boaters from all over the world for a drink and a small dinner. Conversation tended to center on people's triumphs and frustrations (mostly frustrations), with a day spent working on their boats. The highlight of the dinner hour was the anticipation of the sunset. We had an unobstructed view looking west over the ocean. As the ball of fire slips slowly downward to a clear ocean horizon, it grows larger and somehow wider as it sinks, until suddenly only a broad sliver of orange remains. Then, as this last vestige vanishes away, if you are watching closely, you may be treated to a one-second flash of vivid emerald green. Then it's gone; only the dark ocean remains. I have watched for the green flash in many locations around the world, and I have usually been disappointed; no flash. But thanks to some quirk of geography, at the Vunda Point Yacht Club we were treated to a spectacular show of the elusive green flash almost every evening. It became so expected, so common, that we would give a numerical score to each flash. "That was an eight point five," someone would say, while his neighbor might give it a nine point two. No matter the score, each and every green flash was an extraordinary treasure.

Work on *Sundance* was coming along nicely, and I was getting rather eager to feel the wind in her sails. I was just beginning to look into making some serious plans for continuing on when I received an unexpected e-mail from my daughter Kelly. "Dad," she wrote. "If you're serious about having us come aboard, let us know. Kasey and I can clear some time in June."

I was ecstatic. All the girls had been sailing with me from the time they were in diapers, but they had never had the opportunity to spend any time on *Sundance* or to sail offshore. I wrote Kelly back immediately, like a businessman who rushes to close on a good deal before his counterpart comes to his senses. By all means, I told her, please come. Over the next few days, we worked out all the arrangements. I would have the company of two of my beautiful daughters for twelve full days!

Now, in addition to preparing the boat, I hashed out an itinerary that would pack in as much fun, beauty, and cultural interest as I could possibly arrange for. With the girls' visit to look forward to, time sped by.

When the day finally came, I met the girls at the Nadi International airport, wearing a traditional Fiji sari (men's skirt). Once they saw me in my skirt, they laughed so hard they almost wet their pants. This was the beginning of the laughter, and it didn't end until the girls returned home twelve days later.

I thought it would be fun for my daughters to have some idea of what their mini-cruise would entail, so I handed each of them a printout of the following itinerary:

OPERATION SUNDANCE FIJI–VANUATU

Fiji to Vanuatu – 531 nautical miles
Average miles sailed per day – 120
Days of passage – 5
Example of itinerary:

- Monday, June 3, 2002, ETA–Nadi, Fiji @ 0530. Spend the day in Vunda Pt. Marina. Orientation and customs paperwork.
- Tuesday, June 4, 2002, Depart Vunda Pt. Marina in AM. Three-hour run to Musket Cove Yacht Club.
- Wednesday, June 5, 2002, Musket Cove Yacht Club, water activities.
- Thursday, June 5, 2002. AM departure Musket Cove Yacht Club. Day sail to Somosomo. Anchor the bay. Participate in Kava Ceremony with Chief.
- Friday, June 6, 2002. AM departure for island of Matacawa Levu.
- Saturday, June 7, 2002. AM departure for Turtle Island Resort and Blue Lagoon Caves. Traditional Fijian pig roast dinner. Swim with manta rays!
- Monday, June 8, 2002. AM departure (about 0900–1000) Sail to Yasawa-I-Rara Village. Final provisioning for the passage.
- Tuesday, June 9, 2002. Big departure day. AM starting the passage to Vanuatu!
- June 9 to June 13. At sea, en route to Vanuatu. Watch schedule: three hours on—six hours off.
- Thursday, June 13, 2002 (EDL) estimated day of landfall. Island of Tanna. Port Resolution. Erromango Island, Dillon's Bay.

Efate to Pango Point to Mele Bay and finally Port Vila Bay.
- Friday, June 14, 2002. Entry procedures Vanuatu, customs clearance.
- Remainder of island-hopping in Vanuatu, to be determined while on passage.

A disclaimer: this itinerary is subject to change according to weather and should only be used as an example. In reality, we have no schedule and we are going to stick to it!!

It was fantastic to have the girls on board, although I felt an enormous sense of responsibility for their safety. I didn't feel that way when I was alone. That simple recognition made me reflect on the tradeoff I had made decades before, when I became a father. Being alone in the world carries its freedom, and yet, shouldering the responsibility for the safety and well-being of loved ones is a crucial aspect of humanity, one I was very pleased not to have missed out on.

Our island-hopping began with Somosomo, and it was clear from the start that for my girls—both of whom are school teachers—one of the highlights of Fiji would be the children. Kelly and Kasey kept their pockets full of candy for the kids, and sometimes they looked like a couple of pied pipers walking along the beach with a gaggle of laughing children trailing behind.

The Fijians believe that they own not just their islands but also the surrounding waters. Visiting yachtsmen are therefore expected to ask permission of the local chief to anchor in his waters and walk on his island. The traditional custom is called "presenting Sevu-Sevu." When you visit an island for the first time, you pay your respects to the chief by presenting him with a small bundle of pepper root (purchased in Lautoka), wrapped in newspaper and tied with a ribbon. As we anchored off Somosomo, we were rather eager to act out the Sevu-Sevu tradition.

We paddled ashore in the dinghy, where we were promptly met by a representative of the chief who accepted our gift of pepper root on his majesty's behalf. "Please come," he said, "and you may meet the chief in his hut."

Feeling a bit like we were crashing a movie set, we followed the silent representative up a narrow path away from the beach, past chickens, scrawny goats, and staring children, up to a cluster of huts with a trickle of smoke twisting above the trees. Our guide motioned us toward the opening of one of the huts. I peeked inside. There sat the chief (I knew it was him because he enjoyed the luxury of a chair) and three tribal elders. The girls came in behind me and the three of us nodded respectfully and sat cross-legged in a circle on the dirt floor. By his appearance, I figured the chief probably remembered when Captain Cook had called on his island in 1774. He stared down on us, not unkindly, but never saying a word. One of the elders lifted a skinny arm and spoke a few words in a language that might as well have been Martian. The chief nodded and groaned, apparently signaling his approval. It was now time to partake of the Kava.

Back in the day, the Kava drink was made by native women who chewed the pieces of raw root into a soft pulp before spitting the juice into a hardwood bowl, and it was this saliva-inflected concoction that visitors were expected to drink. I had heard that sometimes Kava was still prepared the traditional way and sometimes not. I silently prayed that this particular tribe had discovered the benefits of using a hammer to soften the root. I didn't want to offend the chief and get kicked off his island, but I certainly didn't relish the thought of drinking Kava spit.

Kelly was the first to be offered the cup (half a hollowed-out coconut shell) filled with Kava. We followed the lead of the elders in the circle, and clapped three times with cupped hands to make a hollow popping sound. I had coached the girls on protocol a little bit beforehand, having done some reading on the subject. We knew, for example, that you are expected to drink the Kava with one gulp—no sipping! Kelly did a great job, slugging the drink down in one pull, but the look on her faced afterward was the same I used to see when she was a little girl and had just swallowed a dose of cough syrup. Her nose and lips were curled up and her eyes watered as she forced a smile for the chief. Now it was my turn, and I was wishing I'd gone first. I rushed it a little so as not to prolong it, and it shot harmlessly down my throat, then as kind of an afterthought my taste buds kicked in. The Kava tasted like muddy, gritty water. On to Kasey, who got hers down successfully. We sat grinning up at the chief like fools, and he stared down at us for a moment, and then made a few guttural sounds that must have signaled his permission for us to visit his island.

That evening, we scored an invitation to a traditional Fijian meal of a pig that had been roasted in the ground. Again, we felt like anthropologists, thrilled to have been set down in the middle of this exotic experience. The pork was delicious and the people were friendly and eager to share their customs with us. To our relief, no Kava was served.

Over the next few blissful days, we swam with manta rays, strolled on the beach where the movie *Cast Away* was shot, look-ing for Wilson the volleyball, spent a day on the island where *The Blue Lagoon* was filmed, snorkeled with heaps of multicolored fish, and filled our in-between hours having fun with the local natives and their kids.

The five-day passage from Fiji to Tanna in Vanuatu was delightful—soft trade winds, no storms, millions of stars, and endless conversations filled with laughter. I hadn't been so hap-pily alone with my girls in ages. I had them captive on this boat with no distractions. We were able to carry on long conversa-tions without interruptions, or to drop a train of conversation and then pick it up an hour or a day later when we thought of something else to say. It reminded me of when I used to take the girls skiing; only a father could understand why the ride up the mountain in the chairlift was the part that I most looked forward to—for that brief time, I had my girls all to myself for what we used to call "quality time." Well, this was a lot bet-ter than any chairlift ride. This was the epitome of quality time.

Before leaving Fiji, I had connected to a SSB radio net with the Auckland Cruising Club, out of New Zealand. Each eve-ning, at a designated time, I tuned in to the proper frequency and listened for the nightly schedule to start with a roll call of all the boats participating. When an older-sounding gentleman named John would call out, "*Sundance*," I would respond, "This is *Sundance*, reading you loud and clear, over."

John would say, "Hope all's well on *Sundance*. Give us your position and weather." After responding with all the information, we'd listen as John delivered us a brief report on what weather conditions we could expect for the next twenty-four hours. Every evening, we looked forward to hearing John's deep voice with his pleasant New Zealand accent. It was reassuring to know that we weren't completely alone, and I took a strange comfort in sharing this little ritual with my daughters. It gave them a taste for what it must be like out here for me all the time. As I was thinking about that one evening, it dawned on me that it was becoming increasingly important for my daughters to know things like that about me—to know me as a person, to have some insight about what it was like inside my skin, inside my head. Was that a normal part of aging? And if so, wasn't it particularly stupid of me to be spending most of my remaining time out here on the ocean far away from them? I put those thoughts aside, resolving simply to enjoy our time together. There would be time to dwell on things like that later.

The girls did exceptionally well, considering it was their first experience making a bluewater passage. As much fun as we were having, though, I could tell by our third day out that the girls were really missing their families. I broke out the satellite phone and we all called home. My daughters were thrilled to talk to their husbands and kids from the ocean. Each call ended with happy tears. And once again, I had the rather strange thought, *Now, they have some idea what it's like for me.*

On the fifth day, with our final destination just half a mile away, I started FUJIMO to begin our careful approach to Port Resolution on the island of Tanna. There was something there that I wanted my daughters to see. Both of the girls were standing on the bow pulpit, on reef watch, as we entered the pass. They hollered directions back to me, indicating the safe route around the dangerous reef formations. After half an hour of painstaking effort, we cleared the pass without kissing any coral heads and plopped the anchor into forty feet of dark blue water. Once we were certain the anchor had a firm hold on the bottom, there were high-fives all around.

"Congratulations, girls, on a very successful passage!"

"You too, Dad."

It really was a triumphant moment. I was happy the girls were able to experience the extraordinary feeling of accomplishment that comes after completing a bluewater sail of over 500 miles. I was proud of myself for getting them here safely, but that was nothing compared to the sense of pride I felt in the kind of women my daughters had become. They had handled the boat well, they never once complained, never missed a watch, never got seasick, and they were cheerful and upbeat sailing companions to boot. We celebrated the passage with a swim in the eighty-two-degree water.

The "Port" in the name "Port Resolution" is misleading. To me, it suggests some kind of substantial boating/shipping activity, with docks, wharfs, maybe even a yacht club, and, at the bare minimum, a number of vessels about. To my shock, Port Resolution had none of the above; there was nothing there—zip, nada. No dock in sight and a grand total of zero other boats. *Sundance* was the lone yacht calling on this "port."

"Gee, girls," I said. "I hope you can adjust to all this hustle and bustle after being isolated at sea."

We were sitting in the cockpit enjoying the stillness of the water, sipping on a cold beverage (I had splurged by turning on the little refrigerator for my guests) when suddenly Kasey said, "Look there!"

Kelly and I turned to where she was pointing, up on shore toward the jungle.

"What is it?" Kelly said.

"I don't know. Something moving in the trees. A monkey?"

We looked but couldn't see what she was talking about. Then she said, "There it is again!"

Kelly had reached for my binoculars and was scanning the jungle. "Wow," she said. "That's not a monkey. It's a person. Climbing in a palm tree"

Each of us had a turn with the binoculars to confirm the sighting. Were we being watched?

Kelly said, "So there are people living on this island, Dad?"

Before I could answer, Kasey said, "Apparently there are, because here comes the welcome committee."

Another native was paddling a dugout outrigger canoe across the little bay toward *Sundance*.

"Are they friendly, Dad?"

I shrugged. "He sure looks friendly enough."

It was true. The man in the canoe was beaming at us, conveying his good intentions from fifty yards away. He paddled up alongside the boat, stood in his canoe, and said, "I am Jonathan. Welcome to our island." To our delight, he handed Kasey a large bunch of small green bananas. With that simple gesture of welcome, Jonathan won my heart; I was finally in the traditional South Pacific, having my Fletcher Christian moment, and I got to share it with my girls.

"Will you come ashore with me, to visit my village?" Jonathan said.

There was no way in hell we would be declining that invitation. "Yes, thank, you," I said. We grabbed our things and launched *Butch*.

"Please follow me carefully," Jonathan said. Paddling expertly, he led us through a narrow opening in the reef, and within a few minutes we were standing on shore.

"This way, please," he said.

Now we walked a path up a steep hill whose summit offered a view down through the jungle to where *Sundance* lay, solitary and proud, in the otherwise empty bay. Jonathan saw us looking at our boat. He paused with us and said, "You know, you have anchored your boat in the same spot where Captain James Cook anchored his ship *Resolution* in 1774. This is how Port Resolution gets its name." Hearing this, I felt chills on the back of my neck.

Jonathan turned and continued up the path, and the three of us followed. He was not very tall, maybe five feet at the most, with a lean but powerful build. He spoke English with a New Zealand accent and wore nothing but a *namba* (penis sheath).

After a fast-paced walk of maybe a mile, we came to our destination. With a proud smile, Jonathan said, "Welcome to my village. This is Ireupuow." We looked around in awe. We had visited a number of villages in Fiji, so we thought we had a pretty good idea of what to expect. But what we saw here was in fact a picture right out of *National Geographic*. This primitive community consisted of small *bure*-style huts, clustered within an open field, with the largest hut reserved for the chief. Dogs, pigs, horses, and chickens meandered freely about the place, even wandering in and out of huts. The women wore nothing but grass skirts, the children were totally naked, and all of the men wore *namba* and nothing else. The women sat in small circles, busy with their daily activities of preparing food out of sugar cane, corn, beets, and some stuff I could not identify. Some used stones to crush corn into flour. Everyone was working, with no one observing. Jonathan explained that most of the men were away from the village tending to their "plantations" (their term for a garden). I imagined that the scene had not changed in the last hundred years or more.

These people trace their origin to a tribe of Melanesians. Archeologists have found evidence that humans have roamed these islands since 3,000 B.C. Malakula Island to the north had its last reported case of cannibalism less than twenty years ago. The native people on the nearby island of Pentecost are the original "Bungee Jumpers." Maybe the Bungee jumpers were trying to get away from rivals who wanted to have them for dinner.

We lingered all afternoon, drinking it all in, talking with the friendly inhabitants of this time capsule, honored that they should be so welcoming. Kelly and Kasey took notes and pictures to share with their students. Elated by the experience, we returned to the boat in late afternoon.

That evening, aboard *Sundance*, we heard a sudden enormous boom in the distance.

"Was that thunder?" Kelly said.

"I don't think so," I said. "There isn't a cloud in the sky."

"Look over there," Kasey said. She was pointing toward a red glow above the horizon.

I knew what it was; it had been my primary reason for wanting to visit Tanna Island with the girls. But I didn't tell them what it was.

The following morning, Jonathan appeared in his dugout canoe once again.

"Quick," I said. "Get some stuff together to give him, in case he gives us more bananas."

By the time he reached *Sundance*, the girls had put together a care package: several cans of stew, a box of cereal, a six-pack of Coke. Sure enough, the first thing he did in coming alongside was to hand us up another batch of bananas.

"Thank you," Kasey said. "And these things are for you. We want to thank you so much for showing us your village."

Jonathan grinned. "Perhaps today you would like to see our volcano?"

The girls' mouths dropped open, and they turned to me. "Yep," I said. "That's what we heard last night."

We arranged to meet Jonathan in the village at four o'clock that afternoon. When we arrived, there was a very old red Ford pickup truck waiting for us. Jonathan motioned for us to climb in the back; we sat on the floor and braced ourselves for a bumpy ride over a jungle trail.

It wasn't long at all before we began to smell volcanic smoke and felt particles of ash in our eyes. Now the truck was climbing a steep, rutted incline, which bounced us around the bed of the truck like three ping-pong balls as we shielded our eyes from the ashes. At last, the truck came to a stop and we opened our eyes. We were sitting directly at the base of the volcano. Above us the sky was slathered with a thick gray cloud glowing red at its belly.

"Well," I said. "We made it to Transylvania. Now let's go call on Dracula."

We followed Jonathan as he picked his way up an ash-covered trail, littered with old lava rocks, to the very rim of the volcano. Jonathan walked so far forward that his toes practically hung out over the abyss. He looked back at us over his shoulder and beckoned us forward. Cautiously, we shuffled alongside him until we all were peering down into the huge, belching crater; our hearts stopped at the sight of this awesome display of fire and brimstone. Periodically, a massive boom sounded, so loud that it hammered the soul and sucked all other sound from the air, leaving our limbs jangling with adrenaline. I fired up my video camera, anxious to capture the scene for posterity. I was concentrating on focusing the camera when suddenly I heard a loud thud on the ground right next to me. I stopped the camera and turned to see what had caused the noise. There, not two feet away from me, a red-hot lava rock the size of a bushel basket glowered fiercely in the dirt. I had come within about twenty-four inches of meeting with a quick and rather spectacular end. Was it time to back up a little bit?

After my close call, it became apparent that similar lava fragments were shooting out of the mouth of the crater and flying hundreds of feet into the air. The three of us looked at each other, a bit overwhelmed, unsure whether we should run for cover or stay on the rim of the crater, savoring the rush.

Jonathan gave us a five-second lesson in volcano watching. "Don't run; look up to see where the rocks are going to land before moving." We wanted to follow his advice, but with each new eruption, our panicked legs tried to carry us off to safety. We were thrilled, captivated, a little scared, but giddy with laughter. As the sun set, the show became more intense, with each piece of magma blistering off into the night sky trailing a jet stream of molten red. It went on for hours, mesmerizing, continually shocking, a natural show of infinite wonder and humbling power.

I was as drunk with this experience as I had been swimming with whales—I was not at all sure I was still inhabiting my body, and I had lost all track of time. At some point, hours into our experience, a huge eruption—one that dwarfed everything that had come before—shook the ground beneath our feet and expelled a fiery plume of smoke that rose a thousand feet into the sky. We stood gaping up at it, as if we had been given a one-time-only tour of heaven, or of hell. As we stared, an enormous bolt of lightning seared through the middle of the smoke, accompanied by an ear-shattering crack of thunder. Molten lava came crashing down all around us. Jonathan shouted, "She is angry; we must go now." She certainly did seem angry.

· · ·

After a two-day stop on the island of Erromango, we sailed to Port Vila, on the Island of Efate. This was to be the jumping-off port for my two gorgeous daughters . . . time for them to return to the real world of being wives and mothers. They were booked on an early morning flight from Port Vila to Nadi, Fiji, and then on to Denver, Colorado. It was still dark when we all loaded into the dinghy for the short ride to the town dock, where a cab was waiting to take them to the airport. I was angry with the driver for taking the girls' bags from me; loading them into the trunk would have given me something to do with my hands. Now there was nothing to do but stand awkwardly and fight back the tears . . . another heart-in-my-throat moment. My stomach was in a knot; my throat hurt; tears stung my eyes. God, I hated to see them go. We had had the time of our lives together. We hugged, hard. I told the girls I loved them, and I thanked them over and over for coming. Once they were in the cab and away, and I was again alone on an island in the Pacific that nobody had ever heard of.

Once I got back on the boat, it immediately started to rain. It had not rained the whole time the girls were with me; tears from the heavens, these raindrops. The island children who had laughed with Kasey and Kelly would be crying. Tears dripped off the mast. *Sundance* was crying, the sky was crying, and the sixty-one-year-old bold adventurer was most assuredly crying. There was no more laughter on this boat, no more tall tales to tell, no jokes, no reminiscing. The silence aboard *Sundance* was deafening. My heart ached. Oh, how I missed my girls. This loneliness was worse than physical pain.

I was never meant for life on an island in paradise, alone. Maybe I should think about what is more important in my life, sailing around the world or sharing my life with those I love. Damn it, damn it, damn it. All I want in this world is to go home.

· · ·

CHAPTER 16

Sail on, Sail on, Sailor

Fatigue makes cowards of us all.

—Vince Lombardi

I<small>T'S HARD TO EXPLAIN MY</small> decision to keep sailing, especially since I was at a very low point in terms of my loneliness and dejection. I couldn't imagine any island so beautiful, any new human encounter so thrilling, as to make pushing-on worthwhile. I felt like an exile from my home, as if some power had banished me from the presence of my loved ones—and yet, of course, no one had done so but me. I was here by choice, and I could go home at any time. But if I was to be honest with myself, there was still a tiny sliver of my consciousness not consumed by homesickness, a fragment of my being that spoke up saying, "You've felt lonely before, and you've pushed on and gotten over it. That's part of the growing you still have to do—you have to learn to live with yourself out here." I was getting pretty sick of that voice.

There was one other consideration which seems slight in retrospect, but which had a strong impact on my decision to keep sailing: both Sally and Jungle had made plans to visit me in Australia. I knew that if I canceled with Sally because I was coming home, she would be nothing but thrilled. But with Jungle I felt different. Of course, I could have called or e-mailed him and said to forget it, but I hated to do that to him. He had already booked his flight, probably with a nonrefundable ticket. Anyway, if I make plans with someone, I keep them.

I consoled myself by acknowledging that I had no further commitment than sailing to Australia, which meant only another month or two of being away from home. Surely I could survive that. If, when I reached Australia, I had shaken my funk and felt like continuing, so be it. If not, it would have been a hell of a run.

With that much of a plan in place, I felt a strong urgency to get back out to sea. I wanted to enjoy what I had come to experience as the conviviality of the ocean. On my passage from San Diego to Hawaii, I had thought of the Pacific as a potentially malevolent Sleeping Giant, as if I were sneaking furtively across its surface, hustling to get where I was going before he awoke and crushed me. But lately, the Sleeping Giant had become more of a companion, which perhaps, is one of the tricks of solitude. When you are alone in the world, anything can become a reassuring presence: the vast ocean, the mountains, death itself—even a volleyball named Wilson. I was missing the communion with the Sleeping Giant; it was time to get away from shore.

After re-provisioning and topping up the tanks with water and fuel, I set a course for Noumea in New Caledonia. I looked forward to an uneventful three-day sail of 317 miles to the south/southwest. For the first two days, I enjoyed exactly that. I was within twenty-four hours of making landfall when the Sleeping Giant awoke, shattering my illusions about his geniality.

I saw the massive storm building on the radar screen and instantly knew I was in for a fight for survival. The tempest was blocking my course to New Caledonia; I could see it all on the radar, standing between me and my destination with its arms crossed. There was no way to avoid it—no place to run, no place to hide. It was going to get rough.

I went below and secured everything as best I could. The full mainsail had to be reduced; I quickly put two reefs in, the maximum. I furled the headsail in tight. Next, I shortened the staysail to the size of a child's kite. As I surveyed the preparations, I felt confident that the boat was ready to deal with this storm. However, I wasn't so sure about its captain. It would be my first time in a storm of this size by myself. Ready or not, here it comes.

I felt the blast of cold air first, and then the winds filled in very fast. Within minutes, the wind speed indicator was redlining at fifty-five knots. The seas were not much of a problem, if you don't mind waves of eighteen to twenty feet; these were nice big rollers. Raindrops smashed into my face with such velocity that it felt like gravel being flung at me; it stung like hell and made it difficult even to keep my eyes open. I could have used a pair of ski goggles.

As I stood clutching the wheel and peering forward, with my head angled against the blast of rain, I watched in horror as a sudden violent gust tore the five reef points out of the mainsail like they were made out of spaghetti. *Oh, fuck*, I thought. Without the sail securely tied to the boom, the force of the wind would rip the entire sail to shreds in no time. It was critical that I get the mainsail down and secured around the boom immediately. Which meant letting go of the wheel.

Lowering the mainsail in a powerful storm is extremely dangerous, especially for a single-hander. The boat is moving brutally, bucking and wallowing, side to side, up and down. You can't see. You're rushed and scared shitless. The deck is slippery. In such conditions, the ever-present possibility of getting tossed overboard increases exponentially. Even barring that ultimate nightmare, there's a very real chance of some less extreme accident that still could spell your doom—falling and breaking a leg or an arm, getting whacked in the head by the boom and being knocked unconscious—and none of that is to mention the simple danger of surrendering control of the boat to the autopilot among violent waves, which is like asking a passenger to take your car's steering wheel on a dangerous mountain road while you climb over the backseat to rummage around in the cooler for a sandwich.

I rehearsed in my mind at least a dozen times every step involved, carefully choreographing every move. Somehow, my fear drained away, replaced by a strained caution. I fought the elements long enough to get *Sundance's* bow pointed into the wind, then engaged the autopilot to maintain a steady course. With my safety harness secured, I snapped the tether clasp onto the jack line (a rope secured at both ends of the boat such that, if you've remembered to clip into it with your safety harness, you stand a chance of climbing back on deck if you get tossed overboard). I took a deep breath and began inching forward on my hands and knees until I reached the base of the mast. Hugging the mast like it was Sally on a Saturday night, I eased my way up into a standing position. With one arm wrapped around the mast, I used the other to uncleat the main halyard and then waited for the sail to start sliding down the mast as it normally does. Nothing happened . . . it didn't budge. There was too much wind pressure on the sail to allow it to move. I was going to have to use two hands to pull it down, which meant I would have to release my death grip on the mast. With both hands I reached as high up as possible and, using all my strength, pulled mightily on the sail. It moved, but only an inch at the most. I pulled again; this time, it moved two inches. It required every ounce of my strength to pull down the sail an inch or two at a time. Once it was down, the next challenge was to wrap it around the boom and tie it in place. Again, it would require the use of both hands and great balance to hang on. Finally, the sail was secured and I made my way back to the safety of the cockpit, where I stood triumphantly, basking in my own glory.

I had just done a brave, difficult, and necessary thing . . . and I was still alive; the resulting adrenaline rush was well worth the effort. I felt the confidence of Superman. The sail had been saved and I hadn't broken anything. Suddenly the storm didn't seem so frightening. Within twenty minutes, it had passed on through, leaving *Sundance* and me with nothing but some high seas; it was hard not to imagine we had chased it off. We motored on to our destination.

• • •

New Caledonia is a French overseas territory. Compared to the very rural environment of villages in the South Pacific, Noumea appeared quite cosmopolitan. The locals like to say it is like a small French city transplanted into the Pacific—which, to my thinking, is not a compliment. Perhaps it was my loneliness, but I found the place to be unattractive and crowded, and the French people foul-smelling. I was anxious to leave as soon as the damaged mainsail was repaired.

Fortunately, there was a sailmaker not far from the marina who could do the repair. It took him over a week to double-stitch the reef points. As soon as the sail was fixed, I would waste not another minute saying *Au revoir* to New Caledonia. Australia was my next destination—a passage of nearly 773 nautical miles, as the crow flies, to the west. (Although it would take me over 900 sailing miles to get there, and I don't think a crow has ever made the trip.)

I had been watching the weather on a fax machine in the marina office, and what I saw did not bode well for getting New Caledonia hastily astern. It seemed like every three days another strong storm system would develop in the Southern Ocean and would work its way up across the Tasman Sea between New Zealand and Australia, traveling in a northerly direction, straight for New Caledonia. The Tasman Sea has a worldwide reputation for being a vicious body of water. The bad news was that there was no alternative to reach Australia without crossing the northern portion of the Tasman. The good news was that my course would be west by southwest, so I should not be hitting the storms head-on. Still, there was no way I could make the seven- to ten-day crossing without encountering some adverse weather. No doubt about it: I was going to get my ass kicked . . . again!

I stayed in the marina, hating every minute of it, waiting for a favorable weather window to appear. The best weather forecast is only accurate five days out. After five days, it's a crapshoot. Every evening, I listened to John talking to cruisers on the Auckland Cruising Club radio schedule. Some boats reported favorable conditions; most, though, were fighting their way through frontal systems. One boat reported being dismasted 380 miles out of Sydney and was requesting assistance to help get them to shore. I found such reports to be disconcerting, at best.

Finally, after six excruciating days of waiting, I saw the weather window I had been praying for. With little ado, I untied the dock lines and slipped out of New Caledonia at ten after five the next morning. My first challenge: clearing Dumbéa pass leading to the open ocean. From the harbor, it took three hours of motor-sailing just to reach the narrow pass. It wasn't until I got there that it dawned on me that I'd been so preoccupied with the weather forecasts that I had neglected to check the tide tables . . . and lo and behold, the tide was streaming in through the pass at about six knots; the wind was blowing directly in my face at fifteen knots. I cranked little FUJIMO up to his maximum RPMs, hoping to creating enough speed and momentum to overcome the wind and tide and power through the pass.

It was a useless attempt.

I considered using the wind to my advantage by trying to sail through, but the pass was so narrow that there wasn't enough room to tack. (With the wind on Sundance's nose, I would have had to sail a zigzag course.) I let the wind and tide push us back away from the pass, and stood there watching it recede from view like a little kid who's accidentally let go of his helium balloon. I wanted to cry. My attempt at clearing Dumbéa Pass had been another dumpster fire to add to my record.

I had no choice but to do a 180-degree turn and point Sundance in the direction of the marina. I felt like a complete failure. Nothing in this world even approaches the ocean when it comes to making me look pathetic.

I sulked around the marina, licking my wounds and watching the weather for five more days, until another favorable forecast finally appeared. This time, after checking the tide tables, I left the dock at 9:00 AM with the goal of reaching Dumbéa Pass just as the tide would be ebbing. I got there right before noon, and to my delight, the tidal current was pulling me toward the sea. I was amazed at how easy it was to exit the pass when tugged along by a six-knot current.

In anticipation of eventually encountering some rude weather, I had programmed the GPS with three destinations in Australia. My rendezvous with Sally, and later with Jungle, would be in Brisbane, so its entrance, Moreton Bay, would be my first choice. I wasn't feeling picky enough to argue with the weather, so I'd be happy to land wherever the winds pushed me. In the interest of comfort, I wanted to sail on a reach, rather than beat to weather. With the prevailing winds coming from the south, I selected three towns, each a little more north than the other. The first choice was Moreton Bay, the most southerly of the three; but Bundaberg and Gladstone further north would be just fine by me.

My prolonged layover in New Caledonia had done little to alter my thinking about wrapping up my adventure. Ironically, I had come to feel less lonely when I was out on the open ocean than among strangers, but still, my homesickness grounded away at me constantly. As I made my way toward Australia, I became increasingly certain that this would be my last passage. The girls' visit in Fiji had left me bereft, more like a mourner than a happy-go-lucky adventurer. I found myself fantasizing about making arrangements in Australia to have the boat shipped back to San Diego.

One thing I know for certain: if you decide to chase a dream, it had better be compatible with your personality. Most of the single-handed sailors I have met are introverts. They enjoy their time alone and are not very comfortable around other people. Their family ties are not particularly strong, if they have any at all; and while I was coming to appreciate the solitude of the open ocean—preferring it to being lonely in a crowd—my basic personality makeup is that of an extrovert. I am not naturally drawn to a solitary lifestyle. What I love most about life are my family and my friends. All during my voyaging, I had felt happy only a handful of times that did not involve sharing the adventure with the significant people in my life. There was no question left in my mind as to whether I would much rather be home with the family I love so much than out here sailing around the world.

The final remaining consideration was whether I could find peace within myself if I abandoned this dream before achieving my stated goal of sailing around the world.

In New Caledonia, waiting for the sail repair and then for the weather, I had highlighted a passage in George Day's column, *Captain's Log*:

> The sailing life is among the purest expressions of what's best about the human spirit. Sailing over the horizon to faraway islands involves every aspect of our minds and bodies. It involves a high degree of organization and planning, resourcefulness and problem solving. It engages our practical natures by forcing us to deal with complex sailing vessels and their systems; with navigation, weather forecasting and the intricacies of sail trim.
>
> Sailing teaches us to be ever alert to danger. The sea is an unforgiving mistress and can kill you if you come unprepared.
>
> Along this journey of self-reliance and independence, sailing far offshore stirs deeper pools. The experience may change you. You get that faraway look in your eye; a sense of calm at the center, an uncommon disassociation from the opinions of others. You have become more entirely yourself.

That much was true: I had, through the pursuit of solitude and self-reliance, become more entirely myself. So much so that I was beginning to think I could go home and not feel like a quitter, a coward, or a failure. I was beginning to acknowledge that I had proven to myself the main things that needed proving: that I could hack it out on here on my own, that I could weather storms, equipment failures, and navigational challenges. That I could do something stupid and then get up the next day and try again. That I could deal with loneliness and frustration. With all that under my belt, stopping the trip short was beginning to seem like a practical decision that I could boil down to cold logic: A) What's most important to me is being with my family; B) I'm sixty-one years old and not getting any younger, therefore: C) If I want to do what's most important to me in life, I'd better get home soon before I run out of time.

For the first three days of my passage, the gods withheld any violent weather. The winds were mainly light—too light at times. I had to twist the key on FUJIMO and motor-sail at five point two knots, covering less than a hundred miles a day. It was comfortable going, but agonizingly slow. And then, to my consternation, the wind suddenly filled in, blasting so strong that I could barely control the boat, unfortunately, it didn't last. Just when I'd settled into a new course, the wind would shift direction, still howling like crazy, and pull me off course . . . and then would die, which meant I'd have to start FUJIMO up again. The pattern repeated itself again and again. I was either gritting my teeth and muttering for the wind to blow or clinging to the wheel for dear life as waves crashed over the bow and swells smacked on the beam up and down, back and forth, relentless. There was simply no happy medium.

I had gotten smarter about adapting to life at sea, and had written out a daily routine. At first light, I would:

- Update course on chart
- Check GPS for miles covered last twenty-four hours
- Adjust course for XTE (cross track error)
- Check weather forecast
- Talk on SSB sked
- Listen to Voice of America or BBC news
- Read & send e-mail
- Walk the deck
- Check for chafing, lines, and sails
- Clean the flying fish off the deck
- Wash down deck with seawater
- Check all fluid levels of autopilot, batteries, and engine while running
- Shower with garden sprayer, every day, whether I needed it or not
- Eat breakfast. Eat lots of fruit. Drink lots of water.

For the first couple days, I stuck to it. The routine did wonders for my mental health, even if I had to postpone or interrupt
some of the tasks because of the unpredictable weather conditions.

I was still in touch with the radio sked out of Aukland, and
looked forward to the broadcasts both day and night. It helped
me deal with being so isolated and vulnerable to hear a friendly
voice, to know that someone out there knew where I was and
was concerned with my well-being.

It was during the radio sked on the evening of July nine-
teenth, just two days into the passage, that John announced, "*Sundance*, you have a large frontal system moving your way! You will
feel its effects within the next six hours. Better batten down the
hatches. All of the best to you, mate."

I felt like an unprepared student who's been unexpectedly
called on in class. With a sudden burst of butterflies in my stomach, I replied, "Roger that, Big John. Talk to you in the morning,
I hope. This is *Sundance* and we're out."

I had tried to sound cool, but I wasn't feeling very cool. I
could sense every muscle in my body starting to contract. The
inside of my mouth felt like I'd been snacking on sandpaper and
I honestly thought that I might throw up. This might be a replay
of the storm that had torn the reefs out of my sail—or it might
be something far worse. I hadn't liked John's tone when he told
me about the storm. Was I just imagining it, or had he sounded
like he never expected to hear from me again?

Oh, crap—once again, no place to run, no place to hide. I desperately wanted to be any place but here; I wanted to run home to
my mom. Yet, this was where I was, and the storm was coming
whether I wanted it to or not. I had felt isolated and vulnerable
before the radio call, but now those feelings were magnified a
million times. This was going to be a true test of my resolve.

I went below to make certain everything was tied down
tightly, and I slowly and systematically secured every window and
hatch. I neatly arranged all the necessary foul-weather gear, even
digging out a heavy duty PFD (personal flotation device) that
had not see the light of day for the last 4,000 miles. I checked

to make sure the EPIRB (Emergency Position Indicating Radio Beacon) was fired up and in its position next to the cabin bulkhead, where I could reach it if necessary. I stared at it there. The only time the EPIRB is activated is in a life-or-death emergency. The device sends out the GPS location of the vessel in distress. If the storm smashed us to splinters, at least the authorities would find what was left of *Sundance* and my body. That was comforting!

When I came back on deck, the clear cloudless day gave way to a bright orange sunset in the west. In the east, the top of a yellow moon was climbing up out of the ocean. I was awestruck by the epic ambivalence of such beauty juxtaposed with my human frailty. Where else could one see such an incredibly beautiful sight, all the while holding one's breathe in anticipation of getting crushed by a killer storm?

I shortened sail by putting two reefs in the main, furled in the headsail to halfway and brought in the staysail by twenty-five percent. The mizzen sail was down, secured to her boom. I took a long look at the life raft secured on the stern, and hoped it would never have the opportunity to taste the ocean.

As night fell in earnest, the seas began gradually building, and a smear of cloud cover shrouded the moon, and then blotted it out completely. Now the air felt cooler, and then cold, as the wind steadied up.

Showtime.

I glanced at my watch. Auckland John had been spot-on; it was now 1:00 AM, exactly six hours from when we had spoken. I braced myself, and Neptune threw his first punch, a twenty-five-knot blow of bone-chilling wind just off the port bow. *Sundance* poked her head up into the breeze, seemingly anxious for a run after three days of light wind. I buckled down and guided her along, watching the wind speed indicator slash its way up to fifty-four knots.

I can only estimate the size of the seas, but I'm certain they were at least twice as high as a basketball rim, twenty, or perhaps, twenty-five feet. Their tops blew off in clouds of spray like cotton candy, and the ocean was completely covered with white foam. When I dared sneak a look to windward, out from under the dodger, all I could see was a wall of black water, its summit somewhere high above us, invisible. *Ho-ly shit.* I didn't know if *Sundance* would manage to ride up and over the wave or if tons and tons of water were about to crash down on us, driving us straight to the bottom of the ocean.

I was sailing just close enough to the wind that I could ride up the leading edge of those huge rollers. To my relief, *Sundance* did struggle all the way up to the top of the wave, but once there, she dropped off the back side with such force that it felt like this twenty-two-ton vessel had taken up skydiving, freefalling down the surface of the wave until we crashed into the bottom of the trough like an applecart. We were unhurt, somehow. But no time to reflect: time to do the same thing over again, because here comes the next wave; just as big, and just as evil. If I made even a slight miscalculation and fell too far off the wind, the mammoth wave would smash into *Sundance* amidships instead of at her bow, with all the force of a guided missile, and we would certainly end up with the mast pointing at the seabed.

Every single new wave was a fresh challenge, requiring my full attention. There was a rough pattern to them, but not a true one; no two waves would be exactly alike, and to assume that they were might possibly mean the end. Each time a powerful gust would hit, I would ease the bow to weather (into the wind), spilling some of the force of the wind off the sails and preparing to labor our way up the next edifice.

The roar of the wind and sea were deafening. The rain pummeled my face, making it impossible at times to see what was coming ahead. I was standing in three feet of water, the little cockpit drains woefully insufficient to handle this kind of deluge. A more experienced bluewater sailor may have handled the situation differently, but I had no way of knowing exactly how. This was only my second time sailing through a massive storm alone, so I could only do my best and follow my instincts. Back in San

Diego, *Sundance* had seemed impossibly big; right now, I thought she was ridiculously small to be out here fighting such a huge storm.

I had no choice but to tune out the stream of what-ifs that threatened to drive me crazy. What if a shroud (support cable) gives way? The mast will come crashing down. What if the next big wave breaks on top of me? It will flatten me for sure. What if the rudder falls off? I'll lose control of the boat and we'll capsize. What if a rogue wave washes me overboard? Then I will die a truly awful death, terrified and alone out here in the middle of the dark, churning ocean. I was getting better at silencing that inner dialogue, but such thoughts managed to sneak in at times, despite my discipline. Each of those contingencies was beyond my control, so there was nothing to do but plan for the worst while hoping for the best.

The wind was playing tricks with me. It would slack off, die down a bit, making me think the storm was subsiding. Then, just as I was taking a deep breath and beginning to relax, another sixty-four-mile-per-hour blast would scream through *Sundance's* shrouds, fast eliminating any thoughts of the storm being over. The Sleeping Giant was laughing at me, toying with his victim.

I began sassing him to lift my spirits, to keep up my side of the fight. "Hey, Mr. Giant, why are you so pissed off at me? You're acting like I kicked your dog or said something bad about your fat-ass mother." Another blast of fierce wind. "Okay, just kidding about your mother. I'm sure she's lovely." On and on the storm raged, and on and on I jabbered, like a madman: "Can you just chill out even a little? Come on. Back off, man. Give me a break. Let me get through to Australia, and I'll get off your ugly back once and for all."

The storm finally blew itself out in the pre-dawn hours. Its ferocious winds dropped to a manageable twenty knots, but the waves were not ready to give up the fight. They remained ugly for the rest of the day, with great iron lumps of sea crashing over the bow, combined with vicious cross swells.

After being on the helm fighting the storm for six hours and sleeping for fifteen minutes at a time for the past three days, I was beat, physically and emotionally. I desperately needed some sleep. I wanted to collapse and enjoy my victory over the Giant's best shot. But first I needed to walk the deck to survey the damage. I pushed the button to engage the autopilot, just as I had done countless times before over the past 9,000 miles. There was no response. Nothing happened. Zip. Nada. *What the fuck!*

It's telling of my utter exhaustion that I actually had the thought, *Well, maybe I pushed the button incorrectly.* I shook my head around for a minute like one of the Three Stooges, trying to jiggle my brain back into line, and tried it again, and then again, with still no response. An ominous message appeared on the small screen: RUDDER RESPONSE ERROR!

This meant that the autopilot and the rudder were not communicating. Great. This was a first. I had no idea what could possibly be causing it. Then I remembered that I had a backup autopilot—I had never needed it since leaving San Diego and had nearly forgotten that it even existed. I flicked its switch, but once again nothing happened. Dead. Okay, time to panic.

I tried to swallow down my dread. Above all else, I had to remain calm and assess my situation. What might "rudder response error" mean? Well, for one thing, it could be that the rudder had been damaged during the storm. I turned the wheel, cocking my head and listening. Something felt different, out of sorts; the boat wasn't reacting as quickly as it normally does. Yes. I decided that something was definitely wrong. I felt my concern ratchet up to a mild panic. Fuck: If the storm had done extensive damage to the rudder or the rudder post, was the damn rudder about to fall off, leaving me unable to steer my boat?

This was one of my worst "what-ifs." I knew I had to get down in the water and inspect the rudder, which meant leaving the helm, which meant using the autopilot—which of course, was broken. If I let go of the helm, the boat would be at the mercy of the wind, fall off course, and eventually sit with her beam taking the brunt of the huge waves—maybe even taking one strong enough to roll her over and capsize her.

Think man, think. My head was sluggish; I wasn't feeling very creative. I grabbed two lengths of elastic cord and tied them around the wheel to hold it steady. Then I stood and watched, wanting to make sure it worked before I got down in the water. My cob job managed to hold the wheel in place for only three or four minutes before the strength of the waves forced the boat off course. As soon as that happened, the sails filled with unwanted wind and off we went, crashing through the waves in the wrong direction as I fought to free the wheel from the elastic cord. I got *Sundance* faced back into the wind and tried again . . . same damn thing. Tying down the wheel was not an acceptable solution.

This was unfathomable. I stood there, feeling as though my heart was being deprived of blood. *Try something,* I told myself. There's a technique called heaving to, which is used by sailors in emergencies. To heave to, you sheet in the mainsail and back-wind the staysail such that the bow of the boat rides into the wind and stays locked there. It's not a technique for moving, but rather for treading water, as it were, while you get your shit to-gether and see to your emergency. I tried heaving to.

It didn't work. *Sundance* refused to ride bow to the wind, like she was supposed to. Sitting dead in the water, getting pounded by huge waves was not tolerable. For more than an hour, I tried a series of different sail combinations, always with the same miser-able result: ending up with the beam to the seas. It was painfully obvious that I should have practiced this maneuver to perfection before finding myself in an emergency situation in the middle of the Tasman Sea. *I have been terribly negligent, and now I am paying the price for my incompetence.*

No. Drop the negative thoughts. I can do this. I can do this. Do what, exactly? There wasn't much to do but keep trying to heave to, or simply stay at the fragile helm and keep the boat pointed the right way as long as the rudder remained connected to the boat. At last, hours later, the seas lay down and the wind fell light. I was finally able to lash down the helm and move about the boat.

The first thing I did was call Sally on the satellite phone. I needed to hear her voice and take from it what confidence I could muster.

"Hello Honey," I said. "How are you today?"

"Oh, things are all right. Took Sedona to the vet."

"Everything okay?"

"Just his checkup. How are things with you?"

"Well. To be honest with you, I'm in kind of in a pickle."

"Oh, my God. What's the matter, Michael?"

"Now hold on. It's not that bad. I'm partway to Australia and I just weathered a big storm and I'm tired and it looks like my autopilot is broken and I think there's something wrong with my rudder."

"What does that mean?"

"Right now it just means that I can't leave the helm. I have to keep steering and I'm tired and I need to sleep."

"Oh."

"But there's a chance that the rudder might get worse. So I want you to take down my coordinates just in case I end up needing help, okay, baby?"

There was a long pause, and her voice was very quiet when she answered. "Yes. Tell me the coordinates."

I gave them to her.

"Michael, what else can I do?"

We had made some boating friends in Tahiti, a couple who live in Australia. I asked her to let them know I might need some help, especially if the rudder did indeed fall off.

"I'll call them. What else?"

"Nothing, baby. I'm sure everything will be just fine. But I'll call you back in an hour to see if you've heard from Australia."

"Michael, please be careful. I love you."

"I love you, too, baby. Talk to you in an hour."

I felt better already. Just hearing myself describe the situation had made it seem a lot less dire. I sailed on for an hour, and then called Sally back to see what our Aussie friends had found out. The news was not good. They had been told by the Australian

Coast Guard that I was too far out for them to provide any assistance. I was on my own. I felt my stomach tighten as chills ran through my body, any shred of confidence leaching away. I was scared to death, to think there was no one to help bail me out of this mess.

Still, I tried to sound cheerful. "All right, baby. No big deal. Just a minor crisis that I'll have to handle on my own." We agreed I would check in with her at least once a day.

After I hung up, I was gripped by a feeling of utter isolation and helplessness that manifested in a kind of paralysis, as if all of my major organs had collectively ceased functioning. I wanted to climb through the phone to be home with Sally and Sedona, sitting in my leather recliner watching a football game.

Without a rudder, steering a boat is pretty much impossible. It would be like a car without a steering wheel, or a bike without handlebars. You just can't get from point A to point B without the ability to steer. I had recently heard a report on the SSB radio about a fifty-five-foot sailboat that lost its rudder after hitting a reef. The crew of four improvised a temporary rudder by using the oars from their dinghy and other stuff they had on their boat. But because steering the boat was so difficult with the temporary rudder, it took fourteen days for them to cover a distance that would normally have taken three days. There were four of them, so they could steer in shifts; I was all alone, and was beginning this challenge already stone-tired from three days at sea and a massive storm. The specter of the difficult days ahead sprawled like an eternal torment—no end in sight. Almost any challenge at sea can seem tolerable if it's guaranteed to end that very day, or at least, within the next few days, on the anchor in a flat lagoon. But this sail was far from over, and I was already so tired and worn down that I wanted to puke.

Once the seas finally calmed down, it was critical that I evaluate the damage to the rudder. Again I lashed the wheel and set about the task. First, I would check to see if the rudder post was secure, and I didn't have to get off the boat to do that. The top of the rudder post was located at the very bottom of a stern storage locker, about four feet down. The stern locker was akin to a garage where we store the stuff we never use and want to keep out of sight. After pulling out a heap of gear, some of which I had forgotten was even on the boat, I finally reached the rudder post. Everything appeared to be in proper working order: nothing loose, nothing out of the ordinary. It took me an hour to repack all the gear into the stern garage.

When I was finished, I stood scratching my head, not wanting to contemplate what was next. I had half hoped to find a problem with the rudder post, because the only way to make sure the rudder itself was secure was to go down into the water. Damn, I did not want to go swimming alone.

But I had no choice. There was simply no alternative; and with the seas gone flat and no wind, there would never be a better time than right now. Muttering a constant stream of curse words, I went about securing the mainsail to the boom, furling the headsails in tightly, and untying the helm so that the rudder could move freely. Still cussing, I dug out a pair of diving fins, a mask, a snorkel, and put them on. I tied two dock lines together as a tether, attaching one end firmly to my left wrist and the other to an aft cleat. I stood for a moment on the rail, checking over my setup, and then I looked around me at the vast ocean. Jesus, it was a vast, ugly, dark abyss and looked scary as hell. I jumped in.

The rudder sits four feet below the surface of the water at the very stern of the boat. It's large; maybe four feet long by three feet wide. I eased myself down along *Sundance*'s side, my limbs tingling with the wrongness of being in this water alone. At the transom, I took a deep breath and plunged underwater, using the hull for leverage to get low enough to grab the rudder with both hands. With all my strength, I pulled and I pushed against the rudder, half expecting it to twist free of the boat and disappear toward the ocean floor . . . but it seemed sound. I let go and bobbed up to the surface, where I sucked air. After a moment, I repeated the operation, twisting and yanking the rudder in all directions, searching for any sign of weakness. There were none; the rudder didn't budge. It wasn't going to fall off after all; it was solid. I must have imagined a change in the feel of the helm. I was angry with myself for imagining a problem where there was none, but mostly just relieved that I wasn't going to lose the rudder.

Once safely back on the boat, I took new stock of my situation. I was without an autopilot, but it appeared I could count on having a rudder for the foreseeable future. Best thing to do was get some sleep, and then when my head was clear, I could work on the autopilot problem. I used my handy garden sprayer to take a quick freshwater shower, put on some clean clothes, wolfed down a peanut butter and jelly sandwich, and crashed. I had been awake for the past twenty-four hours; it took me about one second to fall asleep.

Forty-five minutes later, I was rudely awakened by the violent movement of the boat. The lull in the weather hadn't lasted; the Sleeping Giant had grabbed a power nap of his own and was gearing up for another round. The seas were building, the wind freshened. It was time to run up the main and let out the headsails, use this weather to gain some ground. It was 585 straight-line miles to the Australian coast.

I lashed the wheel and pawed around inside the cabin until I found the long-forgotten instruction manual for the autopilot in the stack I had been meaning to read. Frantically, I started scanning the pages, desperately hoping to solve the rudder response error problem. I found nothing there that was of any help.

The autopilot is one of the most essential pieces of equipment on a bluewater boat, especially for a single-handed sailor. It is the equivalent of having another person on board to steer. The autopilot had been successfully guiding the boat every day and every night since setting sail in San Diego. It was only necessary for me to take the helm in bad weather and when entering a pass or a harbor; I only hand-steered when I wanted to. When it came time to purchase a steering device for *Sundance*, I had faced a number of choices. Knowing the autopilot is such a significant piece of equipment, I chose to buy the most powerful, most expensive hydraulic unit available, one that produced enough power to steer a tugboat. The installation was a major operation, taking days for a professional to accomplish. The total cost for parts and installation was $8,334. I am a firm believer in having a backup for everything, even a backup for the backup in some cases. With that in mind, I had an auxiliary wheel-type autopilot installed that cost more than $2,000. At the time, I'd been perfectly happy to spend over $10,000 for the peace of mind, knowing I would never be without a working autopilot. And now look: Both of these expensive and essential pieces of gear were dysfunctional. I was in a heap of trouble, and would be forced to hand-steer my boat, unable to leave the helm, twenty-four hours a day.

I was aware of a maneuver sailors used for centuries to bring a boat under control during a storm and get some relief from the helm. It's called "heave to." It's a relatively simple technique of adjusting the sails and helm so the boat slows down, but keeps moving through the water at a safe speed without the need to hand-steer.

Unfortunately, I had never experienced the need to heave to in all my years of coastal sailing. The only heaving I have done was to heave my lunch overboard. And, mega-unfortunately, I never learned how to accomplish this relatively simple maneuver. I tired adjusting the sails and the helm over and over to no avail. The huge twenty-four-foot waves crashed against the side of the boat with such strength that I was in danger of capsizing. This calamity was not the fault of my boat, but rather a result of operator error. I had no clue how to heave to. I am such a dumb ass! Lashing down the wheel might hold her on course for five minutes, max. In a light wind, while motor-sailing, the lashed-down wheel might maintain a steady course for a max of fifteen minutes. At the end of another exhausting day, so tired that my head felt flattened, I took stock of my situation: Australia still lay more than 500 miles away. How the hell was I going to eat, sleep, read the GPS, navigate, keep the chart updated, make sail adjustments, go to the bathroom, talk on the radio sked, and make my daily call to Sally, all the while staying awake and steering the boat? *Oh, I am in a heap of trouble!*

· · ·

For the next eighteen hours, the wind remained light and variable, with a medium-sized sea of five to six feet. Taking advantage of the benign conditions, I dropped the main, furled in the headsail most of the way, and attempted to sleep, eat, wash, talk to Big John in New Zealand, and make my daily call to Sally to reassure her that I was still alive. Suddenly, it seemed do-able. I could make it to Australia; all I needed was for the weather to cooperate.

And that's about when the first of a progression of punishing storms slammed into my beautiful boat with a vengeance. My peaceful day of being productive was soon a distant memory. I stood at the helm for hours at a time fighting the storms, then steered sitting down until my butt went to sleep, then stood back up as long as I could, then sat back down again. Trimming the sails and steering *Sundance* was the extent of my physical movement in the cockpit day after day. Stand up, sit down, stand up, sit down, steer the boat. Only very rarely could I lie down and sleep, and when I could, it was in fifteen-minute intervals that kept me barely sane but provided no real rest.

This chain of storms coming up from the Southern Ocean would kick ass for twelve to fourteen hours at a time, then subside for a few hours before the next one blustered in. Fortunately, they were not as substantial as the initial mammoth storm that had caused the autopilot to fail. They blew at about twenty-five to thirty knots, with seas of ten to twelve feet, but maintained a nasty swell. They were not epic, but they were big enough to require my undivided attention, and I was beginning to experience signs of severe mental stress. The human body and psyche simply cannot handle sustained life-or-death concentration and immobility for that long without beginning to break down.

Eating was an adventure in itself. If the wind was light, I

would lash down the helm with shock cords, slack off the sheets, scurry into the cabin, grab an MRE and a small bag of instant rice, and then hustle back to the wheel. I generally had less than a minute to accomplish this maneuver before the boat would move off the wind. When I returned to the helm, I would correct the steering, trim in the sails, and get *Sundance* facing the right direction again. Unzipping my foul, weather jacket, I would place the MRE in one armpit and the bag of rice in the other, and then wait about thirty minutes for them to warm up. Taking the MRE out first, I would rip off an opening with my teeth, spit out the little piece of plastic, then stick the MRE in my mouth and squirt in a good-sized bite, then return it to the armpit/warming oven. But it wasn't time to start chewing yet; I had to go through the same process with the rice, out of the other armpit. Once the rice was combined in my mouth with what tasted like Alpo from the MRE, it was dinner time. Mm-mm, good.

Imagine for a moment, if you will, what it would be like to stand or sit in the exact same spot for twenty-four hours a day for five days and nights. My mind would wander off, thinking about anything to take me away from my despondency. I thought about all the cars I have owned; starting with the black 1932 Ford three-window coupe. It was chopped and channeled with a red full race four-cylinder engine. I was fourteen years old and bought it for $200 that I'd earned as a caddy. I was the coolest kid in the ninth grade. Gas cost twenty-four cents a gallon at the Gulf station where my dad worked part-time. Oh, how I wished I still owned that car. Then I thought of the next car, and the next, all the way up to the present day, every car from my past parading down the Main Street of my imagination.

I then threw another parade, this one featuring every woman I had ever made love to. Sweet Mary Anne, a cheerleader at Ann Arbor high school, was the very first, bounding ahead of the pack with her pompoms shaking in celebration. Ah, yes. I spent hours reliving each one of those wonderful experiences, concluding, of course, with my beautiful Sally.

The food parade was almost as good as the parade of women,

although it was less organized. I couldn't celebrate everything I'd ever eaten, so I just let myself to daydream about what my next meal would be once I made it to Australia. The most persistent fantasy was devouring a huge traditional Thanksgiving Day turkey dinner with all the trimmings. I could taste the moist turkey, the pucker of the cranberry sauce, and the steaming spices of the dressing. A chili-cheese hot dog with mustard was high on the list as well . . . and ice cream. Oh, how I love ice cream. Back home, I ate a generous helping of it every night. Chocolate malt would taste great right about now . . . and pizza would be good too! One thing was certain: once I got off this boat, I would never, ever eat another MRE!

I also enjoyed playing a game called "Where Would I Rather Be?" As in, what would I most prefer to be doing rather than suffering on this fucking boat? This was a question that took up a lot of my time, since it was really a question about my future, not just a celebration of the past. It was like two cellmates who talk about what they'll do when they get out. As I whiled away the hours, a primary consideration in my thinking emerged: I didn't want to be alone anymore. I just didn't. No more solo anything. I thought it would be cool to buy a big bus, something like Willie Nelson's old tour bus. Sally, Sedona, and the grandkids would all pile in and we would travel all around the country stopping at rodeos and big balls of twine, eating bologna sandwiches, and going hiking. We could sleep whenever we wanted to; we could eat whenever we felt like it. That was another thing: it was important that I be in control of my environment.

After a while, the tour-bus fantasy gave way to something even more attractive: I would purchase a cottage on a lake in northern Michigan. When I was a kid, the days spent "going out to the lake" were the most fun part of my youth. Imagine all my loved ones gathered at the lake house, sleeping in, and coffee on the deck, taking the kids fishing and waterskiing. Of all the escapist fantasies I entertained, this one was the single most gratifying, the one that served to motivate me to survive this terrifying ordeal.

It was on my fourth night of imprisonment at the helm that I saw the old woman perched up on my boat. She sat with her back up against the mast, her knees pulled up against her chest, and arms wrapped around her legs. She had a large hooked nose, wore a black hat with a big brim, and clinched a pipe between her teeth. I stared at her for awhile, wondering where she'd come from and how she'd gotten on my boat.

That's a ghost, you idiot. You shouldn't look at her.

I tried to avert my gaze, and managed to avoid looking at her for a minute, but it was storming and she was sitting just where I needed to look.

She was still there. What the hell was happening, is she a ghost? "Ma'am," I shouted through the wind, "as long as you're here and you don't seem to be very busy, would you mind taking a turn on the helm? I'm just so god-awful tired."

She didn't answer me. Was she deaf? I yelled at her again, "Hey," I said, "There are no free rides on this boat. Get your ugly ass back here and steer." Bullying didn't help, so I went back to pleading. "Please take the helm," I said. "Please, ma'am. I need to go the bathroom, really bad. And I'm starving." She never even acknowledged me. I couldn't understand why she was being so unsociable; after all, she was a guest on my boat. When I thought of it that way, it really pissed me off. I wasn't going to tolerate this bullshit. So I gave her an ultimatum. "If you don't come back here and take the helm right this minute, I am going to kick you off my boat." The next time I looked forward, she was gone, and I missed her sorely.

Not long afterward, I lifted my emptied-out head right in time to see the red and green navigational lights of a ship just off the bow, seconds away from plowing into us. Holy shit! To avoid a collision, I swung the wheel over so violently that the sails caught air on the back side. I looked up and the lights were gone. I whirled around and scanned the dark sea behind me; no ship. Now I had to struggle to get back on course before I was completely back-winded and heading off in the wrong direction. Just as soon as I was back on course, another mystery ship loomed out of the darkness right in front of me, and I again yanked the wheel to avoid a crash. This continued on and on through the night. As soon as one of the phantom vessels was gone, I would see the lights of another ship. After the third such close encounter, I thought, "I must be getting close to a port to have all this shipping activity going on." I actually used the VHF radio to hail the ghost ships, but of course they never answered. I had surely entered the twilight zone, but the ships appeared so lifelike that I had no choice but to treat them like the real thing, in the off chance that one of them wasn't a hallucination—which jangled my nerves worse than ever.

Then my hat began talking to me. I have a yellow south-wester, a wide-brimmed fisherman's hat that I've been wearing while sailing for over thirty years. Voices started to talk to me from inside my old hat. Actually, they weren't so much talking to *me* as just talking—it was a little bit like being in the bathroom at a cocktail party and hearing the burble of conversation from behind a closed door. I caught little snatches of mundane, ultimately meaningless conversation, things like, "Not enough to really make a difference," or, "That's really my point, if you'd think about what I'm saying."

When I first heard the voices, I took my hat off and shook it like a witch doctor driving out spirits, then plopped it back on my head. The voices continued. "Well, that's strange," I thought. "Thirty years I've had this hat, and this is the first time it's had voices in it." *What the hell is going on?* The voices came and went, mostly during the night, but I never engaged them in conversation. My acoustic system was obviously picking up something from the local stimuli and interpreting it as something that, in reality, did not exist. Part of my brain was trying to convince the rest of my brain that the hallucinations were not a major problem; but with old ladies appearing against the mast, phantom ships looming out of the dark, and babbling voices emanating from my hat, I was finding it plenty difficult to distinguish imagination from reality.

• • •

After five days of storms, even the fantasies tapered off, and were replaced by monotonous agony. I could feel the fight slipping out of me. Physically, mentally, and emotionally, I was depleted. When this trouble had begun, I had taken deep breaths and reassured myself that things were going to be fine. There was a need to put this mess in the proper perspective, and it had become my practice to know the difference between a temporary inconvenience and a real problem. So I told myself to just take it one day at a time. After two days, I had to narrow my focus and tell myself to take it one hour at a time. During the night of the fourth day, fighting my way through the teeth of a vicious storm, I was begging myself to just get through the next moment. Circumstances had collapsed such that I had to fight like hell just to convince myself to carry on into the next minute. Gone was my perspective on this situation as a temporary inconvenience; it had deteriorated into a problem of epic proportions. This was a problem that was quite likely to kill me.

During that night, the clouds off the bow spread open like torn muslin, and I peered through swollen eyelids at a small bit of reflection off of the moon on the water. *Sail to the light*, I kept telling myself. *Sail to the light. Just get through the next moment.* I had not felt a need to pray in some time, maybe thirty-five years. But, as the boat shuddered up the waves and then crashed down the back sides, always one false move away from a capsize, I started chanting Hail Marys and Our Fathers; I was convinced I would not live to see the sun come up.

Not knowing if you are going to live or die, day after day, alone in the middle of the Tasman Sea, is a trauma no one should ever have to endure. This was worse than my situation with DH. At least on that passage, I had always felt like I had a certain degree of control over my destiny. My adversary was made up of flesh and blood; I could see him, touch him, and fight him to the death, if necessary. My predicament at the moment was much more serious. How do I fight the Sleeping Giant? How do I fight complete mental and physical exhaustion? How do I reverse the effects of sleep deprivation? The only way to beat exhaustion is to sleep, and if I fell asleep, I would die. This enemy was simply unbeatable.

I have to face reality. I am fading fast. I am hanging on with my last bit of strength. When you're reading about someone clinging on to life, it's easy to imagine them thinking of their loved ones, their motivations to go on fighting. And it's true that I was not ready to die, that I wanted to live on and be with Sally and my daughters. But you would be surprised at how difficult it is to conjure up your loved ones when you are going crazy from sleep deprivation and your entire reality has become nothing than empty sky, threatening seas, and repetitive tasks. Sometimes I had to squeeze my eyes shut to remember a receding reality that had featured Sally and my girls—I felt like a hundred-year-old man trying to remember and be motivated by his childhood. When I was successful, I could hear my grandkids laugh, feel them hugging me around my neck, see them running and playing, and it was like a shot of medicine to my thinking. *Yes. I need to show Sally how very much I love her and to tell I am sorry for being such a selfish asshole. I can't die until I do that much.*

No, I refuse to accept death alone out here on the ocean.

I had to sleep. After the storm died off, the wind grew light, so I sat down and stabilized the wheel with my feet. I put one boot on the wheel spokes on the left and the other on a spoke to the right. Steering with my feet allowed me to lean back on my favorite large blue boat cushion. In this position, I could nod off and catch some blissful shut-eye, until the fierce movement of the boat would jolt me back into semi-consciousness. When it did, I would make the necessary course corrections by adjusting the position of my feet on the helm, then slip back to sleep for another five, ten or maybe, fifteen minutes. For the time being, I wasn't concerned with direction, speed, or sail trim. My primary concern was to get some sleep—that, and to keep the boat upright. But I knew that in my present condition, it was just a matter of time before I would make a serious mistake that would be fatal. This was the scariest night of my life.

Hours later, I watched ecstatically as pink, and then orange light came moving up the sky from the east. I was mesmerized by the miracle of dawn as if I'd never seen it before, the first blessed orange limb of the sun creeping up from the pewter-colored ocean; maybe this nightmare was coming to an end. Once the sun lifted clear of the sea, I screamed to it, "I'm still here!"

By midmorning, all traces of the storms were gone; the water lay as flat as Death Valley, not one whitecap in sight, not a whisper of wind . . . all of the sails flogged aimlessly. I pulled down the mainsail and tied it to the boom, then tightly furled both head-sails. I turned the key to wake up FUJIMO, and we were off, gliding over the flat ocean with less than a hundred miles to reach Moreton Bay. Now, when I lashed the helm with shock cord, it stayed put for as long as a whopping twenty minutes. This gave me enough time to shower with my sprayer and eat some wonderful MREs. Already I could feel my strength coming back. I was back in the game. I picked up the satellite phone and dialed Sally. "Baby," I said, my voice hoarse, "I'm going to make it into Brisbane tonight."

As I continued on toward Moreton Bay, I made contact on the VHF radio with a boating couple I had meet in New Caledonia that had been on its way to Brisbane. I was pleased to learn that they were indeed in Moreton Bay, and they were anxious to help in any way possible. We selected a rendezvous point and agreed to make radio contact every two hours. Fifteen hours later, at 9:00 PM, having reached the agreed-upon coordinates, I cut the engine and sat bobbing in the water, straining through bloodshot eyes to see through the fog. Presently, a pair of navigational lights appeared, and my friend's voice came over the radio. Oh, what sweet relief. At last, this horrendous ordeal was coming to an end. I was too exhausted and too weak to celebrate. I followed my friend's boat on into the harbor, staring dumbly at his stern lights, too stupid to navigate anymore myself. Finally, on the night of July 25, 2002, at 10:30 PM, I took enormous satisfaction in lowering my anchor into twenty-five feet of blessed Australian water. I was certain my sailing days were over. If I had known what troubles awaited me in Australia, depleted as I was, I would have picked up anchor and sailed on.

CHAPTER 17

. . .

Endgame

There is no such thing as accident; it is fate misnamed.

—Napolean Bonaparte

I THANKED MY FRIENDS, AND they motored away. *Sundance* lay still at her mooring, as if she, too, had been sleep-deprived and had dozed off as soon as we came to rest. I dialed Sally while standing up, afraid I'd pass out if I sat down.

"Baby," I slurred. "I made it. I'm safe."

"You're in Australia?"

"Yes, baby."

"Oh, I'm so relieved. Oh, thank God. Now I can get some sleep—and I guess you can, too."

"Baby, I can't guarantee you that I'm not already asleep."

"Okay. Go ahead and get some sleep. I'm so happy. So glad you're okay."

"Me, too, baby. I love you."

"I love you, Michael."

I peeled off my salty foul-weather gear and let it plop onto the cockpit floor. That was the extent of my bedtime preparation. Without further ado, I staggered below and crawled into my bunk, too tired to remove my clothes. I slept for the next fourteen hours.

My best estimation was that I had slept a total of eighteen hours in the past seven days. If I were back home under normal conditions, I would have slept eight hours per night, or fifty-six hours over the same period. The eighteen-hour total meant I'd slept for an average of two and a half hours per day for a week, while under severe physical and emotional stress. No wonder I felt like a zombie. To expose oneself to constant danger will have a titanic effect on anyone, especially at sea.

The port of entry for Brisbane is a marina in the small town of Scarborough. Using the VHF radio, I contacted the office of the Australian Quarantine Inspection Service, and scheduled an appointment for that afternoon. When it was time for my appointment, I ran up the yellow Q flag (the quarantine flag indicating that the vessel has not yet cleared customs) and motored over to the designated dock for the quarantine inspection service. There I was greeted by not one, not two, but three customs officers, a woman and two men. They were standing on the dock inside a locked gate, dressed smartly in their official uniforms of dark blue slacks and light blue shirts. None of them was smiling. "Hello, sir," the woman said as I docked. She seemed polite in a strained way, but far from friendly.

I handed the older of the male officers a file containing all the proper documentation for the boat, including a clearing-out form from the last country I had visited, New Caledonia. The younger man and the woman looked at me rather grimly and then boarded *Sundance* wordlessly, proceeding directly into the cabin.

"Have a seat, please, sir, in your cockpit," the oldest one said. I was not getting a good vibe from him. He had a high-and-tight haircut and the attitude of a Marine drill sergeant. No exchange of pleasantries, no smiles, especially no how-are-you-this-fine-day. He stood over me, reviewing all of the legal documentation forms, then proceeded to ask a lot of questions regarding where I had been, why I had come to Australia, and how long I planned on staying. By now, I had been through the clearing-in process several times, and I had never felt more like I was being interrogated. This officer had no interest in the perilous experience I'd had to endure to reach Australia, instead making me feel guilty for coming here. I felt like there was a warrant out for my arrest;

had I committed some heinous crime in my hallucinatory stupor? It was tempting to just say, "Hey, lighten up, guys. I'm just an old boy from America"—but something told me that would be a bad idea.

I peered down through the companionway and was shocked to see the two younger officers conducting a no-holds-barred strip search of my boat. They opened every drawer, dumping out its contents on the floor; they even switched on their powerful flashlights to inspect inside the spaces where the drawers had been. They emptied every storage locker, pulled out heaps of provisions, checking each can, each package, to make certain that it contained what was written on the label and nothing else. They pulled the mattresses off the bunks; they crawled into the bilge.

By now I had answered all of the first officer's questions and he had thoroughly reviewed all my documents, but he kept me sequestered in the cockpit anyway. The two of us sat silently staring at each other. I tried not to fume. I had cleared customs in seven countries, and never once had any customs official performed this kind of search. Clearing through customs had certainly been time-consuming in the past, but it had been far from nerve-wracking. This was an intensive, in-depth, in-your-face strip search, and I was in the worst possible mental, physical, and emotional state to deal with it. Worst of all, if I appeared a bit nervous, it was because I indeed had something to hide.

Back in Fiji, one of my boat friends had given me a small bag of pot to use for medicinal purposes. I know that's used as a joke all the time, but as Buck McGee had taught me, pot is the most effective means of relieving the symptoms of the dreaded seasickness. I had never even opened it, but the little baggie of pot was still on the boat! Before entering the quarantine area, I'd taken a moment to hide my stash in the anchor locker in the bow. It wasn't a very creative hiding place, but based on my past clearing-in experiences, I'd seriously doubted any official would be searching in there. And now look: of all the times for a scorched-earth campaign. Why hadn't I just tossed the baggie in the ocean?

I sat there across from the hard-ass customs officer, trying to smile a little, and listening to the other two rummaging around in the cabin. *Oh, shit*, I thought, *if they find the pot, and it looks like they will, I am going to jail. Fuck, fuck, fuck.*

About halfway through the search, the younger male officer walked off the boat. When he returned, he was carrying something that looked like a small yellow plastic suitcase. Trying to sound like some kind of *Popular Science* reader, I asked my unfriendly minder what kind of gadgetry was in the box.

"It's new," he said a little proudly. "It's pretty high-tech. It can detect the odor of narcotics. Not only narcotics that are present, but those that have been on the boat at one time."

"Cool," I said. Inside, I was panicking. *That's it*, I thought. *I am busted.* How in the hell was I going to get the pot off the boat while under the close supervision of this officer?

I waited a few minutes and then, as if I'd just thought of it, I suddenly stirred in my seat and said, "Sir, would you mind if I checked in the anchor locker to make sure everything is properly secured? I just remembered I didn't check in there when I made landfall."

He frowned. "Okay," he said, "but you've got to make it fast. And I'll have to come with you."

With my heart in my throat, I went forward to the locker and got down on my hands and knees. I stretched down, reaching three and a half feet into the recesses of the locker, doing my best to block the officer's view of my hands. I probed around for a moment, grabbed the baggie, and in one smooth motion, as I rose to my feet with my back to the officer, I stuffed it down the front of my pants, inside my underwear, right next to Mr. Happy. *There. I just hope they don't strip search me.*

"That's better," I said. "Got it all secure now." Trying my best to look nonchalant, I slowly walked back to the cockpit and took my seat across from the silent officer. I was still worried about that super-sniffer machine, which they hadn't yet switched on. If it got a whiff of my crotch, I was done for. After a minute or two, I said, "You know, this is taking longer than I expected. I'm sorry about this, but I really need to go to the bathroom. Would that be all right?"

The officer looked disgusted, as if he himself had never had such an urge and couldn't understand people who did. "All right," he said. "Follow me."

We stepped off the boat and I followed him to where he unlocked the security gate and led me to a bathroom next to the marina office. He motioned to the door, and I walked through, wondering if he intended to follow me in and hold my hand while I did my business. To my relief, he instead stood waiting outside the door.

My intention had been to flush the stuff down the toilet. But as I lifted the lid and looked down at the water in the bowl, I hesitated; I could not bring myself to toss the magic weed down the dumper. I knew it would be wonderful to have just one hit after all I had gone through. I deserved one hit. Purely for medicinal purposes, you understand. There was a tall chrome trash can standing in the corner. As quietly as possible, I removed the dome-shaped lid, pulled out the plastic liner, gently placed the baggie on the bottom of the trash can, returned the liner and the lid, smiled, and thought, "You stay right there until I come back for you."

The strip search finally ended after four hours of tearing apart my boat. Either they never turned on the super-sniffer or it wasn't quite as super as it was cracked up to be, because they never mentioned the pot. When the officers were finished, they each gave me a slight conciliatory smile and stepped off the boat. "You're free to go, sir," the senior officer said. Breathing yet another sigh of relief, I moved the boat to a guest slip, tied her up to four cleats, and walked down the long dock to reach a park-like area close to the marina.

Once my feet were on solid ground, I felt an all-consuming bliss. I was alive! Alive and free! I dropped to my knees and kissed the green grass. Words are inadequate to describe my ecstasy.

I inhaled the smell of the leaves, the tree bark, and the soil. I was just so fucking happy to be alive! I felt reaffirmed and filled with joy. It was similar to my feelings after making landfall in Hawaii, yet multiplied by 1,000 percent. I walked along like a rip-roaring drunk, not caring where I was going, just needing to walk. I strolled along slowly, kicking the leaves on the sidewalk in the park. I had never realized how much I loved the trees and green grass, so much more than the huge desert of water, the ocean.

I recalled an article I had read years ago. When I first read the piece, I was unable to fully comprehend its significance. A noted philosopher had been asked to share his greatest joy. His answer puzzled me; I'd been expecting something involving the birth of a child or his wedding day. His answer, though, was "Suffering!" How could suffering give one joy? He'd gone on to explain that without suffering, one can never experience pure joy to its fullest extent; that there was a direct correlation between the depth of suffering one endures and the pinnacles of joy one can experience. At the time, I'd thought, "Yeah, and hitting your head against a wall is great too, because it feels so good when you stop." Today, though, I had a much more immediate appreciation for his theory. The depths of my recent suffering now allowed me to feel a much greater degree of happiness than I had ever known. I was basking in a newly heightened sense of being. I am alive! I am safe, safe at last!

The marina manager stopped me as I was walking back to the boat. "Just wanted to apologize," he said. "You got treated pretty rough, there."

"Nothing I couldn't handle," I said.

"Well," he said, "there's an explanation."

He told me that recently, an American yacht had arrived at this very same dock to clear in. The skipper was a fifty year-old man, traveling with his sixteen-year-old son. Only one customs officer had been assigned to inspect their vessel. All appeared to be in order until the officer happened to check beneath the floor boards, covering the bilge. There he found a large quantity of pure cocaine. The boat was impounded, the father was still in jail, and the son had been deported back to the States. The normal inspection procedures had been changed immediately. Now, any vessel arriving in Australia under an American flag was subjected to the new strip search rules. I was offended because their new procedure smacked of trait attribution, assumed similarity, and stereotyping. All Americans were considered guilty until proven innocent. Never mind that, I, uh, had been carrying some contraband of my own; it was the principle of the thing that got to me.

For the next three days, I slept twelve to fourteen hours a night. When I wasn't sleeping, I was walking around, contemplating what I should do next. The original plan—conceived well over two years ago now—had been to continue the circumnavigation post-Australia by sailing around the northern tip of the continent and then across the Indian Ocean, up to the Red Sea, through the Suez Canal, on into the Mediterranean and to points beyond. Now, the very thought of that itinerary filled me with disgust. Why on earth would anyone ever want to do that? I had absolutely no desire to sail across another ocean. In my gut, I pretty much knew that I had sailed my last passage. However, I also knew that I was in no condition to cement my decision. Sally was coming to Australia for a week's visit. I wanted to talk with her, in person, before finalizing my plans.

No matter what I decided, I'd need to get the two autopilots repaired. The marina in Scarborough was pleasant, but did not have the boat repair people. So I moved the boat across Moreton Bay to a marina in the town of Manly, closer to Brisbane, where there were a number of skilled tradesmen available to work on the boat. There was heaps of work to be done besides fixing the two autopilots: repairing the mainsail, again; installing a new float switch in the bilge; replacing the VHF antenna that was blown away in one of the storms; replacing the fuel filters; varnishing the teak—this was only a partial list. There was enough work to keep me busy for a month, and I wanted to get it all done before Sally arrived in just two weeks.

• • •

When Sally walked out of the customs offices at the Sidney airport, I bounded to her like a child toward Santa Claus. We hugged, we kissed, we hugged some more, making a spectacle of ourselves among the travelers. Being with Sally had the effect of a magic elixir—her presence was rejuvenating; the sky looked bluer, the grass appeared greener, and my life was even more full of happiness and joy than it had been moments before.

Driving the rental car on the "wrong" side of the road was frightening and fun. Sally refused to drive, and I felt like I was sixteen learning how to drive all over again. We laughed and gasped at our near misses. We both loved Sydney; it reminded us a lot of San Francisco. We threw ourselves happily into the role of tourists, visiting the famous Opera House, walking on the Sydney Bridge, and enjoying a relaxing cruise of the harbor on a quaint old ferry. We held hands and strolled through a koala preserve, remarking on the beauty of the animals. We took a trip to Lord Howe Island and the Great Barrier Reef, the largest reef system in the world. There, we viewed the lush ecosystem from under water, snorkeling among thousands of multicolored fish, large and small. The next day we had a spectacular view of the reef from a helicopter—among other sights, we saw a huge manta ray as big as a 747 and a reef formation in the shape of a heart; it was a spectacular experience.

We overspent the budget by staying in luxurious hotels. (I justified the expense by telling myself that I had earned the opulence.) Our evenings were spent sipping glasses of Australian Shiraz over leisurely meals. The conversations were endless; it was wonderful to have someone special in my life to talk with again. Going to sleep in a comfortable, dry, stationary bed, holding Sally in my arms—oh, it was exquisite.

I was relishing the role of tourist, but our time together was rapidly coming to an end. Throughout Sally's visit, I had been purposefully avoiding talking about the elephant in the room:

What was I going to do, sail on or call it quits? Sally would be leaving in the morning; I needed to settle the question once and for all.

As we sat on the balcony of our hotel room overlooking the Great Barrier Reef, enjoying a bottle of local wine, I said, "All right, baby. Time to talk about it. I'm thinking about quitting, but I really want to talk this through with you."

"All right," Sally said. "Let's talk."

And so we did, on into the night. I opened up to her completely, sharing with her not just what I saw as the advantages and disadvantages of each course of action, but also the deep personal feelings that had driven me on this journey and had then kept me at it. I told her about how my father constantly used to emphasize that I should "keep my priorities in order and always keep my eye on the ball." I impressed upon her just how deeply ingrained my anti-quitting attitude was, and how much that meant to me.

"Having said all that," I said, "Solo sailing has given me ample time to sort out my priorities. I don't think I have anything more to prove. I don't think I'll feel like a failure if I quit."

Sally listened closely to what I was saying, reserving judgment, just letting me talk.

"All I could think about out there, toward the end, was all the stuff I'd rather be doing than sitting alone in the middle of an ocean. You want to hear some of the stuff I thought of?"

"Of course."

I told her about the old tour bus idea. "Doesn't that sound like fun?" I said.

"Kind of," Sally said.

"What about this? We buy a cottage on a lake. Can't you see us all sitting on a dock enjoying life on a lake?"

"That sounds more like it," Sally said.

"My point is, the common denominator is always the same—whatever I do next, I want to share the experience with the significant people in my life."

"I really like the sound of that, Michael."

I told her that the pandemonium of the last passage, not knowing if I was going to live or die, dealing with the reality that I might never see all those I love so dearly, ever again, had served as a wake-up call that had shaken me like a sonic boom, driving home the fact that I must go home.

"Then I think you should honor that feeling."

"Yes. And you know, after I did the passage to Hawaii, I couldn't let myself quit. But that was two years ago, and things were different then. I only had 2,700 miles under my hull. Now I've sailed close to 10,000 miles, about half of those by myself. I've endured life-threatening storms. I've called on eight countries. I just don't feel that burning desire to prove to myself that I'm man enough to sail my boat across oceans. Does that make sense?"

"Of course it makes sense, Michael."

"But you know what I worry about, right?"

"Of course. You worry that you'll go home and only then start feeling like a quitter."

"Right. How do I know that won't happen?"

She sighed a little bit. "Do you feel at peace with the decision, right now?"

"Yes."

"Can you picture yourself, five years from now, in your tour bus or your lakeside cabin, looking back on your sailing adventure and being glad you quit when you did?"

"Yes."

"And can you picture yourself looking back on it and cursing yourself for having quit too soon?"

"Actually, no. I think I'll feel glad I got home and got on with spending the rest of my life with my loved ones."

"Then there you have it. Excuse me for saying so, but it would be pretty foolish to put yourself through what's certain to be more years of hell just in case there's a chance you'll have some mild regrets later."

I appreciated her saying that. It was certainly true that right now, I did not feel the slightest sense of being a quitter whatsoever. To the contrary, I felt tremendously proud. I had accomplished a pretty extraordinary sailing adventure, one very few men have achieved, even though so many dream about it. I thought again about what the marina owner back in San Diego had told me: so many dream, and so few actually head offshore. Not only had I headed offshore, I'd done long solo passages and weathered excruciating conditions. It's easy to talk the talk, but I would always know that I had been among the few who had walked the walk.

Sailing around the world no longer felt like a dream—it felt like a self-imposed nightmare: the unrelenting torture of loneliness, hunger, discomfort, fatigue, and the terrors of the treacherous ocean passages ahead. My dwindling passion for this one time dream had jumped ship somewhere between Fiji and Australia. I closed my eyes and rested my head against Sally's neck. I pictured being at home: falling asleep in my leather recliner while watching a football game on television, playing chess with my grandson Alexander, golfing with Jungle, and hiking with Sally and Sedona. I opened my eyes and closed them again and tried to imagine sailing on. Battling through the elements only to be rewarded by . . . what, more foreign countries? I missed the comforts of the great United States, and I was "islanded out." What do you do after taking a beating on a passage once you reach the next island? You work on the boat, you see the village, you snorkel, maybe you spend time with boat friends; and then you sail on to the next island, alone, and do the same thing all over again. Alone. Alone, alone, alone.

I opened my eyes. "I'm done," I said. "That's it. I'm going home."

"Final answer?"

"Final answer."

She pulled me to her so eagerly that it felt like we were a couple of high-school kids with a curfew to beat.

• • •

It was much easier to say goodbye this time, knowing that Sally and I would be together again in six weeks, after I'd taken care of *Sundance* and entertained Jungle. I had heaps of work to get done in the next six weeks. The first order of business was figuring out what to do with this damn boat. I had three choices: A) Sell her in Australia; B) Hire a delivery boat captain to sail her to California; or C) Have her shipped home.

I began asking around. The easiest option would be selling the boat in Australia, so I made inquiries about that first. It didn't take me long to discover that selling her in Australia would involve a hefty tax of twenty percent. At my asking price, that would amount to $40,000. Unless it would cost a mint to hire a captain or have *Sundance* shipped home, option A was out of the running.

I talked to a few delivery boat captains, and what they had to tell me wasn't much more encouraging: they wanted $25,000 to do the trip, and they were pretty up-front about the fact that the wear and tear on the boat would be extensive. Add up the captain's fees and the costs of the subsequent repairs, and you were looking at something like the tax bill for selling her in Australia.

That left option C: Arrange to have her shipped home. I was aware of a shipping company called Dockwise Yacht Transport. They used floating dry-dock ships to transport boats all over the world. I found them on the Internet and was successful in making a reservation to have *Sundance* picked up in Brisbane in five weeks. And, amazingly, it was the cheapest of my three options, at only around $12,000. This was the perfect solution; she would be on her way home without the wear and tear of an ocean passage.

Jungle would be arriving in three weeks for his next—and final—visit. I was looking forward to getting to spend time with him again, but there was a lot of work to get done before he arrived. Fortunately, now that the end was in sight, I found that I actually enjoyed being busy working on the boat. The two autopilots had been removed from the boat to be repaired. I got the mainsail repaired, for the third time. A friend hoisted me to the top of the mast, where I installed a new VHF radio antenna. I gave the bright work (the teak wood) two coats of varnish, replaced FUJIMO's fuel filters, topped off the batteries, and installed a new float switch on the bilge pump. My schedule was simple: work on the boat all day, eat something, read a book, and go to sleep. Get up the next morning and do it all over again. There was no end to the work. I was happy.

When I picked Jungle up at the airport, he looked me up and down and said, "Look at you, Cos. Every time I see you, you look a little more hard-core."

I suppose he was right. Two years at sea will do that. I was tan, lean, straight, and my hands were calloused and nicked— sailor's hands, for sure. I didn't look much like an insurance agent these days.

"Listen," I said. "I know you came here to sail. But I thought it might be fun to spend a couple days driving. What do you say?"

"All sailed out?"

"Just feel like seeing the country a little bit."

"I don't blame you. Let's do it."

That was Jungle, always up for anything. It was nice to stop working and go back to being a tourist. We rented a car; I let Jungle try his hand at driving on the left side of the road while I served as his navigator. Of course he was great at it—go figure that the fighter pilot can handle British driving rules. I wanted to talk with him about my decision to quit sailing. For some reason, I cared a great deal about what he would think of my plans. Once we'd been on the road for a couple hours, I was about to broach the subject when he suddenly said, "I've made a tough decision and I wanted to talk to you about it, Cos."

Bizarre. Those were my lines!

"Go ahead," I said.

"I've just put in my resignation. I'm leaving the Marines, leaving the F-18 Hornet behind. I've taken a job with Delta Airlines as a commercial pilot."

"Yeah? Congratulations! That's great."

"You think so? Think it's the right decision?"

"Well, tell me about it."

He did. He explained his reasons: more money, less stress, and an easier lifestyle for Leslie.

"That all sounds smart," I said.

"You're not disappointed?"

"No way. You've got to do what's best for you and your family."

"Flying fighter jets is *cool*, though. You know? Flying airliners, not so much."

"The hell with cool. It's overrated."

"Yeah."

"Listen. As it just so happens, I've made an uncool decision myself."

"Have you?"

"Yep. I'm coming home after this."

Jungle glanced at me. "Actually, Sally mentioned that," he said.

"What do you think about it?"

He looked a little surprised by the question. "What do I think about it? I think it'll be great to have you home. What do *you* think about it?"

"I think it'll be great to be home."

And then I suddenly found myself telling him in exquisite detail about that last passage between New Caledonia and Australia—the storms, the seas, the broken autopilot, the constant specter of death, the sleeplessness and imprisonment at the helm, the hallucinations, the feeling of utter helplessness, the fantasies, and the loneliness. It was important that I tell him everything, neither embellishing nor leaving anything out. When I finished my story, he was silent for a long moment, shaking his head. Then he said, "Even with all my training, I don't know if I could have handled that. You should be very, very proud of yourself. You can wear that passage like a badge for the rest of your life, Cos."

We spent two days touring the country. One of our most interesting stops was at Steve Irwin's Crocodile Hunter's Zoo. We both had enjoyed Irwin's nature shows on TV, so we drove out of our way to see the zoo, and we were glad we did. It was fascinating to see these monstrous creatures up close, and it gives you a stronger appreciation for the kind of courage Irwin had.

I wanted Jungle to experience an overnight sail, so I'd planned for a trip to Hamilton Island, near the Great Barrier Reef. We spent most of the first day motor-sailing north through the muddy, miserable Moreton Bay, and then toward evening we sailed out to the community of Mooloolaba to spend the night. Unloading the story of my last passage onto Jungle, and hearing him talk about his own decision to give up fighter jets had changed something in my mind; somehow now I felt absolutely certain that I was really done with my voyaging and would never regret going home. The world suddenly seemed like a much easier place to live in. As we sailed along, I felt like whistling—but I didn't. After what I'd been through with DH, I wouldn't do that to my worst enemy, let alone to Jungle.

We took a visitor's slip at the local yacht club, walked into town to enjoy a meal, played a bit of backgammon, and turned in early. When I lay my head contentedly on my pillow, I had no idea that my great sailing adventure, fittingly enough, was about to end not with a whimper, but a bang.

Dawn broke clear and lovely, quickly giving way to the perfect morning for a sail on this broad deepwater bay. The wind was light, running at about twelve knots, just right for a comfortable sail. Jungle was already up and made coffee when I awoke. "You smell that air?" he said. "I smell fine sailing!"

"Then let's go."

We hoisted the anchor and raised the sails. Having Jungle there, I could feel some of my old enthusiasm for sailing coming back—it really was a beautiful thing when the sails filled and the boat clipped neatly along under the perfect amount of wind. For the thousandth time, I reminded myself that I was, at heart, a day sailor.

We cruised along, chatting happily for two hours. I was on the helm (the autopilot was yet to be reinstalled) with a full main, staysail, and headsail all pulling nicely on a close reach. Jungle was standing forward of the helm, next to the mizzenmast, when he suddenly flinched and yelled, "A boat! Watch out!"

As I looked from Jungle up along the bow, I was shocked to see a large sailboat bearing down on us. It seemed to have materialized out of nowhere, and it was already too late to avoid a collision. A split second later, the twenty-ton force of my boat, traveling at five knots, smashed into the other vessel amidships with the force of a cannon blast.

• • •

CHAPTER 18

Hellhound on My Trail

Sometimes paranoia's just having all the facts.

—William S. Burroughs

THE STRENGTH OF THE IMPACT threw us off our feet and slammed us into the bulkhead of the cabin amid the thunderous crunching sounds of the two boats mashing together as *Sundance* rode up and over the other vessel. I was immediately sick to my stomach. As soon as I had recovered my footing, my first impulse was to free my broken boat from the boat that had appeared out of nowhere. I fired up FUJIMO and slacked off the sheets to allow the wind to spill out of the sails and reduce the pressure on the other boat. "Any injuries?" I called out.

"Nothing serious," the other skipper said.

My head was reeling; I still hadn't quite accepted the implications of what had just befallen me.

We had been sailing on a port tack (meaning that the wind was filling the sails from the left side). The other boat had been on a starboard tack (wind filling her sails from the right side), and she was heeled far over, with her port rail close to the water. *Sundance* had been sitting almost level on the water, which is why, at impact, she had crashed on top of the other boat. We'd hit her just forward of her mast; after the collision, the two masts had been looking eye to eye. Neither Jungle nor I ever saw this boat coming; it appeared quite out of nowhere.

Just based on that much information, I knew that I was in a heap of trouble. The rules of the road regarding sailing pretty straightforwardly address situations like ours: "a boat under sail on a starboard tack has the right of way over a boat on a port tack. The port vessel must give way to any boat on a starboard tack." And that wasn't some piece of arcane nautical lore: it is the first rule every sailor learns before they even step foot on a sailboat. I had been traveling on a port tack; I was to have given way! I was in the wrong. Without question, I would be considered responsible for the collision.

I stood there in the cockpit, trying to make the whole thing go away by shaking my head back and forth. Jungle looked at me like he didn't know what to say. I was at least glad he was here for moral support. "Well," I said, "this little morning sail is going to be very expensive." I didn't know whether to cry or throw up.

I hollered to the other skipper that I was going to back my vessel off his boat, and he gave me the okay. With FUJIMO in reverse, we slowly backed off the other vessel. Again, the sound of metal on metal, stainless steel crushing against stainless steel, fiberglass on fiberglass, was ear-shattering. Finally, the bow plopped down onto the water where it belonged.

We did a quick check for leaks. The hull had survived and we were not taking on water. We took down the mainsail, furled the headsails, secured our boat, and then stayed on the scene, circling the other vessel to make sure they didn't need our help. Thankfully, they were still afloat; they were not taking on water and all four people on board appeared to be uninjured.

After hailing the Water Police (the Australian term for its Harbor Patrol) on the VHF to report the accident, we limped back to our slip at the Yacht Club. The Water Police were waiting for us when we arrived; without much preamble, they began snapping pictures of the damage to the two boats, requested all of our documentation papers, and asked both parties to meet in the yacht club in thirty minutes.

So I had half an hour to stew. This was my very first accident. In forty-eight years of driving, I had never been in an accident. In thirty-seven years of sailing, I had never been in an accident. I had safely sailed halfway around the world. I had been all but finished with my ill-conceived sailing adventure and had been just puttering around in the bay like any day sailor. And the worst thing was: I was at fault. How had I let this happen? I was mortified. I felt like I had committed a major crime rather than having had a simple accident with another boat.

The other skipper and I met with the Water Police in the dining room of the yacht club to give them our verbal accounts of the collision. When I saw the owner of the boat I'd hit, I was instantly put off. My first impression was that he looked like a man who had entered the witness protection program . . . or maybe he was a used car salesman. The guy was wearing a bright yellow T-shirt with coffee stains all over its front. He was burly, shorter than average, with a thick build, overweight by at least seventy-five pounds, with small squinty dark brown eyes. His face had not felt a razor in some time. His thinning hair laced with gray was pulled back into a tight ponytail, helping accentuate the profound depth of his forehead (Actually, I quipped to myself, it looked more like a "fivehead" than a forehead). His fat nose veered slightly to the left, presumably the result of a right hook he'd fielded sometime in his past. He spoke in a raspy voice and I detected the remnants of New York accent.

I tried to be friendly. "Are you from New York?" I said.

"Actually, I'm a Jersey boy," he said. "But I've been living in Australia for the past nine years." He pronounced "Australia" the way the locals do—*Ozz-drail-ya*—which I couldn't help taking as an affectation. That's it, I thought, the guy really is in the witness protection program; probably some sort of mob boss back in Jersey. Oh, man, just my luck. Out of all the fine people in this great country, I have an accident with a transplanted "Jersey Boy."

After a negative Breathalyzer, we gave our recorded verbal statements. I went first. As I was talking, I looked up to see a young man being carried past the doorway on the back of another man, who had a shit-eating grin on his face. It threw me off enough that I paused in my testimony, and the others looked out the door and saw them, too.

"That's my son," the Jersey Boy said. "Eighteen years old. He hurt his knee in the crash. Just reflexes, you know—he stepped in front of your boat to fend it off."

What? Was this kid playing with a full deck? Who in their right mind would step in front of a twenty-ton, forty-foot boat traveling at five knots and expect to stop it or even slow it down? It was the same as jumping in front of a wayward bus. It didn't matter what I thought, though. The story of the smashed knee made it into the other captain's official version of events.

The Water Police were polite and efficient. The officer in charge turned off his recording device and said, "That's all we need from you both for now. I'll ask you both to provide us with written statements telling me what you just told me here, and I'll come by to collect them tomorrow afternoon. This wasn't a serious accident, and no further police action is necessary. The two of you can sort out the details."

> Headstay furler bent. Not operable. Needs repair.
> Dolphin striker and bobstay broken. Replace.
> Hull at water line cracked. Not leaking. Repair.
> Bow pulpit timber (new in Fiji) cracked. Replace.
> Bow platform damaged. Replace.
> Navigation lights broken. Replace.
> Anchor bracket bent. Repair.
> Stanchions bent. Replace.

That made me feel better. Perhaps I wasn't such a sordid criminal after all. Unfortunately, my sense of relief would be temporary.

I returned to the boat, where Jungle and I sized up the damage to my poor battered boat.

Poor *Sundance*, my beautiful *Sundance*. She looked like she had been in a heavyweight fight. She hadn't lost the fight, but she'd put in some good rounds and was down for an eight count.

But, as the saying goes, "You ought to see the other guy." Our damage was minimal, compared to that of the other boat. She would require a great deal of work before she could go to sea again.

What about insurance, you ask? Why, that's a very astute question. The answer is: I had researched purchasing an insurance policy before leaving San Diego. And I'd been disappointed—even angry—to learn that the premium was outrageously expensive and that it included numerous restrictions on single-handed sailors that made it unrealistic for me. So, yes: the big-time insurance agent—the sailor who owed his ability to do this trip to his success in the field of insurance—was voyaging without a policy.

As we sat in a bar licking our psychological wounds, Jungle and I spent hours trying to piece together how it could possibly have happened that we hadn't seen the other boat until it was directly in front of us. At last, like a couple of forensics experts, we went back to the boat and stood in the cockpit, behind the helm, reenacting the scene. We soon found our answer. The cockpit is covered by a canvas cover/roof called a "dodger." A small strip of canvas runs from the top of the dodger and connects to the top of the cabin as a support. Our view of the other boat had been obscured by this narrow strip of canvas. The only way for that to have happened is that both boats must have been traveling at the same rate of speed and on a directly converging course. When the accident happened, I'd been constantly scanning the water for any other traffic, just like I always do. But, because of the highly unusual circumstances of two vessels converging on each other at the same speed (as Jungle put it, this was a case of "constant bearing with decreasing range"), I never caught so much as a glimpse of the other boat until it was too late. Oh, and by the way: sailboats don't have any brakes; there's simply no way to stop quickly. This was a one-in-a-million occurrence. Lucky, lucky me.

As if addressing itself directly to our situation, the "rules of the road" manual, right after the part about a port boat giving way to a starboard vessel, goes on to say, "Every vessel must maintain a sharp lookout and avoid a collision at any cost!" Clearly, we had failed at this, too, but we thought we had figured out why. The question was why hadn't the other boat seen us and done its best to avoid a collision? There had been four people on board that boat. It seems logical that at least one of them would have seen my boat bearing down on them and alerted the skipper. The more I thought about it, the more I became convinced that this man from New Jersey had been well aware of my position but was so intent on maintaining the right of way that he refused to change course. It was my responsibility to yield, not his, so he would rather have a collision than give way. To change course, in his distorted mind, would have been a sign of weakness.

Sunday morning, I took Jungle back to the airport. Talk about a ruined trip. Not only had we not gotten to do the kind of sailing I'd promised him, but he'd had to live through this disastrous collision—and to make things worse, he felt like it was his fault. "I was your wingman," he kept saying. "It was my job to keep a lookout."

I told him over and over that whatever happened on my boat was ultimately my responsibility—I was the captain, and I'd been at the helm at the time of the crash. Standing in the airport, he apologized one last time.

I gave him a hug. "Forget it," I said. "Go home and forget it. I'll see you in a few weeks and we'll laugh about it."

He walked through security and I stood there feeling very alone, doubting I'd be laughing about this one anytime soon. The crash had left me both unnerved and unbalanced. I was devastated and seriously doubted I would ever laugh about this accident.

• • •

It was close to noon the next day when I saw the skipper of the other boat come strolling down the dock. "Might I have a word with you?" he said.

"Come aboard."

He settled in the cockpit, looking small and roly-poly. He still had on his disgusting yellow T-shirt. "I just wanted to let you know," he said, "that I've spent a couple hours this morning conferring with my solicitor."

Solicitor is the Australian term for an attorney.

"And?"

"And I guess you don't know, but my son had sustained a knee injury, and he may require surgery. Also my boat was severely damaged."

I said nothing, just looked stonily across at him.

"Per my solicitor, you are totally and without any question at fault in the accident. I'm sure you know the rules of the road. A starboard boat has the right of way over your port tack."

"Let's hear the punch line," I said.

He gave me a dirty look. "Because you are a foreigner, my solicitor strongly recommended he be allowed to file a criminal negligence suit against you . . . in the amount of $175,000."

I felt my heart sink, but I wasn't going to take any shit. "Go ahead and file it," I said.

"Well, listen," he said. "Because you are a foreigner"—it grated on my nerves every time I heard this Atlantic City tough guy refer to me that way—"there's a real possibility you might try to flee the country to avoid prosecution. Just so you're aware, if you do that the police will be forced to arrest you and you'll immediately be put in jail. Your boat will be impounded and held by the authorities until the case is settled. That's how the law here works. And, typically, a case like this can take three or four years before reaching a satisfactory settlement."

While looking me directly in the eyes, he proceeded to tell me he had a solution to my vexing problem. Exactly like he was peddling a used car, he said, "I think I can help you out. What do you say we forget about the lawsuit and handle this man-to-man, honorably. If you will give me $175,000 U.S. within the next forty-eight hours, I'll be happy to call off the lawyers and you'll be free to go about your business. You have my word on that." His tone was low and calm and yet slammed into me like a giant fist.

I felt my fury rising up inside me, and I wanted to choke him. Instead, looking into his beady eyes, I said, "Where I come from, that would be considered extortion."

His response was cold, without the slightest show of emotion. "Call it whatever you want," he said. "But the price of your freedom is still 175,000 bucks, or you'll find yourself in jail before the sun comes up on Wednesday."

I was shocked. This wasn't a used-car salesman but a hard-boiled mobster from New Jersey hiding out down under. He could smell the deep pockets of an American yachtie. For the first time, it occurred to me that perhaps he had not refused to change course out of some self-righteous adherence to the rules of the road; he had crashed into me specifically to collect the cash. Time seemed suspended, but actually, only a few seconds had passed. I was certain I was watching a man who lied with the same capacity that I breathed.

I reacted calmly, like the insurance agent I am, like I was waiting for my policyholder to decide between a whole life and a term life insurance policy. Inside, his extortion demand was causing my pulse to accelerate, and I desperately wanted to alter the asshole's structural integrity. But on the outside, I kept my cool, suppressing my anger.

"I'll need some time to come up with that much money," I said. "It's a little more than I have in my checking account right now. But I'll do my best to come up with the 175,000 by Wednesday afternoon." I was just buying time; there was no way this asshole was getting my money.

He stuck out his hand, waiting for me to shake it. I looked at him, shook my head, and said, "You have got to be shitting me."

"I'll see you in two days," he said, and disappeared down the dock, living proof that someone in New Jersey had figured out how to clone human waste.

As soon as he was out of sight, I rushed to the yacht club manager's office and told him of the extortion demand.

"I wish I could say it surprised me," he said. "I wouldn't take another step without a good solicitor, and I've got one who's a very good friend if you'd like his number."

"Sure," I said.

Two hours later, I was sitting in the solicitor's office. I have a deep-seated distain for all bloodsucking sharks—I mean, for all attorneys—but this guy was not your classic lawyer. I was favorably impressed as soon as I saw his small office: unpretentious, modestly furnished. That was encouraging; maybe he was not the typical ego- and greed-driven lawyer I was accustomed to working with, or against. In a few moments he walked into the room, a tall, attractive fellow in a blue dress shirt with no tie. "Michael?" he said with a grin. "I'm Michael Ferris."

"Nice to meet you, Michael."

I told him my story, and he listened carefully, asking the occasional question in his soft-spoken way. He seemed genuinely concerned with my plight. I felt comfortable talking with him, and my impression that he was the right man to help only grew stronger.

After gathering all the details of the accident, including the extortion demand, he sat quietly for a moment, seemingly weighing something in his mind. At last he said, "Is your boat seaworthy?"

"It floats," I said.

"Could you possibly sail to New Zealand tomorrow?"

"Oh, hell no," I said. "She's not *that* seaworthy."

"Let me tell you what I'm thinking," Michael said. "I don't believe they'll throw you in jail. At least not right now. However, it is possible for the police to impound your boat until the case is settled. And your new friend is right: that could take a couple of years."

"In other words, I'm pretty much screwed."

"You will be if you stay around here," he said. "That's why my recommendation is for you to leave Mooloolaba as soon as possible, get your boat repaired just enough for a long sail, and then get yourself the hell out of Australia."

He agreed to serve as my legal counsel in the case. I paid him a hefty retainer, confident he was the right solicitor to handle things for me. I genuinely liked the guy. I couldn't imagine any attorney I'd ever worked with before who would have been so frank as to recommend my fleeing the country.

One thing was clear: if my boat were to be impounded, she would be landlocked, stuck in a police lot, exposed to the elements. I would not have access to her to take care of her. She might have to sit there for three or four years. The damage she would sustain would be tremendous.

I wasn't going to let that happen.

• • •

Back aboard the boat I worked as quickly as possible, making temporary repairs wherever I could, frantically preparing the boat for a FUJIMO-powered run. At four o'clock the next morning, under the cover of darkness, I untied the dock lines and slipped unannounced out of the Mooloolaba Yacht Club. Once again, I had a terrible feeling in my gut, like I was a common criminal running from the law. Yet, to be clear, I never had any thought of absconding from my moral or financial responsibilities. I had been in the wrong, and was willing to accept full blame for the catastrophe; I was not, however, willing to be the helpless victim of an outrageous extortion attempt. Plus, I told myself that the idea to flee the scene had been on the recommendation of my legal counsel.

I motored across the dreaded shallow Manly Bay to the marina I had left a week before. There, I could complete the necessary work to get my damaged boat ready to return to sea as soon as possible. By the next afternoon, I had two guys working on the boat. One concentrated on the headstay furler while the other was repairing the broken bob stay. When these guys showed up on the boat, I'd asked each of them for a written estimate, including both their projected fee and the amount of time they anticipated taking. I looked over their estimates, and then offered each of them twice as much as their stated fee if they could complete the repairs within the next seventy-two hours. They all jumped at the opportunity to collect 100 percent more than their normal rates. Throwing money around works sometimes: I'd have the most crucial stuff fixed in three days; the remainder of the repairs would have to wait until New Zealand.

Next, I contacted the shipping company and canceled my reservation. They said there was a good chance they would have available space on one of their ships leaving from New Zealand next month. I made a tentative reservation.

I was certain my extortionist would be at the yacht club sometime the next day to make sure *Sundance* was still sitting in her slip. Once he realized I was no longer there, I knew he would hit the panic button and notify his solicitor and the police. My fear was that the police would then issue an all-points bulletin in an effort to flush me out. Nervously, I called the yacht club's manager, hoping I could trust him.

"Yeah," he said, "that jerk came by here this morning. He was furious. Got up in my face. Demanded to know where you'd gone."

"What did you tell him?"

"I told him he could get bent. Told him I didn't even know you'd left the club, and anyhow if I did know where you were, I'd never tell him."

I thanked the manager profusely and hung up. Thank God he was looking out for me. And then it occurred to me: What if he wasn't? What if he had led me to Michael to help the extortionist set his trap? As ridiculous as that thought was, I couldn't help sliding into the grips of paranoia. This was a new experience for me. I had worked with people suffering from paranoia, but I never truly knew how demoralizing it was. Suddenly, it seemed that everyone was out to get me, to capture me. If a person walking past my boat stopped to take a longer look than normal, I was certain they were part of the search to locate me and my boat. It was a miserable feeling to be so suspicious and mistrust everyone. Walking down the sidewalk to a coffee shop, I could feel people staring at me. Even though I hated the feeling, I found it impossible to not justify, in my mind, a total distrust of my environment. The paranoia made it difficult to sleep. I was terrified, convinced the authorities would find us in the middle of the night, come crashing through the cabin hatch, and haul me off to jail. Paranoia was such a bitch to deal with that I found myself thinking I would much rather be in the middle of the ocean fighting off a mother of a storm than dealing with the Australian land sharks.

Wednesday arrived. Deadline day—the day I was supposed to deliver $175,000 to my extortionist. And I was not ready to put to sea. I needed more time to complete all the work.

And that wasn't my only problem. Before leaving the country, of course, I'd have to complete the clearing-out procedure with the local customs officials—yes, those folks who'd been so kind to me on my arrival. Part of the clearing-out documentation was a statement that the vessel was not leaving the country with any outstanding financial debts or warrants. Without such documentation, I would not be allowed to clear-in to the next country. Should I arrive in New Zealand without this official document, I would be required to leave the country within twenty-four hours. And then what?

There was no alternative; I would have to go to customs headquarters in downtown Brisbane to make a request for clearance to leave the country. Downtown Brisbane is not where I wanted to be. Had there been a warrant issued for my arrest? Had the official criminal negligence suit already been filed with the court, preventing the officials from granting my request to clear? If indeed the authorities were searching for me, I would be leaving the customs office in handcuffs . . . that much I knew. I tried to think up schemes for obtaining my clearing-out documents without showing up in person, but there were no two ways about it: I had to roll the dice and stroll into the customs office a wanted man.

That afternoon, my heart throbbing in my throat, I rented a car and drove the seven miles from the marina to the customs office located in a high-rise in the center of Brisbane. The directory in the lobby indicated that the office was on the fourteenth floor. Riding up in the elevator, I was wracked by a new helping of fear that made me shake like a rabbit in sight of an eagle. I was feeling fight-or-flight, particularly flight; I wanted to run as far away as my old legs would carry me. My knees shook; my mouth felt like I had overloaded it with honey. I had to go to the bathroom so bad I was afraid I might leave a puddle on the elevator floor. I was certain that when the bell sounded and the doors slid open, the uniformed staff would take one look at me and say, "Here's that rich American yachtie. Cuff him and book him." I was walking into a lion's den, without a whip or a chair.

No one met me at the elevator door. I found the office and hesitantly walked up to a lady standing behind a window with a small hole to talk through.

"I'd like to complete the paperwork to clear out of country," I said, sounding to myself like a sixth-grader talking to the bully who's about to steal his lunch money.

"Have you made an appointment, sir?"

No way; I hadn't wanted to give them advance notice I was coming.

"No," I said. "I'm sorry. I didn't make an appointment."

She gave me a disgusted look, as if I had just asked her for her age and weight.

"Please take a seat, sir."

The waiting area was a large, old room, cold with high ceilings and a number of hardback chairs. It lacked any ambiance of personality, lest anyone think they were about to charm the officials, I suppose. I sat down and tormented myself for twenty minutes with thoughts of my impending arrest. Finally, a plump woman in her fifties, with undistinguishable features, dressed in the official blue uniform of the customs people, waved me over to her desk. Her demeanor was a perfect match for the lobby—cold, impersonal, and bland. That was fine with me; I'll take bland over eager-to-put-me-behind-bars any day.

"Please show me your documentation papers," she said in disinterested monotone.

I'll bet anything you aren't married, I thought to myself.

She read through each document as if she had to memorize each word. When she was finished reading, she stood up suddenly. *Uh-oh.*

"I'll be back in a few minutes, sir. Please stay here."

Oh, shit. Why was she leaving? Where was she going? Had she recognized my name? Was I on some kind of most-wanted list? After an anxious twenty minutes, she returned. Only now she was accompanied by a towering male officer, bald as a billiard ball. Like "Bull" on *Night Court.* What did she need him for?

She eased back down into her chair. Bull just stood there staring down at me, not saying a word. Christ, what was this guy's deal? *Oh, man, I am going to piss my pants if he doesn't say something pretty soon.*

This is it. The jig is up. He knows exactly who I am. He's going to drag me off to jail any minute. When he finally spoke, it was to utter a single vexing word: "Why?"

Then silence. My palms were springing water and I was sure everyone in the place could hear the percussion of my heart. Jesus. What was he, the sphinx? Why what? Why was I running away? Why did I crash into the boat of an ugly little Jersey boy? Or maybe it was a broader question than that. Maybe Bull was into philosophy: Why does man exist? Or perhaps he's posing a musical question: Why do fools fall in love? Jesus. WHY? Why what?

He must have left me hanging for ten seconds. Finally he said, "Why are you leaving the country when there's such a large storm building off the coast?"

Oh, man, was I happy to hear that some silly storm was his big concern. I could talk my way out of that. I told Bull I'd managed to sail single-handed from San Diego through any number of major storms, without any problem whatsoever (I lied, in other words), and that one more storm didn't concern the likes of me (I lied again).

"Sit tight, then," he said when I was finished babbling.

The two of them disappeared again. *Oh, shit.* Again I sat waiting, wondering was going on behind the closed door. *What the hell were they talking about back there, and for so long?* I pictured them on the phone, coordinating with a swat team mustering on the sidewalk below. The female officer returned, unaccompanied, and handed all the paperwork back to me. "Your request to clear out has been approved," she said.

What? Had she just approved my request? Holy God, I wanted to jump across her desk and plant a wet sloppy kiss on her dowdy mug.

"You should be aware, sir, that that storm front is substantial."

"Yes, ma'am."

"I only hope I won't hear that your vessel needs help from the Coast Guard."

"No, ma'am. I'm sure."

If she only knew; a storm at sea was the least of my worries. I walked out of the office with a spring in my step. But as I looked down at the paperwork, I saw that there was still one small problem. The document was only good for forty-eight hours. That meant I had two days to get ready to sail offshore. The extortionist's deadline had passed while I was taking care of the customs issue.

I devised a brilliant plan. Since I was dealing with such an unscrupulous, dishonest person, I decided to play his game. Without even going back to the boat, I drove the rental car straight to the Brisbane airport, went inside the terminal, and found a pay phone. My first call was to the Water Police. I told them of the extortion attempt and that I had retained an attorney, giving them Michael's name and phone number. I wanted to cover my ass with the police.

My next call was to my antagonist, who had given me his phone number. I got his answering machine. At the sound of the tone, I said, "Hey, asshole. Today is Wednesday. Your deadline has passed. I refuse to allow you to extort $175,000 from me. My boat is currently 400 miles offshore, in the hands of a delivery boat captain. She's on her way back to America. I'm standing in the Brisbane airport and will be boarding a flight to America in twenty minutes. So you can kiss my white *American* ass, you son of a bitch!"

I figured that it was wisest to have made the call from the airport, just in the unlikely event he could somehow trace its origin. I was hopeful this ploy might slow down my pursuer long enough to let me finish the necessary work on *Sundance*.

By Thursday evening, the repaired autopilots were installed, and both the headstay furler and bobstay had been replaced. I topped off the fuel and water tanks. I still needed two more days to complete the rest of the repairs, and then I would be ready to sail again.

On Friday morning, I walked a mile to the closest phone booth to call my solicitor and give him an update on the progress of the work. When his secretary answered the phone, I was surprised that she didn't exchange pleasantries; the couple of times I'd spoken to her previously, she'd been extremely warm and friendly. "Please hold," she said rather formally.

When Michael came on the phone, he answered in a near whisper. "The Water Police are in my reception area," he said. "They've come to my office looking for you. I'm afraid they're prepared to arrest you. It looks like there may well be a criminal negligence suit filed against you. Listen, Michael. I'll try to delay them as long as possible, but understand me: you need to leave the country immediately!"

I hung up the phone and sprinted as fast as my sixty-three-year-old legs would carry me back to the marina. Earlier that morning, I had done a load of wash, and all of the clothes were hanging out on the lifelines to dry. I yanked each item off the line, clothespins flying in the air and plopping into the water. Anyone who saw me would have thought I'd lost my mind. I flung the damp laundry below into the cabin, fired up the engine, released all the dock lines, and left the marina, with FUJIMO roaring at full throttle.

• • •

Jungle always referred to his upcoming maneuvers as "Operation" so-and so. I decided to give my maneuver of eluding (and hopefully escaping) the Australian Water Police the name of Operation Geronimo, the Great Escape. The legendary Apache chief, Geronimo, was a master at eluding the U.S. Cavalry; it took decades before they finally captured him. I was hoping I might have some of his luck in evading my pursuers. (A decade later, the U.S. military would steal the name of my operation, using it for the hunt for Osama Bin Laden.)

There are only three ways to reach the open ocean from Brisbane; all require successfully negotiating an obstacle course through the shallow, muddy, miserable Moreton Bay, before reaching a pass leading to the ocean. Separating Brisbane from the Tasman Sea are two large islands, Moreton to the north and Stradbroke to the south. Going north to Cape Moreton would require motor-sailing for nearly six hours. To head south to Stradbroke Island required working my way through a narrow pass only navigable during high tide; that might take as long as five hours. The third choice was a frighteningly narrow pass that lies between the southern tip of Moreton Island and the northern tip of Stradbroke Island. I could reach it in two hours, if I dared. In conversations with local boaters, I had been quite emphatically warned never to attempt this tiny, treacherous pass. Only small fishing boats ever use it, and with good reason.

Well, as they used to say in the movies, that idea was so crazy it just might work. The Water Police would be on the lookout for me elsewhere, plus it was the fastest way out to sea. That pretty much decided it. I was either going to make it through the pass or end up on the rocks, but I was not going to be arrested.

With only about three miles to reach the pass, I spotted a large powerboat off my stern, skimming along at a high rate of speed. My heart sank. So they *had* thought to look here after all. Fuck. Busted! It took the boat twenty minutes to catch up to my position. As it drew closer, I shut down FUJIMO and sat dead still in the water, all too aware I could never outrun a power boat given my top speed of five knots. As the vessel approached, I watched in amazement as it passed me by without even slowing. Two men stood together near the helm, and they waved jauntily as they sped past. It was nothing more than a fishing boat; paranoia be dammed!

I started FUJIMO back up and proceeded toward the pass. But once I got it within eyesight, I lost heart again. Huge breakers crashed willy-nilly over the coral; it didn't even look like there was a pass at all. Normally, a pass will have some navigational markers to help guide boats through. This one had none, nada, zip. The Coast Guard purposefully did not provide any such markers; they wanted to discourage madmen like me from attempting to use the pass.

Paranoia aside, it really did seem that Operation Geronimo had come to an end. There was no way I would ever make it through the pass without crashing onto one of the reefs. I didn't even know where to begin trying.

Bitterly defeated, I shut down FUJIMO, dropped the main, furled in the headsail, walked forward and stood at the end of the bow pulpit, looking over the pass, to the Tasman Sea, so close but unreachable. God. There lay the open ocean, freedom from the vicious land sharks. The sun was setting, it was getting dark, and I had lost my only hope of reaching the ocean.

But wait. *How do you like that? The fat lady has yet to sing.* There, straight ahead, the lights of a small fishing boat came bobbing their way through the pass. I jumped up onto the bow and started waving my arms in the air, yelling as loud as possible, hoping to attract the captain's attention. Success! The fishing boat pulled alongside.

The vessel carried three middle-aged men, whose well-seasoned faces registered curiosity and concern. "What the hell are you doing out here?" the captain said. "It's almost dark."

"Well, I've kind of screwed myself, boys," I said. "I didn't realize this pass was so small. I've got to get through it tonight, but I see I can't do it without help."

"No. You'll smash your boat apart."

"Listen," I said. "I'll give you $500 cash to lead me through."

The men laughed as if I were crazy for thinking they might turn down an offer like that. "Show us the money, mate," the captain said.

After counting out the bills, I stuffed them in a mason jar, tightly secured the lid, and tossed it over to them. One of the fishermen unscrewed the lid as the others looked gravely on. Then all at once, they all threw their heads back and guffawed. My heart stopped. I braced myself for the sight of them speeding off with my money and leaving me stranded.

Instead, the captain said, "So are you ready right now, mate?"

"Hell, yes. But can I have my mason jar back?"

"Cost you another hundred," said the guy holding it. Then he burst out laughing and tossed me my empty jar, and we were on our way.

It took forty-five minutes to zigzag our way through the pass, at times coming within three feet of the reef. I was glad I hadn't been foolish enough to attempt it alone; it would have been impossible without the local knowledge of the crew on the fishing boat. Once we got through, my new friends pulled alongside.

"There you go," the captain said. "Where are you heading, anyway?"

"Fiji," I said. "I've heard it's beautiful."

The men shrugged. "Never been there," the captain said. He took his seat and got ready to motor off. Before they left, he said, "What's your name, friend?"

I already had my mainsail up and was itching to be off. "My name?" I said. "They call me Geronimo."

There was no time to celebrate. I still needed to clear three more miles before reaching international waters, beyond the jurisdiction of the Australian Water Police. I set a waypoint on the GPS and watched my progress toward it. When I'd reached international waters, I stood on the stern, looking back at the hostile continent disappearing behind me, and shouted, "So long, Australia! You can kiss my American ass!"

It wasn't like my troubles were over, though. Now I was facing a passage across the Tasman Sea of 1,465 miles of open water. Brisbane was to have been the last stop on this sailing adventure of a lifetime. I had absolutely no desire to make another ocean passage, especially across this notoriously treacherous sea. But the mess in Australia had left me with no other choice—

either make another dreary ocean passage to New Zealand or go to jail. This was not a difficult decision. In fact, for the first time I was somewhat happy at the prospect of a bluewater crossing. I was free . . . free and lucky. The storms the customs officer had warned me about had pushed north of my route. Clear sailing, to coin a phrase.

It was a luxury to have the autopilot steering the boat again. Now I had the freedom to move about, to trim the sails, to eat something (anything but an MRE), to sleep for thirty minutes at a snatch instead of fifteen. It was wonderful to talk on the SSB radio sked with Big John from Auckland, and to reach Sally every day on the satellite phone. However, the prevailing wind was from the northeast, mostly on the nose (blowing from the direction I needed to sail), which meant beating into the wind, crashing through twelve-foot waves that seemed to take sick pleasure in jumping over the bow and landing in my lap. The larger waves would lift the bow clear out of the water; We would come slamming down the back side making thunder, the entire structure quivering like a nine point nine earthquake; at times I was genuinely afraid she might break in half. This rough passage felt like the one from Hawaii to Tahiti, forever beating into the wind under the toughest point of sail. But, considering how bad it could have been, the Sleeping Giant was positively smiling on me: a high-pressure system that produced fair winds, manageable seas, and no gigantic storms.

I fairly flew across the passage, covering 1,687 miles in just ten days and eight hours. The only time I found myself in un-expected trouble was shortly after rounding the North Cape of New Zealand. With just fifty miles remaining to reach Opua, in the Bay of Islands area, I was running before the wind with the mainsail sheeted well out on the port side, close to a rocky shore; the autopilot was steering on a course in the direction of the land. I knew it was time to jibe (change direction) before we got too close to the rocks, but I felt the all-too-familiar urge to take a leak. I had been putting it off for hours. I had to go so bad my back teeth were floating.

As always seemed to be the case when the urge would hit, I was dressed in my complete foul-weather attire. I couldn't wait; I located my trusty green bottle and began digging around for Mr. Happy. I braced myself against the mizzenmast, stuck Mr. Happy where he needed to be, and got ready to pee. For some reason, as a last preparatory act, I glanced over my right shoulder, and I didn't at all like what I saw behind me; the sky was dark black, with the clouds touching the water. A considerable squall was closing in. I wouldn't have much time to relieve my bladder before the storm hit. I had to make this fast. But damn it, I couldn't let go.

I closed my eyes and tried to talk Mr. Happy into it. At last, it began to work, but just then, the squall began breathing its cold air down the back of my neck. It came in low, hard, and fast, slamming into the boat like my own private hurricane. In a matter of seconds, the wind speed leapt from a pleasant twelve knots to a rude forty. Mr. Happy was greatly displeased. I imagined him saying, "Put me back! Put me back where I live, you dumbass!"

I did, which was fine for him, but *my* situation wasn't improving: the powerful winds had hastened the boats progress toward the rocks, which now loomed less than fifty feet away. This was serious.

I disengaged the autopilot and attempted to turn the helm, but with no luck. It wouldn't budge, as there was too much pressure on the sails. Crap. I needed to trim in the mainsail and spill some wind in order to take pressure off the sail and change course. With every second, the boat was picking up speed and closing in on the enormous jagged rocks. I braced my feet against the bulkhead, wrapped both hands around the mainsheet, and, using all my strength, managed to pull in the mainsail one inch at a time, releasing just enough pressure to allow me to steer away from the rocks. But the maneuver had put a lot of wind on the back side of the sail, causing an uncontrolled jibe (meaning that the sail had swung violently from one side of the boat to the other,). It was a dangerous eventuality, but we cleared the rocks by less than fifty feet.

I sailed away from the rocky shore, my pulse pounding with

282 •• IMPERFECT PASSAGE

excitement. Shit, wouldn't that have been ironic? After the awful passage with DH, after all the storms, after the collision and
my escape from the authorities, I'd damn near lost my boat and
maybe my life because I had to take a piss at an inopportune
moment.

CHAPTER 19

• • •

Exit Strategy

A man travels the world over in search of what he needs and returns home to find it.
—George Moore

THE S/V *STELLA* OUT OF Toronto, Canada, was in Opua, with my friends from Bora Bora, Terry and Ariel. I easily reached them on the VHF, reported my ETA, and took down their directions to the marina. There, I would once again perform the clearing-in rites, this time with the New Zealand customs authorities. It was eight in the evening on Sunday, October 12, 2002, when I tossed Terry my dock lines to help secure *Sundance*. Especially after my latest ordeal, it was great to see an old friend; we shook hands and hugged.

"Congratulations on another successful passage," Terry said. "Come on board and join me and Ariel for a drink."

I sat aboard *Stella*, telling my friends about what I'd endured in Australia. They were just about speechless. I had almost finished my story when the customs officer arrived. He was an older gentleman with white hair, with a grandfatherly manner and a pleasant smile. The entire clearing-in process took no more than forty-five minutes with no strip search. He was a pleasure to deal with, but as he was standing on the dock getting ready to leave, he made an offhand comment that caused my heart to stop. He said, "You must be a pretty popular guy. A lot of people have been calling our office, asking if you had arrived yet."

"Do you have any names?" I said.

"No, sir," he said. "I assumed it would be friends or family."

I glanced at Terry and Ariel, and they shook their heads to indicate it hadn't been them doing the asking.

Friends or family, my ass. What was going on? Who was concerned with my arrival?

I spent the rest of the evening drinking rum and talking story with my friends. The next day was Canadian Thanksgiving, so Ariel invited me to join them for a traditional turkey dinner, the meal I'd fantasized about on the hellish passage from New Caledonia.

I was walking back to my boat, pleasantly stuffed with good food, when I noticed a beefy woman with short blonde hair, dressed in a full-length black overcoat, striding directly toward me. Why was she wearing an overcoat? She certainly looked out of place among the boats. She smiled and said good evening, so I smiled back and wished her the same. It was a pleasant enough encounter, and I gave it no more thought, except that I remembered her strange overcoat. The following morning, I rose early, looking forward to a long hot shower in the marina bathroom before breakfast. I grabbed my shaving kit and a towel and threw on some flip-flops, shorts, and a T-shirt. I was still exhausted from the ten-day passage, and had no greater post-breakfast plans than to go back to sleep. As I stepped off the dock and made my way toward the bathroom, an attractive-looking young lady approached me; I was immediately struck by the heavy amount of makeup covering her face. Before I could get to my next thought, she had closed in on my personal space and was standing with her face thrust up into mine. It all happened so quickly that it took me a moment to realize she was sticking a photo in my face. I backed up a little and realized it was a picture of a young boy lying in a hospital bed.

"Do you know who this is? Do you know who this is?" she kept saying over and over again.

Of course I had no idea who the kid might be.

That's when I saw the man with a big video camera over his shoulder, and a guy next to him holding a furry microphone on a long boom over my head. *Oh, shit*, I thought, *this is a damn television crew. She's a reporter.*

Enter the mysterious fat woman in the black overcoat.

"This is the boy's mother!" the reporter was yelling. "What do you have to say to her?"

My attention was instantly riveted on the mother. The pleasant smile from the night before was nowhere to be seen. Now she was charging at me, her eyes glazed over; she looked like Dick Butkus from the Chicago Bears ready to sack me for a sixteen-yard loss. Taking the reporter's cue, she screamed at the top of her lungs, "You ran over our boat! My son is in hospital! You tried to run away, but we have found you, you son of a bitch, you scumbag, you arrogant American! You are going to pay! We're going to sue your ass for everything you've got! You can never hide from me! I will follow you all over the fucking world!"

As soon as that rant was over, the reporter fired a barrage of questions at me—Why had I fled Australia? What was I doing in New Zealand? What other crimes was I wanted for? Meanwhile, the large mother was bumping me with her fat belly, continuing to shout obscenities. At first I couldn't speak. I felt exactly as though a large fist had been wedged down my throat. These people were putting on a show, and it was impossible to reason with them.

I would have gladly explained my side of the story if they would have only given me the opportunity, but that wasn't what this was about; this was an all-out frontal attack. They had me surrounded. I tried to step toward the marina office but they moved to block the way. I couldn't budge. When given a brief opening, I blurted two sentences: "Contact my attorney in Australia. His name is Michael Ferris and his office is in Mooloolaba." But the yelling and swearing never stopped; clearly the reporter's only interest was in how sensational she could make her story. They weren't interested in the truth; they were intent on making me the villain in a contrived, exploited misrepresentation of the facts.

In order to get inside the marina office, I had no choice but to push the fat mother away from the door and squeeze past her, on camera. I stepped into the office with the entire calamity right on my heels and asked the shocked office staff to please call the police. The mother shouted through the door, "Yes, call the police! He's a criminal; they'll arrest the bastard." She sure seemed to be milking her fifteen minutes of distorted fame; the camera was rolling and she was committed to the part. The fiasco had somehow grown and was now spilling back out into the parking lot. I stood at the door as the pushing and shouting continued, until, to my relief, Terry sped up in a rental car, nearly running over the cameraman.

I stuck my head outside, and Terry shouted, "Get your ass in the car!" Reliving my football days, I rushed through the door, dodging my antagonists, and jumped into the car. Terry burned rubber getting us out of there. I looked out the side mirror expecting to see a motorcade of TV crew in hot pursuit, or at least see the mother closing in on us slavering like the T-Rex in *Jurassic Park*. But no one seemed to be following.

What an ambush. This had been a major media circus, and I was the starring attraction, center ring. I have never been so humiliated and embarrassed in my life. I wanted to fight back, to defend myself, but I'd never had the opportunity. I was out-manned and outnumbered, and they'd had the element of surprise. All I could do was to stand there with my shaving kit in one hand and a towel in the other, looking disheveled and disoriented, like—well, like someone who'd just crawled out of bed.

After about an hour of driving around in circles, Terry and I returned to the marina. Thankfully, all my tormenters were gone. I stopped in the office to apologize for the disturbance, paid my slip fee and hurried back to the boat. I had planned on spending a week with Terry and Ariel, but staying here was out of the question. Like it or not, I was on the run, again.

Ariel and Terry untied my dock lines, gave me a large bag of homemade cookies, and wished me smooth sailing. I hated to leave the only friends I had in New Zealand. I had no idea where I would go. Once I was back in international waters, I used the satellite phone to call my attorney to tell him what had happened.

"Good God," he said when I'd told him the story. "Michael, I am so sorry. I am appalled at that behavior."

"Can we sue them?" I said. "You know, mental anguish, defamation of character? Extreme humiliation?"

"I understand the impulse," he said, "but that would be more trouble than it's worth. You've got other things to think about right now."

"I know," I said. "Like where to go next."

"Where are you now?"

"Treading water off the New Zealand coast. Can they extradite me if I go back ashore?"

"No. That's not a consideration. It would never happen. We are involved in a civil suit; what happened is not considered a major crime. In fact, you haven't committed a crime at all, or broken any laws."

"What about the kid?" I said. "The kid in the hospital bed."

"That's a fabrication. That boy hasn't been in the hospital. According to the police report, his only injuries were cuts, bruises, and a sore knee."

"What about the picture she showed me?"

"Contrived. The whole thing was scripted, choreographed for the television program. The parents are using their son to embellish their case against you in an effort to gain as much money as possible."

"Jesus Christ."

"I don't want you to worry. Go somewhere where you won't be harassed, but don't bother fleeing New Zealand. I've got everything under control. Try to relax and enjoy New Zealand."

• • •

So that's what I did. Over the next two weeks, I sailed aimlessly around the awe-inspiring region of New Zealand known as the "Bay of Islands." With its wonderfully quiet bays and secluded anchorages, it was the perfect place for me to hide out. Here I felt safe from the land sharks. Over the next few days, I could feel the stress leaving my body. Dipping in and out of perfect anchorages not knowing or caring where I was. At my wits end. With the trees filtering light onto lush green grass, I came to realize that I much preferred solid ground, trees and grass, over the sea. The green rolling hills, dotted with quaint farmhouses, made me feel less homesick; it felt good be out of the South Pacific and see pastoral countryside again.

The land was lovely, and yet, I had no desire to venture ashore. Who knew what might await me there? Instead, I lounged about the boat, reading books, playing computer backgammon, listening to music, and writing. My adventuring was drawing to a close—I had secured a spot for my boat on a ship leaving for home next week—so this was the perfect time for me to sit down with my yellow legal pad and ask myself just what I had learned.

Much of what I wrote was directly contradictory, or seemingly so. For example, it was undeniable that sailing alone around the world had been a stupid idea—I had somehow mixed up recreation with living, and I'd been pathetically naïve to believe I'd be happy doing it . . . and yet, it had changed me irrevocably, and, I was certain, I would be a much happier person over the next few decades for having done what I did. Chasing the dream of sailing around the world had turned out to be my introduction to my second adulthood; it had been filled with hours, days, and weeks of what amounted to a concentrated effort to learn who I was in a more visceral sense. It is remarkable what can happen when you dare to step away from the norm.

Most of the personal growth I'd experienced could be directly attributed to adversity. When confronted with my own mortality in life-or-death situations, I'd had no choice but to dig deep for the strength to overcome the psychological, emotional, and physical challenges. I had never experienced such a magnitude of adversity in my life, and, quite frankly, I would never have believed I'd have the wherewithal to prevail. By merely surviving my adventures, I had come away with a new sense of confidence that would stay with me the rest of my life. I'd thought I was a don't-sweat-the-small-stuff guy before, but now I really knew what that meant.

And age? The more I'd sailed, the less I'd thought about how old I was, until finally the very question had begun to seem absurd. I had always heard people say, "Oh, age is just a number," but I had never felt that way myself until I was living each day to the fullest.

I'd been forced to admit that I'd done a piss-poor job of choosing a "legacy" for my grandkids to reflect upon. Sailing around the world was far too ego-centered to matter to anyone but me. My loved ones had meant it when they'd said I didn't have anything to prove to them. It was great for me to have learned I had the skill to sail anywhere in the world, by myself, on a large boat filled with complicated systems. But *legacy*? Come on.

For me, I'd discovered that, a true legacy cannot be accomplished while separated from my family. I resolved therefore to move forward with my pursuit to establish such a legacy by sharing, interacting, even just playing with the significant people in my life. When it came to relative importance, if my family were an ocean, sailing around the world would be a bucket of rainwater.

And Sally: When I'd left San Diego, the stresses we'd been under had rendered me uncertain of the depth of my feelings for her. Oh, I knew I would miss her, and I'd had that epiphany about loving her just before I left, but was it because we were really meant to be together? The longer we were apart, the more I'd come to appreciate what a special person I had left behind. She had hated this sailing idea from day one, but look at how far she had gone to support me in it: she had put up with months upon months of solitude, had traveled all over the world to be with me, had sailed aboard *Sundance* despite her seasickness, had counseled me on my decision-making, and had comforted me in my hours of danger. I consider myself to be the luckiest SOB in the world to be loved by such an extraordinary lady, and I was done hurting her.

In a more philosophical vein, I'd come away with a new-found respect for suffering, no doubt a valuable insight for someone for whom the ravages of old age were looming on the horizon. Without the luxury—yes, the *luxury*—of suffering, one cannot appreciate the pinnacles of joy. Our ability to feel elation is directly proportional to the depths of misery we have experienced. Maybe we have some sort of meter in our brains that acts like a Richter scale to measure the degree of anguish we feel, and then limits the degree of joy accordingly.

Consider the intense joy and relief I felt when I finally stepped on dry land in Australia after my horrific time without an autopilot, not sleeping, not eating, and fighting one storm after another. Compare that joy with the emotions felt by a passenger on board the *Queen Mary* upon arriving in the same port after a leisurely cruise. There is no comparison! Without paying the non-negotiable price of suffering, it is literally impossible for the luxury liner passenger to realize precisely the equivalent depth of relief and joy I was privileged to experience.

I paused in my writing to look up at an emerald hillside where a cluster of sheep had been a moment before. Behind it, water vapor was rising toward the sun in a slanted pillar against a violet-colored sky, an exclamation point at the end of the long, rambling sentence of my adventure. I wrote:

> *I am thankful that I had the opportunity to sail across the Pacific Ocean. I no longer feel the need to prove myself by making an ocean passage. I have done it and know I could have continued to sail around the world, if I had so desired. <u>I do not so desire</u>.*
>
> *I am extremely grateful I lived to tell my story. Would I do it again?*

I spent my last night as a fugitive in a cove outside Whangaparaoa. The next stop would be Auckland; I was excited to reach the big city, where I could get lost among all the people. I hoisted the anchor at 6:30 AM, in light rain and fog. The course to Auckland would take me across the Hauraki Gulf, which happened to be the location of the trials for the Americas Cup.

Coming through the fog and rain toward the entrance to Auckland, I could see two American racing boats being towed out to the practice area on the Gulf. Each boat was flying a huge American flag in their rigging. I was delighted to see that the boats, one of them the famous *Stars & Stripes USA-66*, were coming toward me. When they were close, I walked to the bow, stood at attention, and saluted as they passed by abeam. There were about eleven crew members on each boat. When they first saw me standing on the bow, saluting, they appeared slightly puzzled, as if thinking, "What the hell is up with this guy?" But as we slowly drew past each other, the sailors could see my large American flag flying off the stern. Once they realized we were an American boat, they yelled, whistled, cheered, flashed me the thumbs-up sign. I knew they were showing their appreciation of the effort involved in sailing from America to New Zealand. Their reaction brought a tear to my eye and sent goose bumps channeling down my spine. I felt tremendously proud of *Sundance* and proud to be an American.

A few days later, I motored to the marina for her appointment with the ship that would be taking her home. She would be riding on a unique, float-on/float-off dry dock vessel, operated by the Dockwise Company from the Netherlands. Her masts and rigging would remain in place while she sat up in a supporting hard-stand cradle. I completed all the paperwork, then backed out of the slip and motored to a commercial pier, where the Dockwise ship was waiting. One of the crew members guided me onto the water-filled ship, where we were met by four more crews in diving gear. They secured *Sundance* to her new cradle while I gathered the last of my things from the cabin. It was a weird and wonderful feeling to slide the cabin hatch door closed, lock it, and climb down into the ship's tender, leaving my boat there all by herself.

She would soon be homeward bound. She had earned an all-expense-paid vacation. On this trip, for once, she could relax, kick back, and not worry about any storms, hitting any coral reefs, or colliding with any other boats. She had performed admirably;

I owed my life to her ability to handle big waves and strong winds. She had delivered me safely across more than 12,000 sailing miles of ocean, calling on eight countries and twenty-one islands. She had been my companion as I'd racked up a lifetime's worth of lessons. It's true, I didn't sail the 21,600 nautical miles required to be considered a circumnavigation of the world, but it gives me solace knowing I tried. *We didn't go very fast, but we went pretty far*, to paraphrase that ancient sage Janice Joplin.

Me? I had an important appointment with a Kiwi 747.

The End

Epilogue

I ENDED UP PAYING WHAT I felt was a fair amount for the damages to my extortionist's boat. I sent him a fraction of what he'd demanded, along with a message that if he ever felt like collecting on the rest, he'd have to come to the U.S. to get it. It's been nearly ten years now without a word, so I guess I satisfied him.

Back in San Diego, *Sundance* and I parted company for good. I sold her, at a loss, and when I drove away from the sale, I was glad I was alone because of the lump in my throat. "May the Sleeping Giant look kindly on you, old girl," I said, gripping the wheel.

I was sad to say goodbye to my partner in crime but not sad to give up sailing. There is a time and a season for everything, and my sailing days were through. I plunged ecstatically into the project of committing to my family with the same abandon I'd given the voyage. Sally and I got married, and our love has only deepened over the years. I'm close to all my grandchildren; we didn't buy Willie Nelson's tour bus, but the kids do spend a lot of time with me here at our lakeside summer cabin in northern Michigan (where I sit writing these lines as a purple thunderstorm drags itself across the far side of the lake).

The young ones don't talk much about their old granddad's swashbuckling, legacy-in-its-own-time semi-circumnavigation of the globe because, really, what's there to say? I was absent, disconnected from their lives, a pushpin on a map of the world. The imagined glory of sailing around the world was just that— imagined. It took 12,000 miles of zigzag, cement-mixer sailing to learn that the greatest legacy is created at home, with family and friends: a grandchild's birthday party, a beautiful sunset with my wife, road trips. I gave up on the voyage so that I could embrace real life alongside those who make it worth living. The ocean helped me to grow up, and not a moment too soon. That cursed and blessed circumnavigation attempt will forever define who I am and what I'm capable of, for good and for bad.

I'm still trying to outrun old age, but she's a tough old gal and she's gaining on me faster than I'd like to admit. But it turns out that the journey of aging is a lot like circumnavigation. I don't know which port will be my last. I don't know how many more islands I'll hail, how many more miles this ship will take. It seems terribly unfair that life doesn't come with a user's manual—not that I would have read it anyway. But, regardless of my age, I've learned that in life, as in sailing, we all chart our course, assemble a crew, and set sail, hoping for fine weather. Then, we add a little prayer that our sunset doesn't come too soon—along with a gentle reminder to enjoy each and every one, just in case.

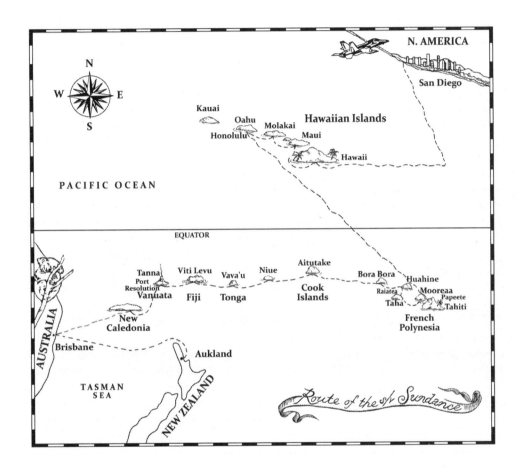

N. AMERICA

San Diego

W N E S

Kauai

Oahu
Honolulu

Molakai

Hawaiian Islands

Maui

Hawaii

PACIFIC OCEAN

EQUATOR

AUSTRALIA

Brisbane

Tanna
Port
Resolution
Vanuata

Viti Levu

Fiji

Vava'u

Tonga

Niue

Aitutake

Cook
Islands

Bora Bora

Raiatea

Taha

Huahine

Mooreaa

Papeete

Tahiti

French
Polynesia

New
Caledonia

Aukland

TASMAN
SEA

NEW ZEALAND

Route of the S/v Sundance

Basic Sailing Terms

Abeam	directly to the side of the boat.
About	on the opposite tack.
Aft	at or near the stern.
Alee	to the leeward side.
Aloft	above the deck.
Astern	behind the boat.
Batten	thin wooden strips fitted into pockets for stiffening the leech of a sail.
Beam	measurement of the width of a boat.
Beam reach	sailing with the wind coming across the boat's beam.
Beam wind	a wind at the right angles to a boat's course.
Beat	sailing against the wind by tacking (sailing a zigzag course towards the wind.
Beating to windward	to sail to windward close-hauled, tacking as you go, to reach an objective to windward.
Boom	spar that the foot of a sail.
Bow	the forward part of a boat.
Broad reach	the point of sailing between a beam reach and a run, when the wind blows over the quarter.

Buoy	floating navigational marker.
Capsize	to overturn.
Chain plate	metal fitting bolted to the side of a boat to hold the ends of stays and shrouds.
Cleat	fitting to which a line is secured, without knotting.
Close-hauled	sailing close to the wind and sails pulled in.
Close reach	the point of sailing between close-hauled and a beam reach, when the wind blows forward of the beam.
Come about	to change course so as to be sailing at the same angle but with th wind on the other side.
Course	the direction in which a vessel is steered, usually given in degrees.
Cutter	single-masted fore and aft boat having an inner staysail and outer jib.
Eye of the wind	direction from which the true wind is blowing.
Falling off	turn away from the direction of the wind.
Forestay	the foremost stay, running from the mast-head to the bow.
Furl	tightly roll up a sail.
Galley	a kitchen on a boat.
Genoa	large headsail, which overlaps the mainsail.
Halyard	line used for hoisting sails.
Hard-a-lee	to put the tiller all the way down toward the leeward side of the boat.
Head	a sail's top corner; also a boat's toilet
Headsail	sail forward of the foremast.

Headstay	a forward stay.
Heel	a boat's angle to horizontal, to lean over to one side.
Helm	tiller or wheel.
Hoist	the length of the luff of a fore-and-aft sail.
Hull	the body of a boat.
In irons	to head into the wind and refuse to fall off.
Keel	centerline backbone of the bottom of a boat.
Leeward	away from the wind; the direction to which the wind blows, down wind.
Line	any length of rope that has a specified use.
Luff	to get so close to the wind that the sail flaps; also the forward edge of a sail.
Mainmast	principal mast on a boat.
Mainsail	booked sail projecting aft from the mainmast.
Mainsheet	line that controls the main boom.
Mast	vertical spar to which the sails and rigging are attached.
Masthead	top of the mast.
Mizzen	the shorter, after-mast on a ketch or yawl.
On the wind	close-hauled.
Port	the left-hand side of a boat, looking forward towards the bow (opposite of starboard).
Port tack	when the boat sails with the main boom to starboard and wind hits the port side first.
Reach	sailing on a tack with the winds roughly abeam, all sailing points between running and close hauled.

Ready about	order to prepare for coming about.
Reef	reduces the sail area by folding or rolling surplus material on the boom or forestay.
Rigging	ropes and wire stays of a boat; securing masts and sails.
Rudder	vertical metal or wooden plate attached to the stern, who movements steer the boat.
Rules of the road	Right-of-way (ROW) regulations to prevent collisions between boats.
Sheet	line that controls a sail or the movement of a boom.
Shrouds	transverse wires or ropes that support the mast laterally.
Spinnaker	a large, light, balloon-shaped sail set forward of the mainsail when running before the wind.
Starboard	right-hand side of the boat looking forward towards the bow (opposite of port).
Starboard tack	tack on which the wind strikes the starboard side first and the boom is out to port.
Stay	wire or rope which supports the mast in a fore-and-aft direction; part of the standing rigging.
Staysail	sail set on a stay inboard of the forward most sail.
Stern	after end of a boat.
Tack	the lower left forward corner of the sail, where the luff and the foot meet; also the diagonal made with the wind by a sailboat when close hauled, (to change from one tack to another by coming about).

Tacking   working to windward by sailing close-hauled on alternate courses so that the wind is first on one side of the boat, then on the other.

Trim   to adjust the angle of the sails.

Winch   a mechanical device, consisting usually of a metal drum turned by a handle, around which a line is wound to give the crew more "help" when tightening a line.

Acknowledgments

I would like to offer my thanks to several people who have given so generously of their time and talents in support of this book.

I owe a huge debt of gratitude to my agent, Laney Katz-Becker of the Markson Thoma Literary Agency, for her undying support.

I want to thank Amy Strong and Derek Burnett for their talented contributions. Thanks to my dear friends, Dick and Karen Brown, for their meticulously informed observations. A huge thank you goes out to my editor, Jason Katzman of Skyhorse Publishing, who, through the editing process, became a good friend. Lastly, but most especially, I wish to thank my wife, Sally. She has been a positive source of encouragement during the good times and the bad. Her contributions to this work are too numerous to mention, but this book is immeasurably better because of her unstinting aid and comfort, sage-like advice, and encouragement. She never once wavered in her support of this enormous undertaking, and for that, I will always be grateful.

I love you, Sally.